A Month of April Firsts

J. Delgado-Figueroa

Writers Club Press

San Jose New York Lincoln Shanghai

A Month of April Firsts

Published by Writers Club Press
an imprint of iUniverse.com, Inc.

For information address:
iUniverse.com, Inc.
620 North 48th Street
Suite 201
Lincoln, NE 68504-3467
www.iuniverse.com

Although the anecdotes narrated in this book are based on fact, all names are fictitious.

ISBN: 0-595-09957-2

Printed in the United States of America

Epigraph

Porque es justo que el hombre no busque su deleite
En la selva de sangre de la mañana próxima.
El cielo tiene playas donde evitar la vida
Y hay cuerpos que no deben repetirse en la autora.

Because it is just that man seek not his pleasure
In the jungle of blood of the following morning.
The sky has shores where life can be eluded
And some bodies should not return with dawn.

Federico García Lorca (1898-1936)

Day 1:

The Misfortune of Nineteen into Nine

His hair was a jumble of black curls. His glance was penetrating and cold. His skin had the texture and hue of hazelnuts. His teeth, seldom stripped of the lips that enclosed them, were the whitest ivory. Years later I would think of him and remember gypsy poems by García Lorca.

According to the file my mother kept on him, he was nineteen, unemployed and illiterate. That was the reason why he was enrolled in the night-school literacy program where my mother taught.

One night he threw one of his arms of steel across my throat, undid my pants and pierced me into the deepest pain when he forced his penis into my nine-year old rectum.

It was one of so many nights when my mother took me along to her night class. Víctor Agosto followed me to the second-floor bathroom of the same school I attended during the day. He grabbed me from behind while I stood at a urinal. I'm not sure how I didn't pass out—every thrust felt like a stabbing. He left me there trying to catch my breath and wondering when blood would start to flow.

Two days later I asked my mother whether Víctor had returned to night school. Her puzzled stare told me she wondered what my interest in Víctor could be.

"No, he hasn't come back."

I told her what Víctor had done.

Her expression hardened into angular granite. It was a lie, she knew it. How could I make up a story like that about that young man? I was a bad boy full of nasty stories from listening to the rest of the ruffians in my fourth grade class.

"You ought to be ashamed of yourself, a boy who just took his first Holy Communion from Father Wilfred and goes to Mass each Sunday! What would the neighbors think if they heard you say something as awful as that?"

For months after that I thought I had dreamt it. One day I saw Víctor staring at me, hiding behind one of the monuments in the park. And I knew it had not been a dream.

Lesson: Mother doesn't always know best. Often she doesn't even want to know.

Day 2:

Husbands and Other Scoundrels

Everyone on our street in Juana Peña, Puerto Rico, knew the Piñeros. Mrs. Marujita Piñero was the social worker at the local elementary school, thundering mutedly at the malfeasance for which pupils from the slums were training and gossiping with other equally concerned teachers about the domestic problems of most of the school's students. She may have been called a visionary of sorts. For instance, when entering notes on the permanent record of a student with discipline problems, she would observe that the child would "most likely become a thief or a convict for life." "Mother of obvious moral turpitude. Future candidate for indefinite incarceration, possibly for murder or aggravated assault."

Her husband, Mr. David Piñero, much younger than his wife, was the neighborhood lecher, or at least that was the reputation he enjoyed, only surpassed by his neighbor, a middle-school teacher by the name of Godofredo Blas. Husbands feared him and decent women avoided him; chambermaids teased him. He bragged about his striking physical similarity to Arturo de Córdova, a Mexican matinee idol of the forties. He did look like Arturo. His macho appearance was bestowed upon him by the work clothes he wore around town at the end of his work day at the family cattle ranch, where he supervised and never did anything that might have made his fingernails dirty.

Mr. and Mrs. Piñero had two children, a boy a year younger than I and a girl three years younger than her brother. Parents in the neighborhood discouraged friendships with the Piñero children, especially with the girl. Rumor had it that her father would get his daughter on the phone to invite little neighborhood girls over when his wife wasn't home, and that his hands could not stay off the little visitors.

From the flat roof of their house we could see baseball games being played in the city park on Sunday afternoons. David Jr. and I would sometimes climb up the ladder behind the house and stand up to watch the games.

One Sunday Don David, still in his bathrobe in the middle of the afternoon, came up the ladder. He stood nearby.

"Ah, I think I have to piss," he said all of a sudden. He squatted to prevent neighbors from seeing him relieving himself while standing on the roof, picked up his robe and gave us an unobstructed view of his voiding penis. The amount of skin hanging from the tip was longer than mine; of course, I was only eleven, so it stood to reason that his organ would almost hit the roof—in a manner of speaking, of course.

He was staring at me all the while he peed. I hadn't noticed until his stream became a trickle and I looked up.

David Jr. was indifferent.

A few weeks later Doña Marujita was off to an evening meeting, perhaps of other visionary social workers, and several of the children in the neighborhood had gathered to play in the Piñeros' car port. Don David told us to move to the porch, since we could scratch his Jeep.

"Children," he whispered a little later with apparent urgency, "come in the house. I hear noises in the backyard. Someone might be back there, some intruder."

Alarmed, we filed into the house.

"Not you, David," he told his son. "Take this flashlight and go find out what's going on back there. I'll watch over the rest of the kids, and we'll look out from the bedroom window."

The obvious did not occur to me until I was an adult: if some danger lurked out there, why was this coward sending out his ten-year old son to deal with it in the dark?

We gathered against the window. Don David was standing behind me issuing directions for his son. "Look to your left. Go farther back. Check the bushes back there."

Don David had positioned himself so that his crotch was pressed against my butt. He rubbed back and forth aping intercourse movements and grabbed my ass with one hand while holding himself against the wall with the other. I stood between him and the window.

"I don't see anything," David Jr. finally said. "There's nothing here. I'm going back in."

The following afternoon I walked past the Piñeros on my way home from a Boy Scouts meeting. Doña Marujita called me into the house. She shut the door behind me. I removed my Scout cap.

"My husband told me what you did last night." Her tone was accusatory and the fist on her hip increased the intensity of her intention.

And what was that? Standing still while he rubbed his dick against my butt?

I remained silent.

"Touching him there? That is a very ugly habit. If your parents knew about it, they would beat you within an inch of your life, you know."

She was right, if my parents took her word for it, which they would.

I looked to the side. Don David was sitting in the living room reading the newspaper as if this had nothing to do with him.

"I don't ever want you here playing with our children again, you hear?" She moved to the side and opened the door for me. Even my badges weighed heavily on my chest.

She might as well have pressed burning coals against my face. I went home wondering whether she would, indeed, disclose my nasty habits to my mother. I knew she had already made the phone calls de rigueur to let other concerned mothers in the neighborhood know about my filthy little secret-no-more. I didn't mind that he did it, but it angered me that he lied about it—and why did he need to tell anyone it had happened, especially since it was not the way he told it? I had been rubbed into becoming every married woman's nightmare.

My ignorance did not allow me to see back then, as I found out years later, that her gossip about me may have shut some doors, but it would have opened several others. Especially when the wife and the kids were elsewhere.

When I was already married and the father of two, I walked down our street past the Piñeros'. Doña Marujita was rocking herself in the porch, getting her daily dose of maleficent slander from María Ramos, the street's reigning rumor monger—Doña Marujita had already retired from her predictive duties. She recognized me and came out to the sidewalk to hug and kiss me on the cheek. Of course, by then I had proved myself worthy of her consideration, siring children and getting a graduate degree. It must have been a phase all those years ago, toying with her husband's yard of skin. Her crystal ball must have been cloudy back then.

A few years later Don David died of prostate cancer. His children then found out about the other three children he had fathered with mistresses elsewhere. On the day of his funeral his daughter had a final exam in college; she took her final and missed the burial. Then she moved to New Mexico. She only came back to that town when her mother died: Doña Marujita was demented and had taken to running naked into the street from the nursing home, yelling that she needed a good fuck. The daughter never came back to claim her inheritance. She said she didn't even want to hear her parents' named uttered.

Lesson: If you're going to be accused of doing it anyway, don't suffer doubly by depriving yourself and then facing the undeserved consequences of your failure to act.

Day 3:

Paco Did Not Have Sex with Boys

Paco García was the first.

Maybe not the first I did it with, but the first I desperately wanted to do it with. He was my obsession, the boy I took furtive looks at during recess and when he walked past our house. Just a year ahead of me in school, he was beefy and popular with girls, played sports, had dreamy black eyes framed in long eyelashes and set against a light caramel skin that I craved to feel. I wanted him to notice me, but not enough to punch my face if I got too close.

So every night I checked his bedroom light from our bathroom window. In the dark I'd wait for him to strip, windows uncluttered by drapery, wrap a towel around his waist and walk out to their bathroom. My heart pounded against the window screen, waiting for him to return, towel himself dry and give me an unblocked view of his penis, barely discernible from the rest of the thick bush around it.

My father tired of my constant nagging about getting binoculars. He finally relented and bought me a cheap pair from one of the stores outside his factory. The binoculars didn't help much. Paco kept moving around the room as he got dressed, and a fraction of a second after he had dropped the towel his dick was in his briefs.

I tried to play butch. Butcher. I'd ask him to wrestle on his parents' manicured lawn, oblivious to the sharp stones that often broke my skin. I pretended to fight him off when he yelled, "Surrender, surrender!" while straddling my butt. One summer my father gave me a BB gun, and I asked Paco to go shoot at the udders of cows out in the fields behind our subdivision. He started giving me shooting lessons. I took the first one. The second lesson involved his rubbing his crotch against my ass while supposedly helping me focus on my target with his hand. I'm sure I pricked him when the hair on my neck stood on end

I had to ask him to stop. He did. I had mixed feelings, but really, what could I do?

One night when my drool made the window screen sticky an erection pointed unmistakably from his towel. I let out a sigh. He must have heard; perhaps he knew I was there all along. Instead of getting his underwear on, he slipped into his pants and a T-shirt and walked out of his bedroom.

My parents were at the Cursillista Tuesday-night Mass in town. Our house was dark. But Paco knew I was there.

The doorbell rang. Paco was standing outside looking threatening and pissed. I couldn't admit to anything. Had he heard my sigh? My gasp? Of course he had: deaf dogs heard it, I was sure.

"Yeah?"

He pushed the door open and came in.

"Do you still have those Superman comics you told me about?"

"Sure. Let me go get them." I was burning with fear and excitement. This probably was going to be it, and I had to decide whether fear of his talking about me was going to overcome my need to touch him.

He followed me silently. In my bedroom I bent over to get the comics, but before I could get up again he was brushing his crotch against my backside. I kept looking. He held my waist and I could feel him swirling his hips. Then I knew that pretending it was not happening was going to be a little more difficult than during the shooting lesson.

He undid my belt and dropped my pants. I heard him unzip himself. His penis was pressed against me. The blood in my body had all collected in my head.

He withdrew to flip the light switch off. In the relative darkness broken only by the car port light outside my bedroom he grabbed my shoulders and led me to sit on the edge of the bed.

I panicked when I felt his bare glans against my clenched teeth. As Granny Chelo used to say, one thing is calling out for the devil, another to see him coming.

"Uh-uh," I whispered, but when I tried to turn my head he grabbed it between his strong hands. I had never had a penis in my mouth and, besides, I had to pretend he had forced me—it was part of a drama where only I had been deceived by my act.

"You've already had it on your lips. What difference does it make now?"

His logic astounded me.

When I was enjoying myself the most he pulled out and asked me to lie on my back. He dropped his pants and knelt over my chest. A pillow propped my head high enough to reach his penis.

My hands were free. I was erect also and wanted relief. But Paco noticed what I was doing and pulled my hands away and above my head.

"You can't do that. I don't have sex with boys, you understand that?"

With his penis still in my mouth I nodded.

I had never had semen in my mouth. I didn't know what to do with it. He squeezed my cheeks and forced me to swallow it. It left an aftertaste of salty castor oil.

This was it? Apparently so. He rose to his feet, got dressed and walked away. The slamming front door told me he had left.

With a few variations, that was Tuesday night when I was thirteen.

Years later, when I had already left home for boarding school and was only around for a few weeks in summer, he tried to start it up again. But by then he had a steady girlfriend, and I felt betrayed. I was not going to have her leftovers.

Lesson: Denying you a kiss or a tender caress is not what makes them straight, no matter what they want to believe.

Day 4:

Arturo's Soap Opus

Arturo and Paco were buddies. I suppose that's how Arturo found out I was game for his own needs.

Though Arturo and I were the same age and in the same class in school, he was much shorter than I. He lived up the street from us, so we rode the school bus together. He was the only male in a family of four children. His sisters all seemed much older than he. They were gold diggers of fame.

Arturo was not our class' brightest star. His English was horribly flawed, and his oral reading risible. His specialty in ninth grade was grabbing girls' asses—which prompts the question: what did he do sophomore year in high school, universal ass-grabbing year? Other than that and leering at girls with his bulging eyes, he excelled at nothing. Our teacher, Sr. Mary Celia, O.P., took special care to mispronounce his last name, Maldonado, stressing the first syllable, giving it a mischievous twist that flew right over Arturo's head. Actually, his last name in Spanish was a compound that originally meant "he on whom a bad gift is bestowed." His was the gift of stupidity, although he was as dumb in some areas as he was too knowledgeable about others.

So it wasn't completely surprising that he should call me to ask me to help him with his algebra homework. After all, I was our class' top student, my English was near native, and no one received more perquisites from Sr. Mary Celia, O.P. than I.

When I got to Arturo's house, he told me to go with him to the laundry room to get his books. It was a cinder-block structure built behind the house, more like a small bedroom furnished with a washing machine, a dryer and a sink.

He shut the door and lunged toward me. Naturally, had I really wanted to push him away, I was stronger and certainly taller to make him bounce against the wall. But I put up just enough resistance to satisfy my belief that he couldn't go around claiming that I had gone down—literally and figuratively—without a fight. He struggled, not much, however, to deprive me of my pants and briefs.

"If you fight me off it's going to hurt more," he warned me, as if I needed his caveat. He made me bend over the sink and went to work.

It hurt anyway. His choice of lubricant was Palmolive soap. It was abrasively fragrant.

Before I walked out to go home he asked me, "Now you know, so tell me, whose dick is bigger, mine or Paco's?"

I guess I could have asked how the hell I was supposed to know, but that would only prolong the game. "You, without a doubt," I said without looking at his face.

"Really?" He was suddenly so smug. "Are you sure? Because he is pretty big."

"Trust me, I know what I'm talking about. He's taller. You're bigger. A lot bigger." Why deny him the pleasure—it was, after all, sorely true.

We repeated my tutoring sessions a few more times. It all ended the day he summoned me to his house during his parents' absence. I walked up the road to his house, and we started to repeat the same scenario on the bathroom floor, when suddenly the door bust open and an alarmed voice behind us whispered, "Damn it, your parents are driving up."

It was Paco. Apparently I had not been alerted to their plans for me that day. I suppose that, given Arturo's obsession with his buddy's anatomical attributes and the impossibility of confirming my assessment without asking

Paco to show him, the threesome would allow both of them to do what they wanted and provide the added advantage of a closer look for Arturo.

But Mr. and Mrs. Maldonado thwarted the tableaux.

I never returned to Arturo's, in spite of his insistence. My fear that he and Paco might be planning something on a grander scale, something that included several other friends of theirs in need of experimenting before marriage, made me stay away.

When Arturo had been married for several years and I was my daughter's proud father, many years later, we coincided at a Rotary Club party. We shook hands; his wife was standing nearby.

"Maybe you should give me a call sometime," he said, winking.

Lesson: You can't count on the wisdom of other people's choices. Be prepared: bring your own water-soluble lubricant.

Day 5:

Hammerhead Cannot Strike Twice

Perhaps it was all the result of the pressures that boarding schools put on adolescents. Or maybe some of us needed to search for creative ways to satisfy our needs without being labeled a faggot, the worst fate anyone can suffer in an all-boys school. It's like prison, except less glamorous.

Luis Héctor was not even handsome. His head was preternaturally big, the disposition of features on his face was not pleasant, and his teeth were crooked. He was three years older than the rest of us, which earned him his nickname, Old Man.

He played football, but wasn't particularly strong or tall; in fact, he was shorter than the rest of us, and would have looked shorter had it not been for the excess of hair on his large head. By the time we graduated high school he was beginning to grow a lot of gray around his temples and in his beard stubble.

Luis and I were on the school newspaper's editorial board our senior year. That meant marathon sessions the last days before the layout went to the printer. I usually skipped sleeping during the two days before final production, then slept through Spanish class, last period. The teacher was our senior advisor, a man obsessed with my football-lineman thighs—when I was doing clerical work for him in my gym trunks he'd walk past me, slap my thighs and say, "Whoa, look at those thighs!"—would let me sleep at my desk in the back of the room. I'd even snore undisturbed by my classmates, and the teacher would shake me awake when everyone left.

We'd all get pretty flaky in the early hours of the morning. I'd start to forget that queer behavior was a definite no-no, and would teasingly rub against some of my fellow budding journalists who didn't mind. Then I'd laugh and go about my business.

Until the night when only Luis and I remained in the newspaper room. When I rubbed my pencil against his arm, he grabbed my wrist and pulled it toward his crotch.

"Hey," I yelled. "Cut that shit out." I pulled away.

"C'mon," Luis said. "Who's going to know?"

I looked at his crotch and noticed the pulsating action coming from it.

It wasn't a particularly erotic sight. Luis had a peculiarity that caused us to joke about his penis. It looked like a long-stemmed mushroom. To others it looked like a hammberhead of sorts. One of the advantages—or drawbacks, depending on your perspective—of boarding school was that we shared changing rooms and open showers. We all knew what everyone had, and Luis' deformity was of general knowledge.

It was time to retire for the evening to the bedroom Luis and I shared with fourteen other seniors. By the time we got back everyone was asleep. I purposely stood by my locker changing clothes in the semidarkness; when Luis came in from the washroom next door, his eyes were not used to the dark and he bumped against me. He knew it was me and grabbed my hand again, taking it to his crotch.

"Let go," I whispered. "You're going to wake someone up."

"You're the one who's going to wake someone up. Be quiet. Come over here," he asked me.

I followed him to the bed in the corner, where his bunk was directly above snoring George Rivas. Luis jumped up and I stood by the bed.

"Touch it," he whispered.

"No."

"C'mon."

"No," I said, and went to my top bunk three beds away.

He started snapping his fingers.

My heart was pounding. This was not the safest thing I should be doing two months before graduation. Several students had been caught that year in flagrante delicto and expelled summarily. After three years of hard work and remaining at the top of my class, I stood to lose a great deal by following my curiosity.

I jumped off my bunk and walked over to Luis'.

"What?"

"Touch it, please."

This would continue all night if I didn't hurry up and put my hand on the hammerhead.

He was wearing his briefs. I squeezed his erect penis twice, certainly no more than thrice. He grabbed my hand by the wrist and withdrew it. I felt the moisture on the cloth. One positive aspect of the touching game was that neither of us had to break a sweat. Andele, Speedy Gonzalez.

Over the next couple of weeks I'd stay up late waiting for Luis to snap his fingers. I'd walk over, squeeze it two or three times, and that was the end of it. I'd go back to bed.

During the daytime we behaved as if nothing were going on. We had successfully sliced out the night from what transpired during the day. Neither of us mentioned anything; even our brief conversations during our nocturnal encounters—I liked him to ask me to touch it; it made me feel less wanton—were eventually reduced to a few words, mostly, "I'm done."

One night I stayed behind in the washroom, standing by the urinals. He walked in.

"What are you doing here?" he asked.

"Waiting for you."

By my demeanor I wanted him to know that I was tired of the touching and wanted to get oral on him.

He pushed me away.

I returned to the urinal. He approached me from behind and, standing on his toes, rubbed against me. It was not something I had enjoyed the times I had done it before, so I really wasn't looking for that.

Then he made the big mistake. He pulled away and said, "I better not go in there. God knows what serious cases of syphilis rot you have up there."

I walked away from the urinal while he went to pee in one of the stalls, left the washroom and went to bed. I felt embarrassed, humiliated and truly offended. Hammerhead—what right did he have to accuse me of something that implied I was a cheap queer who did it with any filthy old thing? As a matter of fact, not since Arturo had I succumbed to temptation.

Luis walked in later and started snapping his fingers. I didn't respond. He started whistling quietly. I still didn't respond. He jumped out of bed, stood on a chair and put his crotch against my arm. I didn't budge. He slapped me across the side of my head and said, "Have it your way, faggot."

School ended a few weeks later. I never spoke to Luis again. One day some eight years later while my wife and I shopped at J.C. Penney's in San Juan, I noticed Luis with his pregnant wife on the other side of the perfume counter. From the corner of my eye I saw him pointing at me to his wife. I looked their way, and he waved and smiled. I suppose he would have walked over to chitchat. I turned away stonefaced.

Lesson: If you want to get some, don't start by ascribing whoredom on the one who might do you the favor.

Day 6:

Brotherly Love

No, not that kind of brotherly anything.

I was a novice in a Benedictine monastery, at nineteen the youngest member of one of the largest religious communities of any denomination in the world. Ours was a medieval enclave surrounded by corn fields and evergreen forests in northern Minnesota, where I had moved to attend college and subsequently become a monk. Our class was the smallest novitiate group ever. The Vietnam War raged on, America was in turmoil, and religious values were undergoing examination everywhere. Among my fellow novices were two who had experienced their religious fervor under the rapture of a mystic epiphany: the possibility of having to ship out to Saigon. Members of religious orders qualified for a IV-D classification, which exempted them from military service.

Spending days without end with them in the same quarters was equivalent to living under the constant threat of air raids in Da Nang. One of the recent converts had a crush on the other one; the other one spent most of his time avoiding the first one, and whatever friendship the other one made with someone else was cause for consternation and long faces by the first one. The other two of the five-member class were a pianist whose every gesture made him a woman with the wrong plumbing, and Howard Friday, a man eight years older than I who had joined the Benedictines after failing to make it with the Franciscans.

We were under the supervision and so-called guidance of a novice master who had survived multiple sclerosis and considered himself God's gift to nonbelievers. "He means well," everyone else in the monastery used to say about him. He may have meant well, but his methods for achieving goodness? Well, put delicately, they sucked.

As fate would have it, in between assignments in the fields picking strawberries and apples and waiting tables in the refectory for the rest of the community, I fell in love with Howard. He did nothing to discourage my feelings. In fact, he taunted me and made remarks meant to let me know he had the hots for me. Unfortunately, that's all he had: heat, like a bitch in estrus.

Howard was a stocky man who had practiced sports in high school; he was an ace at handball and loved to play against other members of the religious community, as I found out later, so that he could leer at them in the locker room afterwards.

Mine was unrequited love, for Howard played with my feelings while flirting with every junior member of the religious community.

Unexpectedly, one day he stormed into my cell while I was getting dressed after a shower, took my hand in his and smeared a gob of Vaseline Intensive Care lotion on it, all the while grunting and pressing his crotch against my naked thigh, and turned around to walk out. He left me wondering what this was all about. I didn't ask and continued to go about my business.

The next day he did it again. On the third day I grabbed his hand.

"What are you trying to do?"

"Nothing," he replied coolly. "I'm just teasing you." He turned around and walked out again.

That night after general silence and bedtime I tiptoed into his cell and shut his door behind me. When I climbed into his bed he whispered, "What are you doing?"

For a moment I wasn't sure myself. When I started to withdraw he got out of bed, held me back, put his arms around me and gave me my first kiss ever. I responded instantly. It was a brand new feeling; I felt

Howard had reached the very essence of my being and I would be his forever. We made out furiously. He dropped to his knees and fellated me and, when he sensed I was about to have my orgasm he pulled me out of his mouth and masturbated me.

I dropped to my knees and took him in. His penis had a remarkable bend that fascinated me; he was too developed for my physical capabilities, and perhaps because I had not been satisfactory, he pulled out.

"God, now I'm going to have to do something," he said. "See what you've done?" He walked out of his cell ahead of me and walked into the washroom. I went back to bed, but I did not sleep.

In the months that followed he sneaked into my cell frequently at night. His kisses were what I wanted most of all; the rest was proverbial icing on that cake.

But as the physical activity in the middle of the night increased, so did his flirtation with several of the young monks in the juniorate. Howard was the first man to arouse in me feelings of jealousy, and they made me feel ugly. His despondence during the day led me to find comfort in brandy, which I started putting in my morning coffee. I was desperate. Nothing I did at night seemed to make any difference to make him closer to me during the day. My smoking increased from one pack a day to three. I was a wreck.

While I had been a student at the university that the monastery operated, I had enjoyed the friendship of an upperclassman by the name of Perry Asheman, himself a candidate to enter the novitiate the year after mine ended. He lived in the diocesan seminary across the road from the monastery. In my despair I thought I could trust Perry, who seemed sensitive enough to listen to me without becoming judgmental. I wasn't sure of his sexual orientation, but he seemed safe enough.

I emptied out my emotional guts. I sobbed and made a mess of myself while I confided in Perry what my problem was. He listened attentively and even told me about his own story of unrequited love with a classmate of his during his junior year. I felt better after talking about it, but once I returned to the monastery reality again struck me in the face.

On the verge of a breakdown, I decided that the best course of action was to reveal my feelings directly to Howard in the event that he had not noticed and thought my interest in him was only physical.

"I love you, Howard," I whispered in his ear one night when I slipped into his cell.

"You're crazy," he replied, and turned over to sleep.

On Thanksgiving that year the monastery held a get-together in The Beer Keller, a small pizza place on campus that was impossible to get into during the regular school year. The monastery invited its candidates who had stayed on campus for the holiday, and Perry Asheman came along. When I walked in with Perry a priest was at the piano, playing corny old songs from his college days in the seventeenth century. Other older monks sang along.

We sat together in a booth, where Howard joined us for beer and chips. Howard sat next to Perry, across the table from me. Perry started feeding Howard chips with his fingers. My discomfort started to grow. Soon Perry was putting his fingers into Howard's mouth when Howard took the chips. I gave Howard the dirtiest look he ever ignored. Just before I stood up to leave, Perry was putting his beer mug to Howard's lips.

I had confided in Perry and now it seemed that I had only provided him leads as to who the sure bets were in the monastery. I retreated to my cell and pulled out the bottle of Christian Brothers brandy I kept in my armoire.

The following Wednesday at our midweek buffet I had so much wine I had to go to bed and was unable to make it to evening prayers.

The next few months I was half dazed most of the time, contemplating suicide and unable to come up with a viable way to gain Howard's affection. Physical activity had ceased altogether.

"Man, you stink of booze," Howard told me one day. He didn't see that I was doing it because he was indifferent toward me. I knew I was driving him farther away with my traumarama, but since nothing worked anyway, the least I could do was to anesthetize myself.

Brother Andrew at the student infirmary helped me with that. He gave me a jar of pills, a tranquilizer cocktail that I started to down with brandy-laced coffee. I wasn't sure where I was any longer. One morning I slept through morning prayers and missed serving breakfast. Another time I forgot to ring the bells that signaled rising time. The novice master called me to his office. He had smelled the brandy, he had noticed my acts of irresponsibility and lack of piety. I had even laughed at a monk who sat behind me and fell asleep during prayers, hitting his head with a loud thud. It was obvious to him that I was often drunk or stoned.

It struck me as interesting that he hadn't noticed that the other love birds and the pianist had been laughing uncontrollably every night during recreation since they had been buying pot from a pusher on campus. But that still didn't excuse my nineteen-year old failings.

Late in January, seven months after I had been invested as a novice, I walked into the novice master's office and announced my impending departure. He was preparing for a trip to Israel the following day.

"Do you think I should stay for that?" he asked.

"Oh, no, absolutely, by all means, go on your trip." As if he needed any encouragement from the little drunk I had become.

I returned to the university a year later to finish my degree. Howard tried to invite himself several times to my room, but I never had time for him.

Some years later Howard also left. Only one person remained with the order from our novitiate class. One of the love birds had quit and moved to San Francisco; the other became an instructor at the college after he made temporary vows of poverty, stability and obedience, but when he overdid his pot smoking with students in his office, he was asked to leave both the university and the monastery.

Howard returned to Ohio, his home state. Nineteen years after my unsuccessful bid for his love I was living in Pittsburgh and drove out to visit him. After I went to bed that night Howard came into my room to ask, "Would you like some company for a while?"

He had lost neither his touch nor the denial of my opportunity to witness his orgasm.

A few months later I went to see him again. While we stood atop a yuppie infested hill overlooking the city, he told me that when Perry Asheman was a first-year junior he would invite Howard to sunbathe on the church's flat roof: the main church was the tallest building on campus, and only someone flying overhead could have seen them. Perry waited for Howard to stretch out in his chair, then pulled Howard's bathing suit off and sank his face in Howard's groin. Apparently it was the best part of summer for both of them over the last six years Howard was in the monastery, when Perry had been appointed to an administrative job at the high school on campus. A sex-abuse scandal broke in the unit Perry administered, some business between one of the priests who taught religion and several under-aged male students, and Perry resigned before being transferred to some other monastic mission elsewhere in the world.

I reminded Howard of what our relationship had been. He seemed confused. I gave him details about his incursions into my cell after my shower, of my visits to his in the middle of the night. He didn't remember any of it. He didn't remember my drunkenness, my depression over his indifference, my pleas for his love. He had developed a terminal case of fellato-amnesia, but he could remember everything he had done with Perry Asheman, my friend the vulture, who used the information I gave him about my pain to identify his next convenient trick.

I never returned to visit Perry. We're still in touch; he sends me a card for Christmas and calls me on my birthday. I know his is in January: I remember the special catalog order for two shirts I placed with J. C. Penney's just before I left the order, paid for with the little money I had saved from my mother's gifts over the seven months I was a monk. All

Perry ever gave him was a pair of red bikini briefs that Howard had to model at his birthday party the last year he was a monk.

Lesson: If you ever consider self-destruction, think first of who will remember your worthless sacrifice two months after you're gone. Certainly not the impious rooftop fornicators.

Day 7:

The Religious Wrong

The bank branch had been where I kept my passbook account when I had worked in the same town in Puerto Rico some four years before. I expected them to reactivate my account so that I could cash my paycheck at the end of the month, now that I was once again employed in the area.

The officer at the third desk from the front, facing the customer line, was staring at me and smiling. He'd lower his eyes and pretend to be working on something, and a few seconds later he was again staring my way with the bedroom eyes and the seductive smile.

"What can I do for you?" he asked. He had left his desk and was looking at me, ignoring the rest of the clients.

I explained my business that day. He asked me to walk over to his desk. I sat down, and he walked into the vault to retrieve my inactive file. He brought it back, sat down and called someone else to update my account with the information I had already given this gentleman, who had introduced himself as Alfredo Robles. While the other person did the paper work, he informally interviewed me regarding my line of work and place of origin. He was from San Leandro, a town I detested: I had spent five years in its parochial school and had nothing but contempt for its provincial, gossipy people. Nonetheless, it was better to set my biases aside and ask about prominent people in the town whom I knew from my elementary school days.

I quickly noticed his wedding band, which produced in me a deep sense of irony. I had spent four years chasing from my mind the ghosts of desire repressed and love dismissed—my uneasiness with myself was what a dream deferred and squelched had become. Now this man, married like me, represented the opportunity to carry out what I had not been able to do since my monastic disappointment, the reason why I had decided that family life was far preferable to the treachery and disappointment I had experienced in attempts to practice what the core of my being had yearned for. My choices had been risking disenchantment or taking up with someone like one of the queens I had seen one night leaving a bar on Halloween in Minneapolis. Neither option seemed as desirable as repression and denial.

Now, six months after marriage, this man was fate's loud mockery of my decision.

I started shopping in town at stores close to the bank. In the morning, before going to work, I'd walk past the bank several times, until Mr. Robles noticed me. He'd wave and I'd smile back. I made sure to park close by, so that shortly after walking past the bank I could drive by and smile again at Mr. Robles, who always stood by the door and waited until I had turned the corner.

One afternoon while I sat on the porch at my in-laws' Mr. Robles drove by. I wondered what he was doing around there: the house was on a cul de sac, and unless he was coming to see someone in one of the three houses, he was either lost or looking for something. He drove away after waving at me. Since then I recognized his car in the bank's parking lot, and one day left a note clipped under his windshield; it was a love poem by a romantic Spanish writer, and I signed it with the poet's name, Gustavo Adolfo Bécquer.

The next day I walked past the car, wondering whether he had kept the note. He had. It sat on the dashboard. He had folded it and written on it, "I could be very interested."

During the next week I left a note every day. Afterwards I would walk past the bank to make sure he made the connection between the note and its author. After all, I figured that a man who had stripped me with his eyes and been so forward the first time we met, probably had several other suitors panting for him. I wanted to put in my bid.

He kept all my notes folded on the dashboard. One day I walked past the car, and the notes were gone. Evidently the banker had changed his mind. I ran to my car and wrote another one on the same type of paper I had used for the previous ones: "I guess you're no longer interested. No more notes, then."

The next day I walked past his car again. Every one of my notes was folded and spread out on the dashboard, on top of which he had left his reply, "What are you talking about? Why don't you call me?"

"This is Gustavo," I said when I called him later that day.

We agreed that we had to meet. I was teaching a night class at the college, and I invited him to come to my office around six that evening, if that was possible—I was trying to make allowances for his own domestic demands.

My office had a large transparent window pane that made it impossible to conceal anything to anyone passing by. Mr. Robles, Alfredo, was very nervous, he said; I was too. He swore that this kind of thing was completely new for him, and he didn't know why he was giving in to it.

Whether or not he knew, obviously we both wanted to do more than sit in my office complaining about what we couldn't do in there. I offered to pick him up the next day at eleven in the morning on a corner a couple of blocks away from the bank, and we'd go to my house on the beach.

Alfredo may have been a novice, but what he lacked in technical refinement he more than made up for in eagerness.

Three and a half years after meeting daily at noon, when we substituted lunch for sex, I had met his family and he had met my wife. He had been one of the first visitors when my first child was born and was at my side during the child's illness and until the boy died a year later. His was one of the many flower arrangements in my wife's hospital room when she had our second child—by then I was the second in command at the college and many of my colleagues had sent favor-fishing flower bouquets.

Alfredo's father had opposed his attending college and made every possible effort to stop Alfredo from going to school, including denying him financial assistance and shutting off the electrical power in their house so that he couldn't study at night. After two years of hardship he decided it was too much of a sacrifice, quit college and became engaged to another girl from his church.

Yes, from his church. Alfredo, who was thirty when I met him at twenty-three, was one of his Baptist church's most loyal members. He was the congregation's treasurer and was on its board of deacons. While we were a closeted item, one time the church had a recognition dinner for him and his wife, believing us to be good friends who had met through his work at the bank, had sent me an invitation—the event was a surprise for him, so he had no idea that I could have been one of the many people in attendance. When he found out about the invitation, while he was sitting at the head table during the reception, he began to sweat and prayed that I had decided not to come. His prayers had been answered well before he elevated them to heaven.

On the fourth year of our lunchtime relationship the bank was bought out by a larger banking group and Alfredo was replaced; in fact, Alfredo was dismissed. His problem was that the bank was increasingly relying on college graduates, and Alfredo had made no attempt to complete his degree after he started working for the bank as a teller thirteen years before.

I needed a bookkeeper for one of the federally-funded programs I was directing at the college and brought Alfredo on. It proved to be a mistake I would regret during the next year. His office was on the opposite side of the building where mine was. Whenever a man walked into my office and I shut the door for privacy, Alfredo seemed to have some kind of sensor that alerted him I was in possible danger of being unfaithful. Within minutes he'd be at my door holding one of the accounting books under the pretense of having to clear up a doubt with me. Lunchtime meetings, shortened by his work schedule's requirements, became tense: I felt I was always under his scrutiny for possible disloyalty. He swore that the new professor in the Math Department had his eye on me; what was the chair of the English Department, the faggot, walking in and out of my office all the time? When I had to travel to Washington, D.C. for a meeting with the dean of administration, a man I had never looked at as anything other than a lousy administrator, Alfredo was furious at the thought that the dean and I were going to share a room at the Sheraton Park.

I thought that he would be able to occupy his time more profitably if he started taking classes at the college. He could transfer some of the credits he had taken at the junior college and at least finish an associate degree in accounting, thereby securing all credits and using them to complete a bachelor's degree right at the college. As an employee he was entitled to take one course at the college during regular working hours, and whichever he could in night school, without paying tuition or fees.

When he brought a transcript of his academic record for evaluation, the academic advisor told him that except for a couple of courses nothing would transfer. Alfredo was discouraged: he didn't want to start all over again to finish a two-year degree. I talked to the advisor and, resorting to my administrative clout as assistant to the chancellor, convinced her to allow the equivalent of a freshman year for transfer. He needed to complete just the core courses for the associate program.

He took business communication from me, which meant that regardless of the quality of his work he would pass. Most of the time he went home instead of attending class, because his wife was complaining that he was spending too much time in school.

Alfredo finished his associate degree. Early on the fifth year of our decreasingly satisfying engagement he started his bachelor's degree course work. His wife started to talk about her plans to go on leave from her teaching job, so that she could finish a master's degree. You see, Rebecca had graduated high school with top honors. When she married Alfredo she had just been granted a teaching degree, also with outstanding grades. After ten years teaching English, she felt her many talents deserved development. She felt educationally unfulfilled.

In the spring term Alfredo signed up for three courses, and Rebecca started attending graduate school at the state university's main campus, thirty miles away from San Leandro. She was going to night school.

Over our lunch break late in January Alfredo informed me that he was going to drop his evening classes. Rebecca was driving to school in the afternoon, but it was dark by the time her second class was over, and driving on the freeway after dark scared her. She was enrolled in two classes, both of which met the same nights as Alfredo's. He would drive out to the main campus and wait for her until her class was done, then drive home behind her.

"Do you know all the trouble I went through to get you registered at the college so that you could finish a degree? Does your wife realize that she doesn't need a graduate degree nearly as much as you need to finish your bachelor's, so that you can go find a job that pays better than that crappy bookkeeping job you have at the college." To say I was furious would be like saying that Hitler had reservations about Jews. That Tammy Faye Baker was partial to eye liner. I had gone out of my way to twist an academic advisor's arm to do me a favor that was clearly beyond acceptable regulations. Alfredo was obviously in greater need of earning his degree than Rebecca, who was tenured and could wait until her husband was done to resume her unnecessary education.

It was crystal clear to me that Rebecca could not stand the thought of her husband being her educational equal. She knew that he had not completed a degree, perhaps because his father was a jerk or maybe because he simply was not as bright, brilliant, outstanding and gifted as she. How could she let him outdo her?

Several years later, when Alfredo and Rebecca had plans to migrate to Wisconsin, I visited with them. "I'm really a house body," she said to me. "I don't intend to go out of my way to find a job once we move. I'd love to stay home sewing and doing crafts and taking care of the children, and let Alfredo get a good job somewhere."

The irremissible bitch. He never finished the degree he was going to need to get that great job she thought he was going to get in Milwaukee, because she had to stroke her own ego by going after a degree she didn't need, and now she didn't even want to use it?

My wicked ecstasy was superior to my expectations when I learned that the only job he was able to get was at the bursar's office in a small vocational college, a job that could not support the family of four, and she had to take a job teaching Spanish in a high school smack in the middle of a very deprived school district. This was double punishment for her: she was also bigoted against blacks, and her district bussed black students in from the rest of the city. She was going to be up to her neck in them darkies she disliked so much

But the nature of my relationship with Alfredo had changed long before then.

At the close of almost five years of hiding and staring at the watch to make sure he wasn't late for work after our lunch break, I asked him, "Do you think you'll ever be able to leave your wife?" The thought had been spinning around the darkest recesses of my head for some months.

"Are you insane?" he yelled back. He sat up in bed and picked up his briefs from the floor, as if the question had suddenly made him aware of his nakedness—like Adam after Eve fed him forbidden fruit. "Whatever do you think you're talking about?" He was so disturbed that I wondered about the wisdom of continuing the conversation.

"Do you think that we'll grow old doing this, meeting for half an hour of intimacy and rush to orgasm because you have to get back to work? Will we ever get out of serial quickies"

"What's wrong with that?" He was standing now. I decided it was best to stand up and throw a robe over my shoulders. I felt strange talking about the future with him while standing around naked.

"It's going to get very tiresome after a few years."

"Maybe for you," he snapped back. "What are you telling me, that your feelings for me have changed?"

"No, I'm saying that at some point we are both going to have to deal with the fact that we are gay."

The color flushed out of his face, which blended with the egg-shell paint of the wall behind him.

"Gay?" The word got caught in his throat. He had to clear it. "Gay? I'm not gay, and neither are you."

I reached for his chin and wiped off what seemed like a small drop of semen.

"Oh, yes, I am."

"No, you're not!"

I was afraid the neighbors would hear his counterclaims.

"Please, lower your voice," I asked him calmly. "Alfredo, I have known about myself for a long time. I am gay. I operate heterosexually and feel the deepest affection for my wife, and the greatest love for my baby daughter, but I can't deny to myself that my preferences tend toward members of my own sex."

"You are not gay, and neither am I," he repeated. He had put his shirt back on and was trying to slip into his shoes.

I was beginning to feel uncomfortable.

"Then what the hell have we been doing for the past five years? When you've had my dick up your ass, Alfredo, what the hell was that, gender confusion?"

"I don't know what it is," he replied, shaking his head as if to unload the monster from it. He walked into the bathroom and combed his hair. Then he stood in front of me, avoiding my eyes. "It's the devil, I tell you. The devil is loose in the world. He's the one that makes me do this. And you are possessed if you think you're a damn faggot!"

It was so ridiculous a statement, even for someone who had been a member of a religious order, that I had to look at him to make sure it wasn't a joke. It was no joke.

"You—you," he said, searching for the next absurdity and to continue the biblical line of self-loathing reactionary mythology, "You're just like an apple, soft and shiny on the outside and rotten to the core."

And there and then I knew that no matter what happened between us from that point on, I would have no respect for him. I could have gone on letting him suck my dick, I could have given him some more difficult-to-explain rug burns on his ass after lying on the floor with his legs in the air and me deep inside his wiggling ass, I could have let him kiss me as if he had never kissed anyone before, but respect he'd never have again.

I remembered how he spoke of one of my colleagues, one of the sweetest men who walked the earth and who had been so supportive when I had gone through the tragedy of losing my first child. He had stood in a corner with maintenance people and some other clerks mocking my friend and his partner during the college Christmas party. Now I could not pretend that his disdain was only for the obvious queens, that he held me in the same contempt he had for someone who dared to live his life free of the oppressive secrets that were crushing his and mine.

"I think we need to stop seeing each other," I said.

He had regained his color, but once again it disappeared.

"What do you mean?"

"What do you think I mean? I don't think this relationship—whatever the hell this has been that we have shared, this can't continue." I was already planning to return to Minnesota, at any rate, and the breakup would come with my departure sooner than he expected.

"You can't mean that. That would devastate me," he said, as if he had just told me that while he would never admit his sexuality to anyone, it was stupid to deny it to the man who had been fucking his ass and face for five years. "You need to calm down and think this over."

"No, I have nothing to think over, Alfredo. You better leave now."

He left, but then he showed me the wisdom of the prosaic aphorism, "Never shit where you eat." From that day and until the day I resigned my position to return to Minneapolis he made me regret ever writing one of the stupid notes, he made me so sorry I had ever chosen his damn bank to open a checking account in. He would come to my office two or three times a day, sit down and try to speak, but his weeping made him choke and he remained speechless. I started to let him go on and went about my work as if he weren't there. Eventually he would get up and leave.

Two years later, when I came out to my wife and moved out of the house to live with another man without whom I thought I couldn't live, I called Alfredo and told him. He was horrified.

"How could you have done this?"

"It beats living a lie and exploding at your wife and children for reasons that have nothing to do with what's really going on. I did my family a favor, even if they don't see it that way right now. I didn't just disappear, anyway. I see them every day."

"My Lord," he replied. "You didn't by any chance tell her everything?"

That was so typical of Alfredo. At the moment when I wanted to share my newfound emotional freedom with him, his concern lay elsewhere. It was time to squeeze him.

"Such as?"

"Other stuff about you."

"Stuff?"

"You know what I'm talking about."

"That I never wore her clothes? That I had had sex with other women before I married her? That I have a secret desire to be an astronaut and suck dick in space?"

"Don't think that because you have made that mistake you can drag others down with you. That's what I mean." He was getting tired of my cat and mouse delight.

"I alone am responsible for my own acts, Alfredo. You're afraid that I may have told her about you and me. I'd be embarrassed to tell her that I spent five years of my life taking for granted the love of a person so full of disgust and hatred for himself and for me. Have no fear."

"You know I still love you very much," he said. Talking to him had become an illustrative exercise in non sequiturs.

"Thank you. I'll remember that."

A week later he called me at work. He wanted to suggest that rather than me moving out—which I had already done—he and I could meet once a week halfway between where we lived. That way I could satisfy my need for sex with another man and wouldn't feel the need to leave my family.

The preposterous nature of his solution to a nonexistent problem was beyond his comprehension. Not only did he miss the point completely, but the impractical aspect of skipping work once a month to drive to some motel 200 miles away to be with a person I had no physical interest in was lost in him.

"That's sweet of you to offer, thanks, but I'm already living elsewhere. I can't very easily go back to my wife now and tell her it was all a misunderstanding. She's not as stupid as others."

My choice of a mate for whom to abandon my family turned out to be less than wise. A year later I was trying to avoid his attempts to persuade me to reestablish the relationship, broken six months before, and took a quick trip to Chicago. I was curious about Alfredo's life in Milwaukee and drove up for a visit.

He would stand behind his wife and give me seductive stares while shaping his lips into a kiss. We sat down for dinner, and while his wife passed around dishes of greasy Puerto Rican food he entertained himself playing footsie with me under the table; no matter how far I moved my leg, he continued to find it and scratch it with his toenails.

"Rebecca made a wonderful banana cream pie," he said. "Rebecca, you've got to bring some out," he asked his wife, and then addressed me, "You won't believe how delicious this pie is."

When she left to get the pie he reached under the table and grabbed me by the crotch. "I want you," he said under his bated breath.

I left a couple of hours later. I needed to get to bed early and still had to drive back to Chicago. It had been a long time since I had felt so great about myself. The doubts I had had about the choices I had made in life during the previous year dissipated as soon as I waved at the happy couple standing in the porch. I sang along with the radio all the way into Chicago and wanted to get out to every bar on the North Side and hug every queen there.

Lesson: If he doesn't respect and love himself for what he really is, don't expect respect or true love back; the sex may be great, but hustlers provide the same service at a much more reasonable price.

Day 8:

He Forgot to Tell His Partner That Their Relationship Was Ajar

At the time Donaldson's was still open at the Roseville Shopping Center in St. Paul. It was one of the mall's anchor stores, at the opposite end of the building from Dayton's, although the Dayton-Hudson emporium was much more elegant.

I had been back in St. Paul for little over two months, starting the final phase of my doctoral work and looking for full-time employment. My teaching assistant salary, even when supplemented with a meager stipend from the college in Puerto Rico, was insufficient to support a family of four. I only had minor-program courses to take, and I could do that late in the afternoon while holding a full-time job elsewhere. Eventually I would have to repay the financial aid I was receiving, because I had no plans to return to the Isle of Fright.

While walking around the men's underwear section at Donaldson's, someone behind me asked, "May I help you find something?"

He was a man shorter than I, with graying hair and deep blue eyes. His name tag's golden stripe indicated that he was management, and his name was Tom Gandy.

"I'm looking for some briefs," I lied.

He guessed my waist size and led me to a display of mesh bikini briefs that I would have never bought.

"You can try them, if you like," he suggested.

"Really? I thought that state law forbids that."

"You can't return them once you've bought them, but you can try them on at the store."

He pointed to the dressing room. I went in, opened the package of briefs and stripped. I put a pair on and soon after that I heard his voice.

"How did those work out?"

Before I had answered he had pushed the curtain to the side and given my crotch a good look. He then looked at me in the eye and nodded. He approached me and gave me a tug.

"I can't stay here now, but meet me outside the store in ten minutes," he whispered.

I got dressed, put the briefs back on the rack and walked out.

Tom was an assistant manager at Donaldson's. He was originally from California and had moved to Minneapolis with his wife Eddie, a flight attendant based in Minneapolis who was originally from West St. Paul. He missed Los Angeles, but he really had no choice but to follow his wife where it was more convenient for her.

Would we meet again? I told him we could and asked for his telephone number.

"Hmmm. Let me give you my work number. That's a lot safer than my home number. My wife could pick up the phone, and she's very nosy. Why don't you give me yours, and I'll call you tomorrow?"

I gave him my office number, and the next day he called. We agreed to meet later in the afternoon the following day at a motel downtown Minneapolis.

We sat in bed talking afterwards. I told him the highlights of my life and why I was back in the Twin Cities. He revealed that he was from San Jose, California, but had spent most of his life in San Francisco. During the last two years in California he had been a vice president with an insurance company in Los Angeles. He and Eddie lived in the Marina, but she had to fly to Minneapolis for work and was tired of all the commuting time, so they decided to move north.

The following week Tom and I met for dinner at Bullwinkle's, a restaurant on the West Bank of the University of Minnesota.

"Rather than sitting here eating, I'd like to take you home and rape you," he said.

Within seconds we were riding his Mercedes to his townhouse in Apple Valley. Later in the evening he drove me back to Minneapolis to pick up my car at the Bullwinkle's parking lot.

During the next months Tom and I met on Saturday mornings when his wife was out of town and I was supposed to be doing research at the library. When we couldn't get together because his wife was home, I'd drive up to Roseville to have a quick lunch with him or we'd talk on the phone. It was working out alright: he was married also, and he could understand the difficulties that married life imposed on a gay man.

I called him at work every morning, and sometimes a sales clerk by the name of Phil answered the phone. Phil was also married to a flight attendant and had moved to Minneapolis from Wisconsin after resigning from his position as a Presbyterian pastor. When I first saw him on a day when I stopped by the store to pick up Tom for lunch, he struck me as the biggest little queen I had ever known: a skinny frame supported by platform shoes, excessively flared slacks, over blow-dried bleached hair and the gestures of a professional drag queen.

What woman had married that?

When I called Tom the next time and Phil answered the phone, he wanted to know who was calling. I made the egregious mistake of giving him my full name. I would soon find out how small the world really was, at least as far as the Land of 10,000 Lakes went.

Early in December, while Tom and I were lying in bed, he took my hands in his.

"I hope I don't scare you by telling you this," he said. "I have fallen in love with you."

I felt tears welling in my eyes. "You're not scaring me. I've fallen in love with you also."

"Please understand that this doesn't mean I'm going to ask you to leave your family or that I'm going to leave Eddie," he clarified right away.

"That's okay, Tom. Let's take it easy and see where this leads us."

"Maybe some day we could take it a little farther," he was quick to point out.

"Let's wait until we get there." The previous disappointment was still fresh on my mind, and I didn't want to pressure myself into something.

After Christmas, during which he and Eddie apparently had a full party schedule, including the big party they had hosted at the townhouse, I returned to school for the winter quarter. One morning I had a message on my desk: "Call Tom."

"No, I haven't," he said when I asked him whether he had called.

"That's odd," I replied. "But as long as you're on the phone..."

The following morning again I had the message on my desk: "Call Tom." And again Tom had not called.

The following day Tom did call to ask me to meet him for lunch. We sat in the car instead, he again with my hands in his; I knew this was important.

"I have a confession to make. I can't hold this back anymore, because I love you, and I need to tell you the truth."

What the hell could this be? I was beginning to fear that he would tell me he had a bad case of venereal disease that I could have passed on to my wife—this would have been a horrible mess for me, not to mention my wife, who would have had to deal with the reality of a sexually-transmitted disease and the knowledge that I had been unfaithful. With another woman, or course. I was sure that Tom was monogamous regarding gay sex, but I had no idea what his wife was doing.

When a closeted gay man is married, the threat of disease can tear him apart. If he is sexually active with his spouse, which usually he is, it is a very real danger: unless he is using condoms with his wife for contraceptive reasons, how else can a man explain their use with his spouse? He performs the sex act that his desire impels him to carry out and then, on top of the feelings of guilt he has to deal with the possibility of getting crotch rot. Crabs can hide in pants you try at any store, but gonorrhea is much more difficult to explain. Back then the worst would be genital herpes—bad enough, but at least you weren't going to kill your wife the way you could today. Regardless, the concern is real and the cause of terrible anxiety. Insanity can set in at the mere suspicion that a slight urinary irritation or a common ingrown hair could evince a case of something that requires penicillin and a better excuse than the one you can provide.

But that was not Tom's problem.

"I've been telling you about my wife, Eddie. Well...The name is really Ed. He's a flight attendant with Northwest Orient."

He might as well have told me that the world was flat and he was going to push me off the edge. How could I respond to that?

I still couldn't understand something. Whenever I was at Tom's and the phone rang, usually some other flight attendant's husband or friend of Tom and Eddie's, he'd refer to her absence. "She won't be home till Thursday," he'd say, for instance, or "When she gets home I'll ask her if she wants to go to the party."

It would take me another year to figure that one out. Tom took advantage of the ignorance he had already noticed in me regarding camp.

"What else is not true?'

"Everything else is true. I just didn't feel comfortable telling you that before. I didn't know whether you were going to be a trick or whether something else was going to happen, so I kept that information to myself."

"So I'm no longer a trick, I'm something else."

"Oh, please," he said, his usual tears welling in his eyes. He seemed to be in complete command of his tear ducts. "I do love you, and I don't want to keep anything from you."

"This is the time to come clean," I said. "Anything else you need to tell me?"

He looked away, then turned toward me.

"I never finished my degree at San Jose State." He had gone to school for four years, although he had been dropped since the first semester of his sophomore year. His father gave him tuition money—Tom never had a job until after his mythical graduation from college, and his father was always bothered that a man with an accounting degree had to take such low-paying jobs—and Tom left for school every day. When his father asked him for his grades Tom would throw a tantrum. "What, don't you trust me? You see me leave for school every day and what do you think, that I'm not doing well?" His father would relent. The next day he'd be at the student center playing cards again.

Tom did that for two and a half years.

"So how does this business of the male partner affect us?" I asked him

"It doesn't. You have to understand, he and I have not—well, I don't want to be indelicate, but we have not been intimate for a long time. We've become more like gay brothers than anything else."

So I had stopped being the male lover and in a few seconds became the other woman. It was not a role I was prepared to assume. However, I was in love with him and it was late to turn back.

The following week I got home in the evening. My wife told me that someone had called and left me a message, "Tell your husband to call Tom."

I pretended to be unconcerned about it. Two of my colleagues were named Tom, and I explained it as such. Then the phone rang. I picked it up.

After a brief moment of silence the voice at the other end said, "Yeah, call Tom" and hung up.

I told my wife that this was some prankster, and to avoid being exposed to the assholes I'd have the number changed, unlisted and unpublished. The following day I did just that.

But by then the caller's identity was pretty certain to me. I called Tom and told him what had happened.

"I suspect it's Ed," I said.

"Oh, no, couldn't be. How would he know? Besides, Ed would be incapable of something like this. No, can't be."

But who the hell could it be?

Later that week, when Ed was home, Tom called me from work. I was getting ready to quit my teaching job and start a job with a large computer company.

"Do you know a guy by the name of Dylan James?" he asked.

Before answering anything I asked back, "Where is that fruitcake now?"

"So you know him," Tom said.

Dylan James had joined the monastery the year before I did. He was a nervous wreck; he'd forget he had lit up a cigarette and sometimes had two or three going simultaneously in different ashtrays in the recreation room at the juniorate. He had suffered from the same ailment as I at the hands of a fellow monk by the name of Jim Wilson: apparently he had been taken advantage of and ended up falling in love with the bastard, who had then wanted to dump him. But unfortunately for both of them, screwing among monks is like doing the nasty with someone at work: when you want out, you still have to see the person every day and be reminded of the bad blood between you, except that it's worse, because, at least for Benedictines, whose motto is "Ora et labora," pray and work, you have to pray, work and live with the person you'd rather never see again. Or in Dylan's case, with the man he wanted to hold on to forever.

Eventually it got so bad that Dylan left the order; Jim Wilson remained in the monastery a few more years smoking dope, dodging the draft and living off the fat of the abbey's land.

Dylan was another flight attendant with Northwest Orient. His lover was Phil, the Donaldson's troll. Phil went home with the gossip of the mystery caller, and Dylan immediately knew who I was. He had left a note in Ed's mailbox at work: "If you don't know anyone by this name, maybe Tom does."

I didn't know what this flight attendant could do. It was clear that the person behind the calls was, indeed, Ed.

"I suppose this means that we are off," I said.

"Don't be hasty," Tom replied.

"I don't want to have to look over my shoulder all the time to make sure Ed isn't walking behind me with a gun in his hand."

"Oh, you're overreacting. He wouldn't do something like that," Tom was quick to say.

"Like he wasn't the person calling my home number?"

"Well, we're okay for now. He's mad and took off to San Francisco. Probably getting in trouble all over town, I guess, but that's okay."

"I can't deal with this, Tom."

But Tom, with his usual ability to color reality a much brighter hue than it obviously was, talked me into sticking it out.

It's tempting to speculate about the psychology of the cheater, of which, to the extent that I was betraying my wife, I also was. I'd rather not engage in useless questions. Suffice it to say that Tom—well, a category was created exclusively for him. He liked to live dangerously, take on the challenge, and trust his unique skills in bullshit artistry to get out of the mess he'd invariably make.

Ed was simply not the person for Tom. Or perhaps they were perfect for each other. Maybe Ed enjoyed the game just as much.

One time Tom came home from work and found Ed waiting for him.

"Did you have any guests over this week?" Ed asked casually.

"No...," Tom replied after putting his finger to his lips, knitting his eyebrows and cocking his head.

"Did you change your cigarette brand?"

"No..."

"Then I wonder whose cigarette butt this is," Ed said, picking up a crushed filter off the ashtray.

Why would this be unusual? Because: (a) Tom smoked Winstons, (b) I smoked Marlboros, and (c) before I'd leave their house following a

Saturday visit Tom would empty all ashtrays into a paper bag and push it to the bottom of the trash bin outside. This particular butt sat all by itself, no ashes around it, in an ashtray in the kitchen, where I had not sat.

"Oh, wait," Tom said as if hit by a bolt of mnemonic lightning, "Bill stopped over the other day." Naturally, this was an easily verifiable fact, not worthy of Tom's elaborate imagination.

"Hmmm. No, this isn't Bill's…Bill smokes Vantage. This is a Marlboro."

"Then I don't know," Tom said as he walked into the bathroom.

As usual, Ed would not pursue it. He was satisfied that Tom knew he was busted. That's how he built his ordnance magazine for B Day. Breakup.

We lasted one more year together under the same circumstances. In the spring of the second year, while I prepared to take my doctoral exams, my wife and children went to Puerto Rico to give me room and quiet to study. They'd be gone for the summer.

Friday and Saturday nights I'd take a break and go to The Grand Finale, a disco downtown St. Paul. It was my first time in a gay bar. It was my first time in any bar, actually. The noise, the music, the apparent availability of so many gorgeous prospects made me realize everything I had been missing.

I felt terrible about keeping the information of my escapades from Tom. He never went to The Grand Finale, the only bar downtown St. Paul, because most of their friends gathered at The Happy Hour or The Gay 90s, both clubs within a single complex on Hennepin Avenue.

And he had assured me that when Eddie—then Ed—was out of town and I was home with my family, he stayed home watching television or reading.

I felt like a scumbag, but I wasn't out to do anything I couldn't tell him about if I had to. What difference did it make? He was home with his companion and I wanted to be out meeting other people, not for sex, but just to have someone else to talk to.

Toward mid-summer my life had changed considerably. I had passed my exams and had decided that I was going to catch up with everything I had missed during all of my years as a monk and then as a husband and father.

I came out to my wife over the phone. She flew back, and we talked about my revelation. She had harbored the hope that once we were under the same roof again—she blamed herself for leaving me alone to go fall under the thrall of perverse attractions—we would return to the same life we had before, even if that life had been full of arguments due to my emotional frustrations.

I had told Tom about my plans. What was he going to do, if he was so unhappy with Ed?

"Oh, I don't know," he replied. "You have to understand that we have been together for almost nine years now. We can't just walk away from our relationship like this."

I was stupid about a lot of things, but some were so transparent that I would have had to be embalmed not to understand. Tom had filed for bankruptcy. Overspending on expensive furniture, and other luxuries that were far beyond the reach of a man whose salary was in the lower tens of thousands, caught with him.

He blamed Dayton's for letting him charge, just like he blamed payees for cashing his checks when he was, as he put it, underdeposited. They should have known better and cut him off before he ran such a bill.

The truth was that his townhouse was furnished with the fanciest pieces. I always wondered how he could afford that if Ed was not participating in the charging fest. Apparently he couldn't, but it didn't stop him. Ed would take half of the furniture anyway, now that bankruptcy had taken care of the bill.

Then we had the issue of transportation. A true Californian, Tom lived by the motto, "You are what you drive." The Mercedes wasn't his: he had talked Ed into trading his Olds Cutlass for the car. Ed couldn't charge much more, because the car payment alone ate a large portion of his paycheck. And Tom couldn't afford a car of his own, so he was stuck in an alleged nonsexual relationship he didn't want for the sake of the luxury vehicle. And the furniture.

I suspected he had the same problem with living quarters, and eventually I was able to confirm it.

But overall Tom reminded me of something my father used to say: "Nothing is ever too expensive for deadbeats. They don't expect to pay for it anyway."

Tom may have loved me, but he heeded the call of the humming money bag.

I called the whole thing off. He blamed me for his breakdown, which consisted of constant crying over the phone, before heading out to The Happy Hour.

By the time he finally told Ed he wanted to leave, I was involved with someone I had met at The Grand Finale. He came to my office holding a white towel in his hand. I didn't know whether he was going to toss in the towel or unfurl it as a symbol of surrender. It turned out to be his extra-large handkerchief. He broke into tears, wiped his eyes with the towel, then with his head up high as if battling the pressure of agonizing pain said, "I feel like a kid who's had a candy bar in his hand for two years, Now someone else has taken the candy and left me the wrapper. Now Ed is moving back to California—he, he who's the one from his hell hole and the one I moved here for, and you have your new friend, and what do I have?" Then he cried some more, and I told him I was in my place of work and couldn't listen to him.

Some months later I met one of his closest friends at The Brass Rail in Minneapolis.

"So you're the home wrecker," he said.

"So it seems. At least Tom was faithful to me," I said, meaning every syllable of my words.

"Oh, please," he laughed. "Tom can't even be faithful to himself. When he was seeing you and still living with Ed he was next door at The Happy Hour every night picking up whatever he could."

I felt so much better.

Ed moved to San Francisco and changed his base to Seattle, since he was working trips to Asia. Tom rented a room at Kris Swenson's mansion in what TV ads called prestigious West Bloomington. He was unsuccessfully trying to sell real estate and writing his parents for money. He invited me a couple of times to dinner, which he was in charge of cooking at Kris Swenson's in lieu of rent, for Kris and his two children when they were visiting, and for Maury and Herb, the other two roomers.

Somehow he made up with Ed and flew out to San Francisco to drive the Mercedes back to Minneapolis before driving it out to California again. The day before leaving, while Kris was at work, Tom was washing the Mercedes out in front when he received a visit from a Hennepin County sheriff's deputy.

"Mr. Gandy, you have twenty-two unpaid traffic tickets, and I'm here to either collect the money or take you in."

Tom slapped the hood of the car with the wash rag, splashing soapy water everywhere.

"Can you believe this?" He turned away from the sheriff, hand in hip. "Look at my house. Look at my car. I live in this huge mansion, I pay taxes through my nose, I obey the law and pay my bills. And what do I get in return? Do you have any idea how much I paid in property taxes alone last year? How much do you make? How much do you think a trip out here to get me for a few lousy tickets is costing taxpayers? Do you think it's worth your time to come and get me when you consider how much I contribute to this lousy state?"

Histrionics were undoubtedly Tom's forte.

"Sir," the lawman said with his tail between his legs, "Do you promise you'll come to city hall tomorrow and pay these off?"

"I could go right now, if you wanted me to."

"No, sir, that's not necessary. I'm going to rely on your word that tomorrow before close of business you'll stop by and take care of this, and I'll just forget about it. Is that alright with you?"

"Of course."

"I have your word."

"Absolutely," Tom said, and shook hands with the sheriff's deputy.

Early the following day he was driving south on I-35 on his way to California. Of course, it was too early and city hall was not open for business when he left.

The following year I flew to San Francisco on business. Tom and I we agreed to meet for drinks at The Lion Pub on Divisadero. Tom was working as an independent home renovation contractor, which I took to mean he was hanging paper around town, otherwise unemployed, and living off Ed. He and Ed were renting a two-bedroom renovated townhouse on the Haight; Ed was traveling that week.

A guy by the name of Robert kept hanging around. Soon it became obvious that he was with Tom, who had been careful not to introduce us. It didn't stop Robert from walking up to me and pulling my shirt and undershirt out from under my sweater.

"Look," Robert said in a drunken stupor, "he must be from Minneapolis. He's into layers!"

I tucked my clothes back inside my pants.

Not that I really cared, but it was the polite thing to do, so I asked Tom, "How is Ed doing?"

Tom's eyes were about to pop. He rolled them to the side.

"Uh?" I asked. I thought he hadn't heard me. "I said, how's Ed doing?"

He rolled his eyes again toward Robert, shaking his head a little in the same direction.

In a world that's always in flux, it's reassuring to know that some people never change. Even when they should.

When I last saw Tom he was tending bar in a restaurant on the Oakland marina and complaining that his zip code was in Oakland rather than in more affluent Martinez—what a social disgrace. He had gained an unflattering amount of weight, mostly on his midriff, and his curly salt and pepper hair had turned completely gray. He was still the

world's greatest bullshitter; funny, too, unless the bullshit involved something he was trying to get from you.

He was sharing the socially incorrect house two streets away from
Martinez with the man who was astounded at my layers. "Going back to
Ed was a mistake," Tom said. But it paid your way back to the Bay, I almost
said, and he probably paid you off to get you to leave once and for all.

Some years ago he sent me a post card from Palm Springs. My last
Christmas card was returned unclaimed. Like McTeague in *Greed*, he must
have ridden an ass into Death Valley and was never heard from again.

Lesson: Never underestimate the power of vested interests to overcome
feigned affection.

Day 9:

Three and a Half Dog Years

That Saturday night in late June I had arrived late at The Grand Finale. I was clad in a pink Izod polo shirt, Levi's and penny loafers.

After having a few beers at the bar I drifted toward the dance floor on the other side of the dividing wall. There he stood, to the side, black hair, moustache and beard, fine features, a narrow waist supporting a ribbed chest and strong arms. He wore a tight gray T-shirt, faded jeans and cowboy boots. A beer in one hand, he was trying to light a cigarette with the other. Under the influence of a hormonal rage and alcohol, I walked toward him and loud enough for him to hear over *Call Me*, I asked him, "Who let you loose to come out all alone and looking so good?"

He chortled delightfully. Years later I would have sneered at the lack of originality, had anyone used the line on me. However, at that particular moment I really meant it. I was hoping he was alone and not engaged in anything else; I was trying to break away from someone who had a live-in lover and had lied to me for two years, and I didn't need the complications I had experienced. Besides, home wrecker was not a name I wanted associated with me. I didn't know whether this man had ever heard the line, but it must have pandered to his love for himself and very healthy self-image.

"I don't have anyone at home to stop me," he laughed. He simultaneously grabbed my waist and pulled me close to him. His name was George Massey, and he seemed both anxious and interested.

"Do you dance?" he asked.

"You tell me," I replied, pulling him by the hand to the dance floor. He stopped to set his beer on a table and put out his cigarette.

He was a good dancer, but he was a better kisser—were it not for the stale ashtray taste of his mouth. Suddenly, before the song was over, he led me off the floor. He asked me to go to the bar side and bought me a beer; we stood against a mirrored wall for a while. Soon he was leading me into the dance area again.

We chatted a bit, mostly about what we did for a living. He was a warehouse clerk for an auto manufacturer in Edina. The information fanned the fires of my fantasy. He was no interior decorator, no hair burner, no antique dealer, all specimens I had met during the few weeks I had been going to the bar.

He asked me whether I wanted to stop by for a drink. The words flowed out of his mouth like the sweetest melody my ears had ever heard. I followed him home, where he asked me to park in front of the house, a two-story early-forties structure on a mound overlooking Como Avenue.

"Normally I park in the back," he said cryptically. I didn't care: I was in a rush to get in the house and find out whether the rest of him was as great as what I could already see.

We sat in the living room, a cluttered area that opened into an equally cluttered dining room. Boxes and crates sat in stacks on the living room floor. In a corner by the living room's French doors sat an unusually plush leather wing-back chair. Both sides of its back were decorated with brass tacks.

"Usually you don't see tacks on the back," he said. "My former lover made it for me. He's an upholsterer. He does beautiful work."

The mere mention of an ex-lover who did something so well, and something I couldn't do, aroused feelings of jealousy in me. How dare that ex whatever? I wanted this man, and I wanted him with amatory amnesia—no one before me, no one after me either.

George poured me a glass of bourbon from a bottle he kept in an incredibly ornate bar in the living room. He had bought it in Viet Nam when he was in the Army; it was beautifully carved and every inch of it opened into a functional compartment. I was pleased to hear that he had brought it to America himself and it wasn't a gift from an ex-lover. I could not deal with his past: I wanted to have a go at his present, and I wanted it fast.

George stood up and took out an ABBA album from a haphazardly stacked pile of records and covers. He played *Andante, Andante.*

"Listen to it carefully," he said, staring into the ice dissolving in swirls in the glass of bourbon.

When the song was over he took me upstairs. We stripped and lay in his brass bed after he picked up, one by one, a dozen grocery paper bags full of documents and set them on the floor.

After sexual activity whose mediocrity I attributed to drunkenness, we fell asleep.

The following morning he brewed coffee and we talked some more. He was a year older than I and had just broken up with his lover. It wasn't the first time. Brad was very violent: a couple of times George had gone to the hospital with serious bruises from their fights. The previous night Brad was at the bar, standing behind me, following us around and making fists in the air. That was why we kept changing locations. But this time it was over for good; George had returned Brad's door keys. No more leather jackets ripped by stilettos in pool halls, no more glasses broken on his face leaving ugly scars on his forehead, no more being kicked out of bed in the middle of the night for no reason.

"Was he the upholsterer?" I asked.

"No, that was Jim. Jim Wells. Brad is an elementary school teacher in Maplewood."

None of it meant much to me. I was curious about this rugged man who seemed tender, vulnerable and abused by the aggressive low-life. Thus, I was happy when George invited me to return that evening.

During the next week I met Cindy, his lesbian roommate who did maintenance work at the University of Minnesota, a twenty-two year old recovering heroin addict. I also met Chrissy, her lover, a hairdresser who spent so much time in the house herself that I had initially believed both roomed in the house. Chrissy was generally there even when Cindy was at work, from four in the afternoon to midnight.

The following Saturday George and I were minding our own business at The Grand Finale when I saw Tom Gandy walking toward us. Ed, the spitting image of the picture I had seen on a table at their townhouse some two years before, stayed at the bar. Tom introduced himself; it was obvious that he was not thrilled to see George leaning between my legs while I sat on an empty barrel by the dance floor.

George walked to the bar to get us another beer.

"So this is why you had to break up with me," Tom said, tears again in their usual place.

"So that back there is why you could not stay with me," I replied.

"You could have been more honest," Tom said with a straight face.

George was approaching us again.

"Nice seeing you again, Tom. Say hello to Ed," I said.

Monday morning Tom called me at the office. He had asked some of his friends with whom he and Ed had very serendipitously decided to stop by the St. Paul bar and found out a lot of unpleasantness about George.

"He's not a nice boy," he said.

"Well, Tom, in your own self-absorbed way, neither are you," I replied.

A month later I was moving in with George. He cleaned out the third bedroom, where I was to keep my bed and desk, since when his mother visited she was to see where I presumably slept.

Every day after work I went to see my children for a couple of hours, and headed for my new home. George usually came home a little later, unless he had stopped at his parents' house in West St. Paul for dinner. When he and I ate together, it usually came out of a Van Kamp or Hormel can. Monday and Wednesday evenings I was enrolled in an accelerated MBA program that my company was paying for. I got home tired and hungry, and went to bed immediately. Around nine in the evening, just before my children went to bed, they would call me to say good night, unless I had warned them that I was going to be busy. Friday and Saturday night we'd head for the bars. We had switched to downtown Minneapolis.

Making love had become less of an occurrence shortly after I moved in. After dinner I sat at my desk to do some research for my graduate work, and George sat in his room watching TV, going through some of the many grocery bags where he kept documents of various types for four or five years waiting for some kind of organization, and drinking whiskey or vodka. One night while he lay on his belly with me on top I heard the sexiest groans and moans I had heard so far from him. It excited me that he was so passionate. Then I heard the snoring, which I had confused for sounds of pleasure.

It happened again several times.

About three weeks after I moved in George waited for me one night to tell me that he had been laid off. I was surprised, but I figured we could live on what I was making—a layoff was not forever, and I was not going to abandon my partner in his moment of need.

"That's alright," he said. "I'll be paid 90 percent of my salary while I'm laid off."

"Oh," I replied, somewhat disappointed. I was going to miss out on the opportunity to show him I was serious about my commitment to him and our relationship.

"But I have a problem," he said. "I've been sort of tight the past couple of months."

I wasn't sure what that meant. He didn't seem to have extraordinary debts other than mortgage payments and utilities, and he was making annually almost as much as I. His money was sure not going to clothes: his jeans and his underwear were full of holes, and the boots had needed new soles and heels for a long time before I first saw them. Groceries could not be the culprit either: I had been buying those since shortly after moving in. It would remain a mystery.

"How tight?"

"Well," he said, rubbing his chin and pulling on his beard, as he usually did when he couldn't come right out to say something. "I'm two months behind in my mortgage payments." He snorted.

"How big are your payments?" I asked.

"Two-hundred and forty-two a month." He was still rubbing his chin.

"That's not a problem," I said. "Do you want to borrow them to bring your payments up to date?"

He stared at me. "You would do that?"

"Sure. Don't worry about it."

"You know, I could ask my parents, but I've bothered them enough and—"

"It's okay," I said. "I'll have the money tomorrow."

The next day he stopped by my office to pick up the money. That afternoon when I got home he wasn't there. I looked out the window when I heard his car behind the house, by the garage. He started unloading a chest of drawers from the trunk; he rolled up the garage door and took the chest into it—where I didn't know, because the garage was filled to the ceiling with what I considered nothing but junk. He also unloaded some smaller pieces of furniture and, after putting them in the garage as well, rolled the door down and came into the house.

A few days later he waited until I got home, poured me a bourbon and water, and sat down to rub his chin.

"Is something wrong?" I asked.

"Hmmm. Gee. I really don't know how to say this."

"Go ahead and say it." I feared that he had gone back to Brad and I was on my way out, while I, dreading that so soon after I had moved in with him would be forced out of the house when the bank foreclosed on his mortgage, had hoped that my contribution to the financial health of the household had helped him get over Brad.

A few days earlier he had been listening to James Ingram singing *Just Once,* and suddenly had waxed nostalgic about Brad, pointing out that the song was just like Brad and him:

Just once, can we figure out
what we keep doing wrong,
why the good times never last for long,
where are we going wrong.

It did nothing to reassure me that his feelings for the hoodlum were completely dead.

"I got a letter from Northern States Power. I'm really behind in the gas and electricity bill."

With most of his paycheck still coming in, my $250 and Cindy's $100 monthly in rent should have made him very comfortable. I really was at a loss.

"How much?"

"Four-hundred." He looked at me with something that could have been interpreted as a sneer, but it was just George's expression for occasions when he was about to make an unreasonable request. That, and the chin thing.

"Oh. Well, don't worry about it. I'll take the money out of the bank tomorrow morning. You can stop by my office to pick it up around noon."

"Oh, okay," he said. "You know, maybe after a while you can buy into this house, and..."

"That's not necessary, George." I still owed a beach house in Puerto Rico; the last thing I wanted was another property, especially one I wouldn't have bought for myself.

"Well, I don't want you to think I'm taking advantage of you."

"I live here too, George. If they shut off power or foreclose on your mortgage, I'm out also. Besides, I'm your partner. I'm glad to help."

"I was thinking. Maybe tonight when I'm done working in the kitchen we can take a long shower together and—you know, have a romantic evening. What do you think?"

"Sounds good to me," I said, but I wasn't sure it was going to happen. George had said that he needed to work on his kitchen. He had been refinishing it for over a year. So far he had stripped the door frames, but he still had to paint walls and cupboards and replace the floor. All of the materials were in the house. He just needed to get going on it. In the meantime, he had disconnected the stove, which sat in the enclosed porch. This meant that nothing could be cooked unless it could be heated up in the microwave oven. Often I'd bring some frozen dinner to warm up, and he had yelled at me, "Can you wait on that? I'm still sanding here, and I don't want you to walk in here and track the dust back into the rest of the house." It seemed like a silly reason, considering that he had not dusted in weeks: he had sawdust in his hair and face all the time—often he went to bed without washing—and I had developed a serious sinus infection from inhaling the dust in a house completely shut to outside air because it was already cold.

I had lost twenty-some pounds and looked sick.

By the time he came up for the shower I was fast asleep.

The following afternoon George arrived home later than usual. He asked me to help him carry a pie chest into the house. He had spent the afternoon going to junk shops, looking for what he liberally called antiques.

By this time I was becoming concerned about the final destination of the funds I was withdrawing from my savings account.

"I paid half of the bill," he said. "They're okay with that, then next month I'll pay the other half."

"But next month you'll have this month's bill plus half of the pending one."

He lost his patience.

"You don't have to be afraid. I'll pay you back. You know, you should trust me a little more," he said.

It was not to be the last time I would hear someone asking me to place my trust in him, even in the face of evidence that trust should have been the last valuable I should have surrendered to him.

"I know you'll pay back, but I wouldn't like you to get so far over your head again that you won't be able to recover."

It was the wrong statement to make.

"Just because you're a company executive and have all those degrees, you know, that doesn't mean that the rest of us don't know how to manage our bills. I've done it for thirty-three years without you."

"That's right, George," I said sheepishly. "I'm sorry for my presumptuousness."

Another phenomenon had been developing during the previous month or so; it may have been happening before, but I only noticed it then. George's friends never called before stopping by. He felt it was rude to tell them we were busy. After all, I was only supposed to be rooming there, so it would be strange for his friends from work that he couldn't receive him in his home because he and I were doing something.

But it wasn't just friends from work. It was Peggy, his hair stylist, who often after work would stop by for a beer or a dozen with George. It was Sherry, one of Brad's closest friends, who showed up at all hours. And invariably, if we had made plans to go anywhere, sometimes to eat, since I was close to emaciation from inanition, our plans were canceled on the spot. Work on the kitchen would stop. George ran out for beer or whiskey and frozen appetizers, and within the hour the bass from the stereo speakers was cracking the foundation of the house. The visit had turned into a full-blown party.

A man from work, Juan, often stopped by with his girlfriend. Juan was supposedly straight, but from the dancing spectacles I started to wonder. George would crank up the volume to some Grace Jones album, and soon the girlfriend was sandwiched between George and Juan, bumping and grinding around the living room. Juan's eyes were fixed on George's, as if to say, "Hey, bitch, get out of the way so that I can get to whom I really want."

If I left to go eat something by myself, by the time I got back George was drunk and angry that I had gone out instead of staying in the house. If I stayed in the house I had to go into what was supposed to be my room, where instead the bass vibrations rattled my brain. When the visitors left, George would pass out on the sofa downstairs, and I was still hungry, but it was too late to go out to get something to eat.

When my birthday rolled around, George threw me a surprise party. I was particularly surprised, because none of my friends had been invited. The guests were people only George knew. Sherry and a fellow speech therapist enthralled the rest of the partygoers with their impressions of tracheotomy patients.

When the guests were gone George and I went to bed for another attempt at sex, and again he fell asleep while I was in him.

His drinking increased. Often by the time I got home from school or work he had already passed out. He drank everything he found, including a bottle of pineapple champagne that my parents had given me some years before from one of their trips to South America, and which I thought too vile to even open.

Nothing was going very well, but this was my first experience living with a partner, and, by God, I was going to make it work. It was up to me to get used to things I had not been exposed to before; it was most likely part of a same-sex relationship and with time I would learn to accept it as natural. The problem was my bad attitude and my inability to accept what was, after all, part of living with a gay lover.

One Saturday morning when Chrissy was sitting in the living room drinking coffee I sat down with her. George was playing the same ABBA album I listened to that other night in June.

When *Andante, Andante* came up, I remarked that it was the song George had played for me the first night I came over.

"I wouldn't be so excited if I were you," she said, paging absent-mindedly through some magazine. "He plays that song for all the tricks he brings home."

I foolishly told George later in the day, when he was drinking from a pint of some Jamaican rum whose brand was unknown to me.

"You shouldn't pay attention to Chrissy." He looked at me in anger. "What, now you're going to judge me by what she says?"

Cindy was less forgiving. She broke up with Chrissy, and then showed up two days later with Martha, a cab driver about a foot shorter than Cindy and with the meanest puss I had seen in years. Cindy moved out to live with Martha, but was back within a week after Martha gave her a beating for forgetting to bring home dinner from Kentucky Fried Chicken.

Three days later George rubbed his chin again. The bank was reminding him of another late payment. I made the usual trip to the bank, he made the usual junk shop rounds.

The next day Cindy made up with Chrissy, who again roamed the house and went through everyone's dressers.

The night of December eighth was my last night of school, and I'd be home early. Before I left for work that morning, and prior to George's first drink of the day, I told him that I'd be done with my degree that night, and I wanted to take him out to dinner to celebrate.

The streets were covered with snow that had been falling relentlessly throughout the day. I was approaching Como from Dale Street, a busy artery that I figured would be more difficult to drive on than some of the other side streets. On University Avenue I turned left onto Victoria and then right to Sherburne.

In front of a house down the street I noticed a white Firebird with a dented fender and a rusty bumper. I slowed down, but didn't stop. It was George's, who had called me late that afternoon at work to tell me that he was going to visit with his parents early in the evening, in case he wasn't home when I got there. But his parents lived on Sherwood Avenue in West St. Paul, not on Sherburne.

I drove on home, picked up the telephone directory and looked up Brad Pembroke's address. Though I really didn't need the confirmation, it hurt my eyes to see what I had hoped was not what I suspected.

I was disappointed, enraged, anxious, and it was difficult to separate one emotion from the other. I walked to the corner liquor store and bought a quart of whiskey, which I took home and drank like water.

I picked up the phone and called George at Brad's. When he came to the phone I asked, "So your parents moved?" I hung up before he could reply.

I went to my room and sat on the floor with my half-empty bottle of whiskey. A few minutes later George arrived. He stormed into my room.

"What the fuck was that about?" His nostrils were flaring up, his eyes were out of their orbits, and his voice sounded like something not of this world. "You made a fool of yourself, calling Brad. I wasn't doing anything, you know. I was there picking up some material I left there when I moved back here."

"Why didn't you tell me you were going there?"

"Because it's none of your fucking business. I was going to tell you anyway. You want to control me, uh? Is that what you want to do? I was bragging about you, how good you were to me, and like an idiot you call there and embarrass me and make an ass of yourself."

He was towering above me. In my drunkenness his body looked bigger and his biceps, above the finger he was pointing at my face, looked stronger and very threatening.

"I don't want to control anything. I expected honesty."

His face was turning purple, and the finger was getting closer to my nose.

"Honesty? What the fuck do I have to lie about? I was going to my parents' house and thought I'd stop over at Brad's to pick up some material I had left there." I wondered when the material evidence would surface, but I never did see it. "You have made a fucking fool of yourself. And I'm tired of it," he said as if it had been a habit of mine to make a bigger fool of myself than I had been by making frequent trips to the bank. "I'm tired of this shit, and I'm tired of your fucking jealousy, and I'm tired of your fucking children calling here every fucking night, and I'm tired of your fucking wife calling you whenever she fucking feels like it, I'm fucking tired of it."

"I can understand, George," I said when I felt the tip of his index finger actually pressing against my nostrils. "I really can. I would be tired of all that myself if I were you. Hell, I get tired of all that calling all the time. I know how you feel."

"That's fucking right."

"I'm very sorry, George. I know I made an ass of myself, and now I know how stupid it was of me to offend you by calling there. I'm so sorry."

"You damn well better be. And that shit better not happen again."

The following morning I was busy in my office looking at apartment ads. I spent four more days waiting eagerly for the Sunday want ads, where I was hoping to locate a place to move to, no matter how small, as long as I could feel safe again. I had thought when I moved in with George that I was not going to be able to support my family and pay for a place of my own, but after almost five months of spending more than if I had rented a luxury penthouse, I figured I certainly could pay for a clean place where I could be by myself.

December twentieth I finally found a studio apartment on Lincoln Avenue, about three miles south of George's house of mirth. I came back to George's at noon, sat with him and explained that although I wanted us to pursue our relationship, I felt that we had moved in together too soon and had not had a chance to determine how that would work.

He seemed to understand. At least he didn't make any remarks. He only wanted to know when I'd be moving.

"December twenty-third," I replied. Actually, I was not going to be able to move until January second, but I had decided to get out and sleep on my wife's apartment floor until my place became available.

That evening when I walked up the steps I could have sworn he was waiting by the door to make sure my entrance coincided with his departure. He stepped out wearing leather chaps over worn out jeans torn at the crotch, a leather vest over a black T-shirt, and a leather cap. He turned the corner of the house; had he really wanted to simply leave and head for the bar, he could have left by the kitchen door. This was an act meant to put me in my place and show me that he didn't need me.

I stayed up until I heard his car, which he parked in front of the house instead of next to the cluttered garage. When I looked out the window I noticed another car parked right behind his. I recalled that normally he parked behind the house. Only when he wanted someone to know that he could still go out and pick anyone up to bring home did he park in front of the house. He had done it to Brad, in case he continued to stalk George the night he left the bar with me. He was doing it now.

I felt as if I had been sitting under a dump truck that had opened the gate and let manure slide down until I was totally buried under it.

Andante, Andante piped out of the speakers.

A while later the two of them walked up the stairs. George locked the door behind him. When I started to hear moaning that was only for my benefit—unless he had fallen asleep again—I turned off the light, slipped on my earphones and turned my stereo's volume up. About an hour later I heard the front door slam, and I knew the trick was leaving.

On the evening of December twenty-third I packed my belongings in my car. I left a box of small potted plants that George had given me on the porch, to load last and thus avoid bruising them.

George's car was parked in back, but he wasn't in the house. I wanted to say good-bye, but I assumed he had gone to his friend Pat's, a retired gay naval officer who lived down the street. I left the door key on a table in the foyer and locked the door behind me.

A month later George called me around two in the morning to accuse me of busting his windshield while it was parked behind The Happy Hour.

"No, George, I wouldn't do something like that."

"Yes, you would and you did, because you hate me. I'm going to send the cops out to get you, too."

I remembered that I was dealing with a nut. It was necessary to control myself, soothe him and bring him down.

"George, you are the man I have loved the most in my life, and even if we didn't work out, I still have strong feelings for you." Strong feelings indeed.

"No one else could have done this," he insisted. "I had to drive all the way from Minneapolis with cold air blowing in my face."

And drunk, I thought of adding, with pieces of glass blowing into the car.

"There are a lot of crazy people out there, George. Who knows. And even if I had wanted to do something as horrible as that, I haven't even left my apartment today. My car didn't start." It was true: for the first time that winter my engine had not started. It had been so cold, and so many people had had car trouble, that I couldn't get a starting service to come out.

"Then you paid someone to do it."

"George? I don't know anyone who would do something like that. Besides, you know that my financial situation is pretty bad right now. I don't have enough money to have people running after you to damage your property."

"I know I owe you money. You don't have to rub my nose in it. How much do I owe you? About 500. I know it. You don't have to throw it at my face."

Five-hundred?

"That's not what I'm saying, George. I'm saying that I don't have any desire to hurt you like that, and I lack the means to go do something like that even if I wanted to."

He quieted down, but only for a moment.

"You hate me. You know how I know? The plants I gave you? You wouldn't even take them when you moved. You left them in the porch so that the cold air coming into the mail chute would kill them slowly. That was twisted."

The plants! It was true that I hadn't missed them. My apartment was so small that even plants would have cluttered it up worse than it was. But the truth was that I had meant to take them with me. I had placed them by the porch door, but when I opened the door to take some other bags out, the plants were hidden behind the door and I forgot about them.

Good God, now George thought that I had tried to finish them off slowly, painfully, until they screeched and withered before exhaling their last gasp, burned by the cold air that blew agonizingly frigid through the mail slot.

"I'm sorry, George. I meant to bring them with me. I just forgot them behind the door."

Another uneasy silence.

"After you left I sat down and wrote down this poem about you. I have it right here: Now you want to be loved, but you want to be free..."

The poem was the theme song from *Live for Life*. Now he was plagiarizing also.

"I guess the timing was not right, George. Neither of us was to blame."

"I guess you're right. I was going to send the police over to get you, but it doesn't sound like you did it." Pause. "Well, I got to go to bed. The windows are open in the kitchen here. I'm using the heating element to strip the walls and took out the windows, and now I can't shut them." He was yawning. His next electricity bill was going to do him in.

"I'm sorry that you've had to go through this, George."

He hung up. I took a deep breath, but didn't sleep the rest of the night.

As usual, when friends find out that the relationship has ended, they come to tell you how relieved they are that you are no longer involved with that cuckoo bird and how much better off you are without the jerk, because it just wasn't right. Ian Scott told me that George, Cindy and Sherry had mocked me behind my back for wearing preppie shirts. Jerry Burbee told me that George's lover Jim, the upholsterer, was a married man. One day when George was angry because Jim wouldn't stay longer with him, George had called Jim's wife to tell her that he was her husband's male lover. Jim Well's wife threw him out, and he lost all contact with his daughters. And Kris Swenson had the juicy stories about George in S&M orgies in Joe Gunther's basement.

The following June I was coming out of the building where my wife and children were living in St. Paul. I found George hunched over the list of tenants. I thought he was looking for some trick he was coming to visit and whose name or apartment number he couldn't recall. I wasn't far from the truth.

"Hi there, George," I said, meaning to walk past him.

"Oh, hello. I was looking for you."

He might as well have said he was looking for the Prophet.

"Oh?" What had happened to his windshield now?

"I was wondering if, well…" O-oh, there was that chin getting rubbed again. "If we could get together again."

Now he really had gone totally bonkers.

"Uhm—could we talk about this?"

We sat in his car. He had been thinking about us, and perhaps it was time to see whether we could go back together. He had missed me a lot. What did I think—hmm, uh—about it?

You must be absolutely, definitely, undeniably bonkers—that's what I thought. Perhaps the best response would be to tell him that I would gladly go back to him if he repaid me the thousands of dollars he owed me or at least paid it back in sexual sessions in which he remained awake without the need of a cattle prod. And if he stopped drinking everything short of turpentine. Maybe then I would consider it.

He invited me over to his house that Saturday night. Everything was pretty much the same, with the stove in the porch and the kitchen as if a tornado had gone through and left the dust undisturbed. We sat in the living room—I was praying to God almighty that *Andante, Andante* would not blare out of the speakers. I really didn't know what I was doing there, but I suspect I was hopeful that I would see at least some of my money again.

The addition of a fish tank to the living room puzzled me.

"That belongs to this guy," he said, and his hand went back to the chin. There was a story here. "He's a teacher in a small Catholic school around here somewhere."

This stranger was dumping fish tanks around town?

"He went home to Iowa for the summer and left some of his stuff stored here."

A-ha.

"Is he going to be rooming here in the fall?"

"I don't know." He was going to grow calluses on his chin. "This guy." He paused and snorted. "We met about two weeks ago and, I don't know." He squinted and shook his hand horizontally. "I—I picked him up at The Gay 90s, and we came here. When he walked into the house his eyes popped, and he said, 'I can't believe I walked into all this.'"

That alone told me what he had not walked out of.

I was keeping quiet and encouraging George with my facial expressions.

"He wants a relationship, but I don't know." Again he squinted and contorted his face. "He said that if I didn't want a relationship he'd want to room here anyway. I don't know what to do."

This prompted the unarticulated question, what is my role in all this?

"I told him that I still had feelings—" he paused, looked at me and held my hands. "I said, I said, 'I just broke up with someone, and I'm not sure I'm ready for a relationship with someone other than him.'"

"Oh?" The picture was becoming clear. "Oh."

We went upstairs and sat in bed, watching television and eating canned chili he had heated up in the microwave oven.

I still didn't know what I was doing there. Perhaps it was curiosity about this bizarre twist in a relationship I no longer thought about except in terms of hurt and insanity. Around midnight I went home without even an offer of sex, which was quite alright with me.

The next day was Father's Day. George invited me to come over in the evening, after he had had his parents over for a barbecue party. When I got there he still had some charred hot dogs and some of the same chili that had made me sick the night before.

George summoned me to his house the following Thursday night; I had not heard from him since Sunday.

After we were done eating the third iteration of chili he started to rub his chin.

"Uh-her-uhm." He chuckled. "I have to tell you something. I'm really torn between you and this guy." The guy was still a party that was to remain nameless. "He called me this morning, and I told him that you and I had been together Sunday night."

Where this was going was a total mystery, but it was getting so weird that I could not take my ears off it. It was like a hideous road accident that would imprint itself in blood and guts on your brain forever, but you still had to look. I only knew for certain that I did not want to have anything else to do with this psychopathic drunk, and I was letting myself get dangerously close to a dead end in a very dark alley.

"So, George, what exactly do you want to do?"

"I don't know."

It suddenly struck me what he was trying to accomplish. I was going to be of use again, just like I had been during the most grotesque five months of my life, to push away someone whom George feared was after his unrivaled mansion. What was so difficult about his decision? Could it be that George had actually fallen in love with the mystery meat?

"I don't know if I can have him stay here. He doesn't make any money." And it was a well-known fact that whoever lived in that house and shared George's bed needed a substantial bank roll. Suddenly and very surprisingly George said, "He has a cock this big." His hands were about a foot away from each other.

I figured I was nothing more than a sounding board for George to weigh the advantages and drawbacks of a relationship with the horse-hung teacher. On the one hand, poverty; on the other.

"Do you think you've decided then, George?"

"Uh-her-hmm. I'll tell you what. I need a few days."

It was true that I had no interest in this travesty, especially since I had already had a bitter taste of what was in store for me if I made this mistake again. And I could even end up sharing the house with the would-be lover. If I were that stupid all over again. But I was in the vortex of pure absurdity: George was going to decide whether I had better attributes than the fish-tank man. George was going to decide. George had attributed that power to himself.

"I'm going to Chicago tomorrow," I said, although I had just then decided to make the trip. I'll be gone for the weekend. When I get back Sunday night I'll give you a call. Do you think that by then you'll have made your choice?"

"Hmm. I don't know. And, you know, I don't want to leave you hanging, but I don't want to rush into any decision. You understand, don't you?"

Me? Would I understand? I was nothing if I wasn't understanding.

On my return from Chicago I called George. He had made his decision. The school teacher had won over me. He was sorry, but he had really thought about it and it was the best for all of us.

I tried to sound disappointed, but not too disappointed. I didn't want him to go on another spin, wondering whether he had made the right choice.

I wished him luck—I hoped that this guy would be everything he deserved.

"I mean that," I said, and hung up.

Lesson: It's not up to you to go out of your way to perpetuate your own misery. If it smells like dung, feels like dung and tastes like dung—don't spend so much time trying to guess what else it could be.

Day 10:

Whine and Dine

Before it disbanded due to excessive bickering over the comparative worth of home-cooked meals vis-a-vis supermarket deli victuals that members were picking up thoughtlessly, CAMP was the place to be the evening of the third Sunday of every month. Its members met for a pot-luck dinner and to socialize with other gay men of diverse occupations and age groups. CAMP (Cities' Association of Male Professionals) was Minneapolis' answer to the more exclusive and decidedly snobbish ARMS, St. Paul's Alexander Ramsey Memorial Society.

CAMP was a true rainbow, ethnically, occupationally, agewise, a testimonial to the diversity that negates any attempt to place us in a monolithic category. We had our retired theater professor, who upon widowing came out with a tempestuous blast, and grabbed his twinkies along the way. We had married men who told their wives they were "going out with the boys" when they were really going out with boys. We had a Mormon pediatrician whose wife hated his lover but was not about to leave their eight children fatherless just because he occasionally needed a taste of male genitalia— she'd page him constantly when she knew the two men were together. We had bank vice presidents, financiers, attorneys, cooks who fancied themselves chefs, and hustler apprentices. We had Bruce Brockway, who later became the first known casualty of AIDS in Minnesota, and his Mariel boatlift boyfriend. And we had Maury Weinberger.

Maury was a high school art teacher who was also trained as an actor. He had deceivingly sad eyes that followed my every more around the buffet table during a CAMP meeting on Sunday, February 14, 1982. He got a mutual acquaintance to introduce us. We chatted amicably; suddenly he started to pressure me to go home with him. The party was a bust, it would be quieter at his place, not too far from there, we could have a nice conversation, enjoy a glass of wine, listen to jazz.

Our rainbow included those who didn't bother to conceal their attendance at monthly CAMP gatherings to drop off a Jell-O mold and try to pick up someone soon thereafter. Maury was in that camp.

"I'm sorry," I said. "I just got out of a harrowing experience and I'm not sure I want to jump into bed with someone this soon." CAMP had been an alternative to hanging out in bars meeting jerks and possibly running into the person I had just broken up with.

"I'm not asking for a relationship. It's only sex."

At least when we met he was honest enough to say so. Actually, his problem was not honesty, it was the brutal indiscretion of his honesty. I, on the other hand, believed that other people could be honest or brutal with me, but not simultaneously.

I looked at him and said, "It doesn't matter. Tonight is just not the night I want to do that."

"Will you find another night when you might? Like tomorrow night?"

I didn't want to reply. I was not responding well to ultimatums. Had I wanted them I wouldn't have left the relationship I had just blasted out of. Standing in a corner and feeling as if Maury had both arms around me to restrain me I felt smothered.

"Right now I just know it's time for me to leave."

I looked at the clock across the hall. I had only been there ten minutes, if that.

"May I walk you to your car?" Maury asked.

"I think the neighborhood is safe enough, but thanks anyway."

"Just to say good night."

"I don't think that's a good idea."

"You won't know unless you've tried it."

"Okay."

I thanked the host and left with Maury trailing behind me, the way johns rush to their cars after agreeing on a price with a hooker. It bothered me. Walking out with my catch on the hook, or impaled in someone's harpoon, what the hell—that's not what I was there for. Leaving a party so soon after getting there with someone I had just met, how gauche—worse than a deli party tray. Perhaps Maury was used to it. I felt like a tramp.

I stood by the driver's side of my car without opening the door as he walked to the passenger's side. From my side he looked like a rendition of the devil with his parka hood covering his head and the contoured thin beard running from one ear to the other. I realized he had expected me to drop the coy act: I couldn't be that dumb.

But I had been.

I let him into the car, he grew several arms and wasting no time plunged into my mouth with his tongue.

"I'm uncomfortable doing this here, Maury."

"The windows are steamed up."

"Wait!" I pushed him back. "I meant it when I said I wasn't ready for this. I can call you tomorrow, maybe some other night. But tonight I just want to go home."

He looked like a love-starved puppy. A Rottweiler puppy. His voice changed to the tone I was to get to know so well, one meant to make me feel like the world's biggest louse for depriving him of the pound of happiness he so richly deserved. Except that he really demanded a couple of tons.

"If that's how you want it." It was clear that he was at least forty, but his hair was jet black. The lines around his eyes became deeper with his disappointment.

For a minute he had me. But I dug myself out.

"I have to go home."

On a promise that I would call him the next day he got out of my car.
At nine Monday morning Beverly, my secretary, took his call.

"If the mountain won't come to Maurice…"

He confused me for a second. Then I realized that was his full name,
except that he pronounced it with a decidedly francophile accent that I
found ludicrous. I recognized the trained tenor who was determined to
make sure I would not resist him. It wasn't resistance as much as the need
to get it over with. I had a feeling that Maury was simply in need of a good
roll, and I happened to be an easy target.

I suggested getting together the following evening, but Maury was
busy. A former student of his who was now attending the University of
Minnesota at Duluth was in town and Maury had bought tickets to *The
Cookie Jar* for the two of them. The young man had just graduated high
school the previous spring. Maury had been waiting for this opportunity.
Maury had been grooming him to be an artist, giving him special attention and nurturing his talent. It would be the boy's graduation present.

Back then I was ignorant enough to buy the line.

We settled on Friday night that week. I spent the night hoping that
some other student needed special treatment and Maury would call to
postpone indefinitely. It didn't happen.

His was a small house on a postage-stamp lot some blocks away from
Lake Nokomis. He had finished the attic into a large bedroom. One of the
two small bedrooms on the first floor was a miniscule den where he had
squeezed a love seat and a TV stand.

Everywhere we turned we were followed (I was also sniffed constantly)
by his Cairn Terrier, Picasso. Picasso could not stop licking any patch of
exposed flesh on my arms.

The window curtains were so heavy and dense that at noon it felt like
dusk. I noticed how disproportionately big the living room was, furnished
with Ida Morgenstern's sofa.

"I chose this house to fit a grand piano."

"You play, then?"

"No. Someone else's piano." His eyes glazed over.

He had been involved with Alex for over six years. He wanted Alex to move in with him, but Alex always had some excuse, the last of which was that he wouldn't move in with Maury unless it were to Maury's own house.

Maury examined his assets, contacted a realtor and started out on the house hunting venture. Alex came along. Just when Maury and the realtor thought they had found the ideal house, Alex came up with some objection. The most consistent was that the house was too small for his grand piano.

Alex had majored in piano performance in college, but was a clerk at the University of Minnesota. He considered his training important enough to maintain it, even if his only performances were at wedding receptions and piano bars around the Twin Cities.

Finally they found this house where Maury now lived. It was perfect. Maury would have the upstairs room to maintain a flimsy semblance of heterosexuality when his parents came to dinner, and Alex could have the larger of the two bedrooms downstairs. The living room was large enough to accommodate the grand piano and a sofa.

Alex approved of the house and Maury signed his life away on a mortgage. After closing he asked Alex when he'd be ready to move in.

"I'm not going to move in, Maury. I'm sorry, but I just can't."

Maury was completely dumbfounded.

"You're telling me that now after I bought the house to your specs?"

"I can't."

Maury continued to pressure him for a better explanation.

"I've been seeing someone else for the past six months."

Maury froze to his seat.

"When have you been seeing this other person?"

"During the week."

"When you were busy practicing your piano technique and didn't have time for me."

Alex nodded without raising his head. "It just happened."

"What's his name? What does he do? Is he better looking than me?"

"That's not fair."

"Okay, what's his name? What does he do?"

"His name is Jesse. He's a waiter at the Lincoln Dell."

"A waiter at the Lincoln Dell. He must do something better than me. What is it?" He was pissed now.

"He's my age. Close, anyway. Twenty-six."

"Oh, so now I'm the old fart. Why wasn't I the old coot before? I bet he has a car."

"That has nothing to do with anything."

"Of course it does. You wouldn't date anyone without a car to drive you to your fucking engagements."

"If you're gonna get ugly I'll get up and leave."

Maury got ugly. Alex got up and left, and Maury just sat there lonely and hearing the loud hiss of air escaping his deflating ego.

His curiosity got the best of him and the following Saturday he went to the Lincoln Dell to see who this Jesse was. He must have worked weekends when Maury and Alex were spending time together. When he saw Jesse his ego felt like a Mylar balloon after someone has sucked the helium out of it and its wrinkled walls stick together.

"Where does he shop for clothes, the boys' department at Dayton's? The man wears Garanimals, for God's sake," he told Alex over the phone. "He's got the body of a ten year old."

"Stop deriding him, Maury. It doesn't become you."

For a couple of weeks Maury and Alex stopped talking to each other. Then Maury asked him to dinner. Nothing was going to happen. He just wanted to get together and mend their friendship. Something had to be worth saving after all the time they had spent together. From then on they had gone out to dinner once a month. Alex had gone on with his life, and he was stuck in his. It was a sad story of betrayal and broken promises, but I was beginning to understand that the world was full of them and Maury's wouldn't be the last one I'd hear.

Three glasses of wine later we ended up in his converted attic. Maury was about four inches shorter than I, but he decided that he was going to prove himself a sexual giant. He failed, but I pretended it had been wonderful.

He went downstairs to wash off, and I lay in bed face down. Suddenly I felt him licking my ass. And then I heard his footsteps up the stairs. I turned around and found Picasso panting between my legs.

I let out a yelp. Maury knew exactly what had happened.

"Picasso, no! Get down. Honest, I don't know how this dog learned that. It's so embarrassing."

I had grown up in a household full of Dalmatians and Alsatians, and none of them had ever climbed in bed to lick anything other than my face. This was not genetically imprinted in canines: this was the product of training.

I should have picked up my cue from Picasso and never returned.

But I did return. Two weeks later anyone would have thought we had been in item for years. He started buying theater tickets without consulting me, as if he knew my tastes and took my availability for granted. He would also expect me to reimburse him for my ticket.

No movie premiere could escape him. It was a religious duty that transcended Sabbath rites.

"Do you have to attend every movie that first opens?" I asked him one day when he insisted that we go to the first screening of *Quest for Fire* in Bloomington and then go to the Lincoln Dell for dinner. I really didn't feel like a movie that night. And I felt that he wanted dinner at the Lincoln Dell for show and tell purposes. I guess I should have felt flattered that he wanted to show me off to Jesse so that he could go back with gossip to Alex, presumably at home practicing his chords.

"Yes, I do."

At the theater he would often run into other members of a failed and frustrated thespian community in the Twin Cities, which he seemed to preside. He introduced me to one of the women one night at a performance of *True West* at the Hennepin Center for the Performing Arts. She had just returned from Spain and, being a country I had spent every child-hood summer visiting, she and I established a dialogue to which Maury could not contribute.

After the show he was sullen and disagreeable.

"What have I done?" I asked. I was still in that stage where everything negative had to be my responsibility.

"Why do you always try to steal my friends?"

"I beg your pardon?"

"You did it tonight. You took over the conversation and left me out. You did it with Eileen at The Rainbow Café last week. Every time you meet a friend of mine you end up monopolizing them."

"Are we competing for friends?"

"That's what you're doing."

"Why do you introduce me to them?"

"What do you mean why do I introduce you to them? You're with me."

"And then after I'm introduced I'm supposed to do like an Arab wife, step back and live under your shadow? What the hell is that about?"

"No, you can participate. Just don't monopolize."

It wasn't the only time we'd have a similar exchange. I opted for doing exactly what I thought he had wanted me to do, receded to the back-ground and only said, "Nice meeting you" when we were walking away.

I thought he'd notice I was overreacting and call me on it. On the contrary, he seemed more content than ever.

"I think we should buy a VCR," he said one fine day.

"I don't need a VCR."

"But think of all the movies we could watch at home."

"I don't need a VCR."

"Why not? Don't you like movies?"

"Yes, but I don't need a VCR." What I didn't need was the expense, which at the time was more than my budget could handle. All those the-ater tickets started to make a severe dent on my resources, especially since

I was never consulted before they were purchased and was just stuck with the bill, sometimes for shows I had no interest in seeing.

"Okay. I'll pay for half, you pay for half. Then you can have full access to it when you move in, and we can watch movies together." Maury had already decided that I was going to move into the empty room downstairs and in preparation for it I had to change my mailing address and notify the bank. I wasn't sure I wanted to do that, but I didn't want to make waves and risk losing the only thing I had going.

"How much is a VCR?"

"Five-hundred."

He went out and bought the VCR he wanted to buy where he wanted to buy it. I handed him the two-fifty.

The first movie we watched together was a porn tape we got at a rental place on Lake Street. He specified which to get and asked me to run in to get it. I had never rented an adult film and foresaw the awkwardness of taking it to the counter where the clerk would know I was queer from the type of films I was renting, as if I were the first and only one to rent them.

"Why don't we both go in? I'm not the one who wants to see it."

"I can't go in there. I teach here. The store clerk's son could be one of my students. They know me around here."

"But I don't want to watch the stupid thing. You go get it."

"Why are you becoming so difficult?" he asked almost with sincerity.

"Fine, I'll go in."

The movie was a grainy copy of an eight-millimeter reeler featuring dirt-blonde scrawny teens letting their hormones control them in some isolated beach. I watched it with interest, not for its prurient value, but because I couldn't believe that the advances that filmmaking had made in the '30s had not yet reached the film's producers. Maury couldn't have enough of it.

Just as I had rented it, I had to return it while Maury waited in the car outside. I was to collect the ten-dollar refund.

"We're charging you two bucks for not rewinding," the clerk yelled out at me. I felt that the multitude of four or five people in the store turned their accusatory eyes at me and were ready to stone me for being queer and not being kind enough to rewind.

In mid-April, while driving to Chicago in the middle of a freak snow-storm that blew one of the headlight covers off my car, Maury notified me that he was going to China in August and would need me to move into the house by then so that I could sit both the house and Picasso.

"How long are you going to be gone?"

"Two weeks."

"You know, sometimes I have to travel for business. What if your trip coincides with a business trip I can't postpone?"

"You're the businessman. You know how to handle those things."

"But—"

"This is a once in a lifetime opportunity for me. I really want to do this, and I already made the down payment. If I cancel now I'll lose the 500 bucks."

I quickly noticed that I had not been asked to come along, which I was thankful for—after all, if a few theater tickets were eating up my savings, a trip to China would force me into Loring Park to join the throngs of male prostitutes. Nonetheless, I immediately realized that if I were to come along neither house nor rimming dog would have a sitter.

"I suppose I have no problem with that."

In Chicago we stayed at the Radisson, which shared indoor athletic facilities with the Chicago Athletic Club. I was thrilled to be able to go swimming while a late winter storm raged outside and asked Maury to come along.

He gave me a dirty look. "I don't swim in swimming pools."

"Hmm. I hope you don't mind if I go down for a while."

I enjoyed my time by myself in the water, doing a few laps and enjoying the view of so many fit men exercising their buff bodies. It was not something I had enjoyed before when I had been involved with someone:

once my eyes focused on my partner I lost all interest in other potential candidates. Maury made it necessary for me to feel I needed to look elsewhere. Or maybe it was just a cheap excuse I gave myself for looking at everything I was depriving myself of. Something was wrong with the picture. I wondered when I'd get enough courage to straighten it out or at least get another hook to balance it with.

Late in May Maury asked me to go to Odegard's Books to buy a picture book for a birthday present. While he chose, I wandered off to the gay and lesbian rack to take a look at the new titles.

"I wanted you to help me pick a book out," he came back and fired off at me.

"I'm sorry. What are you looking for?"

He was looking for a book on Hungary, one of those Time Life wannabes with lots of pictures on the bargain table, of which Odegard's had precious few.

"For whom are you buying this?" I asked.

"For Alex. It's his birthday next week."

Alex? Grand piano Alex?

"Why are you buying him a present?"

"It's his birthday."

"That part I got. Isn't this the guy who did you dirt by betraying you with someone else and screwed you over after you bought a house for the two of you? That Alex?"

"Oh, I don't hold a grudge. We've been able to mend fences. That's why we go to dinner once a month."

"You've been taking Alex to dinner once a month since we've been dating?"

"Didn't I tell you? I thought you knew."

Obviously this was happening on those nights when I had decided I needed time to myself. What else was going on while I was on the other side of the Mississippi?

"I hope you don't think anything funny's going on. It's strictly platonic."

Naturally, it didn't escape me that platonic meant that no one did anything physical, although the attraction was present.

"At first we did, but not anymore," Maury said.

"You did what?"

"He and I had sex after he and Jesse moved in together."

I hadn't eaten yet, but I was beginning to feel the overwhelming urgency of revulsion hitting me just below the diaphragm.

"I told Alex that he owed me. He had pulled this surprise on me without giving me a chance to adjust to the change. So he agreed to come over to my house and we'd have sex, and then go to dinner, and I'd drive him home afterwards."

"And Jesse knew this."

"Oh-oh, no, no, no. No way."

"So Alex cheated on you with Jesse and then fucked you out of pity until you could get back on your feet? So to speak."

"He did owe me, don't you think?"

"I don't know what to think."

The night before the Wednesday when Alex was to be feted I still had not been invited to share the evening and deliver the present I had helped find—not at Odegard's, but at a Waldenbooks downtown St. Paul where I had found the book one day during my lunch hour. Surprisingly enough, I had not been asked to pay for half of it.

Before I left for the evening Maury said, "We won't be able to see each other tomorrow."

My expectation of an invitation was thus responded to. "Why not?"

"After school I have to pick up Alex at work. He doesn't have a car, you know. Then we're going to a Chinese restaurant in Wayzata, one that he really likes. Afterwards we're coming back here for dessert and to watch *All About Eve*, that I'm going to rent—it's Alex's favorite movie."

It happened to be my favorite movie as well, but Maury had never asked me which mine was.

"After the movie I'll drive him home, and then I'll just be too tired and will want to go to bed."

So not only was I not going to dinner, but I had to stay away lest I contaminate the pristine experience of Alex's excellent adventure.

"Am I ever going to meet Alex?" I asked.

"I don't know. I don't feel comfortable with that."

"There's nothing between the two of you, he's moved on, I'm your lover and I can't meet him because you don't feel comfortable."

"I can't explain it."

The man who could rattle on and on ad nauseam about Loni Anderson's acting disabilities—they had been classmates at the U and she only got good roles because of her tits, don't you know—and every insignificant high school production of *Our Town* for hours couldn't explain why I couldn't meet his ex-lover.

"And when I move in here, am I going to have to leave for the night until Alex and you are done with your dinner?"

He shrugged. "I don't know what I'm going to do then," he replied in earnest.

Again I had to give it to him that he was honest in his creepiness. At least he wasn't leading me on with a more considerate yet dishonest statement more along the lines of what I would have preferred to hear.

The early-June night he was out with Alex on their platonic rendezvous I threw on my jeans and polo shirt, slipped into my cowboy boots and headed for The Town House on University Avenue. It was Wednesday night, cheapie night, and the jumpiest night of the week. I had plenty of fifty-cent bottles of Miller Light, and while I was spinning around under the disco lights with a friend I had not seen in over a year, I caught a glimpse of a very sexy man smiling at me from the sidelines.

When *She Works Hard for Her Money* blended into some slow song meant to cater to the female element and to some brand-new male couple, I walked toward the back to unload some beer. I turned around and met the sexy man face to face. Without thinking I sank my tongue in his mouth—he did likewise.

"Meet me outside in about five minutes," I said, "and I'll follow you to your place."

And that was exactly what I did.

The next day while Maury was at work I stopped by his house to pick up the few items I had left there: three of Nat King Cole's Spanish albums, a couple of shorts and a T-shirt. I left the house key on the kitchen table with a note telling him I was no longer interested in seeing him, and reminded him to forward me my half of the VCR money as soon as possible.

He called; I refused to take his calls.

He sent me a cassette tape wrapped in a money order for the VCR. The tape featured a cavernous voice asking, "Why, Joe, why have you done this to me?" He had tried to crack his voice, but it hadn't worked. No wonder he was an unemployed actor who needed to thank his lucky stars that he had a full-time job teaching high school art. The recording made me laugh. It was creepy and hammy.

Why? What bothered him the most was the loss of a sitter for house and dog while he went to China, I figured. And if he couldn't figure out why, I wasn't about to waste my time explaining. I remembered a saying I learned from Dominican nuns in parochial school, "Never try to teach a pig to sing. It wastes your time and annoys the pig."

At the Sun Disco the following week I saw him following me around, standing in the shadows playing a silently plaintive song I was supposed to hear, the way dogs hear what humans can't. I laughed at his face.

My friend Ian was with me. I pointed him out as the man who had tried to convince me that I was unfair for expecting him to respect me.

"The one with the rug?" Ian asked.

"What? No, no. That one over there by the column."

"Yeah, with the rug."

It was the first time I had noticed that Maury wore a thick rug. No wonder he had never allowed me to touch his head. I thought it was just a kink of his. And that day in Chicago—of course he couldn't swim! He probably dyed the rest of his hair that wasn't woven to a stinky pad. His vanity would have suffered a real blow if people had seen his peroxide strands turn orange, sticking out from under the roadkill on his head.

And I thought I had already seen it all.

Lesson: If he's not comfortable with you by his side, perhaps comfort is not the issue. Could it be that he wants to have his birthday cake and eat it too?

Day 11:

Off the Meat Rack

Milwaukee was behind me, and I was getting closer to Chicago. It was late on a Saturday night.

My relationship with George had been over since December, my five-month mistake with Marty Weinberger was also over, and I had just witnessed how my closeted lover of five years was living a life of inauthenticity and denial that I didn't wish on a dog. Well, maybe on the dog he was.

I didn't want to go back to the Holiday Inn. It wasn't too late to take a stroll on North Clark Street. I had heard a lot of nastiness about The Gold Coast, and that night I wanted to see some of it first-hand. A second hand would be alright too.

It was nothing more than a butcher shop. Many of the patrons were in leather. Some confirmed that it was a pity to undress one cow to dress another. Others were selling both the steak *and* the sizzle. The air was thick was cigarette smoke and the stench of booze, but the most persistent odor was that of human skin glazed by the sweat of an early-summer heat. I was not out for romance that night. I was out for sleazy, no-strings-attached sex with one of those gorgeous men. If I had to go into The Pit, where only leather or Levi's was accepted attire, I was wearing just the right stuff for it. But I would not leave that bar without a side of beef. On the hoof.

The walls were lined up with men. Some cruised by, stopped and unhooked their slab, then walked out with it. I got a beer and stood against a spot recently vacated by some lucky hunk of beef. Shortly afterwards one of those hunky black-haired guys with an abundant moustache and a body that screams at you, "Take me here, take me now, then get off me and get lost forever," stopped across the way from me at the bar. He was taking swigs of his beer, standing with his back to the bar and staring at me.

I played coy for about fifteen seconds, then smiled. He really was, after all, smiling at me, not at the other two men standing beside me.

He walked over and unhooked me.

The view from his apartment was spectacular, but I suspected only at night, since it was the unobstructed panorama of the West Side of Chicago. But the lights looked nice against the night sky. Not that I had much time to notice any lights. In a couple of hours I had made up for snores and bum lays and parasites and dog licks and fleecing and rejection.

Lesson: That was then, and this is now. Don't get unhooked or much less unhinged unless you are carrying that ever-important little foil packet.

Day 12:

My Carro Is Your Carro

"Tall, dark and handsome, he seduced with just a glance, a Svengali, a Valentino of the prairie. His pectorals bulged against his tight polo; his sinewy thighs rippled through the fashionable chinos. His every movement exuded sensuality. Women desired him; men envied him and even secretly dreamed of exploring the recesses insinuating themselves impudently between his legs."

Had Jackie Collins described him, that's probably how she would have painted Jack Humphrey. It might have been drippy with clichés, but even she would not have been able to escape the presence that inspired them.

When he walked past me at The Brass Rail and then turned back as if he could not believe he had missed me the first time through, I became weak at the knees. This hunk considered me worthy of giving me a chance? A smile, even? Had I died and gone to dog heaven?

He had driven downtown with a friend, so he didn't mind if I drove him back home and stopped by for the proverbial drink—wink, wink.

"I work across the street," he said as we walked into his apartment. I could see the Texas Instruments building across the street, where Jack was an engineer.

He then eclipsed the blinding light that his beautiful everything emitted when he took out a joint and lit it. He offered me a drag, but I had not indulged in the stuff since my senior year in college, when the campus pusher gave me several freebies before starting to ask for money in exchange for reefer. I felt uneasy in places where people did drugs: I was afraid of a raid that would drag me to jail as a suspect, leaving my children to fend for themselves while their father paid society a debt he didn't owe.

But soon the joint was too small even for the roach clip, and Jack and I retired to the bedroom. After the required romp I got dressed, but before I left he asked me for my phone number and wanted to know whether he could call me later in the week.

He called Thursday night, five days too late for my nerves. Would I be able to pick him up around nine thirty Friday night? We could then go downtown for a while?

When we walked into the bar he told me he wanted me to meet Wilhelmina. It turned out to be a washed-out, bleached-hair, scrawny man, about fifty going on seventeen, whose real name was Bill.

Jack made a beeline for the bar. He came back with a couple of beers, and we stood for a few minutes with Bill and some other men I had never noticed before, but from the sound of their conversation they were there every waking moment. They knew who had been there before the beginning of gay history. Every so often Jack would excuse himself to go to the restroom. He'd come back five or ten minutes later.

Eventually we left The Happy Hour and walked down the sidewalk to The Brass Rail. I got us two beers, compliment of Pat, my bartending admirer. But first I had to perform the ritual.

"Come here," Pat ordered. "No, to this side of the bar. You know the drill." Whenever Pat was tending bar he'd make me go back and kiss him. He said it improved his image. Then the rest of the night, unless I was in someone's company, he wouldn't charge me for drinks. The first one, though, regardless of who was with me, was always free—but I had to kiss him first.

When I got close enough to him that night he whispered in my ear, "What are you doing with him? Don't you know anybody nice?"

"Now, now," I said and returned to my place next to Jack. He must have had a very small bladder, I concluded. He excused himself several times to go pee. Luckily I knew other people there and didn't feel like an outsider, the way I had felt with Bill and the other loudly dull denizens of The Happy Hour.

Before the night was over we had also been to The Sun Disco and back to The Happy Hour.

On the way home he said he was tired. I took the hint and dropped him off at the building door.

"Do you want to go out tomorrow night?" he asked before getting out of the car.

Maybe we'd have a better time.

"Do you want to go to dinner first?"

"Sure," he replied. "That sounds good. You want to pick me up around nine?"

That was somewhat late for dinner, but I agreed.

When I drove up to the apartment building he was already standing outside waiting. We drove downtown, exchanging light chitchat about our respective days. I had planned to go to The Nankin, a great Chinese restaurant on Hennepin, within walking distance from most bars.

"Let's go to Plantation Pancakes," he suggested after we parked. I had never been there. It was an all-night fish bowl on a busy corner on Hennepin Avenue, reputed to be a hangout for pimps and their stables. It served breakfast on a twenty-four hour basis, but I wanted dinner.

"My treat," he said, and it sounded important enough to him, so we went to the pancake joint.

It was all it looked like from the street and even less.

After our nocturnal breakfast the night turned into a repetition of the previous one. Wilhelmina and the rat boys, Pat and the question, Paul at the piano.

The Sun Disco was busier than usual. I opened up some room at the bar to get us a couple of beers. Mark, a man I knew from The Town

House in St. Paul, came over to talk. Jack's bladder struck again. Mark
stayed by me. After ten minutes or so I felt Jack's arm around my waist.
He seemed restless.

"Do you want to leave?" I asked him.

"Ooh, oh, no. I'm having a good time. Aren't you?"

I hadn't thought about it. I was having a time. Of some sort or another.
I nodded anyway.

Shortly after that Jack asked to be excused. The urinal beckoned like
Lorelei to sailors. Then Mark also left. I turned around and saw Jack slowing down, looking toward a corner on the opposite side of the bar beyond
my field of vision. He looked my way; I pretended to be staring elsewhere.
From the corner of my eye I saw him dash across the crowd and head for
the corner.

Avoiding any sudden movement that might reveal my curiosity, I
turned toward the spot where he was standing.

Not really standing. He was making out with someone, probing the
other man's esophagus with his tongue and every other exterior part with
his hands.

What should I care? This was someone I had dated a couple of times.
He owed me nothing. Why should I mind? He was free to do whatever
he pleased.

I noticed Jack ungluing himself from his catch and heading for the
bathroom, then turning around at the door and walking toward me.

At least I was happy to know he wasn't afflicted by some urinary deformity or infection. Or if he did, his frequent treks to the pissoir were not
due to that. Wow, that was a relief.

"Do you want to dance?" he asked.

"Do you have a boyfriend?" I came back.

"No. Why do you ask?" He took a swig from his beer and started to
move to the rhythm of the music, looking away from me.

"No reason. A great looking man like you—it's difficult to think
you're free."

"Well, I am," he said. "Don't you want to dance?"

"No, not right now." I momentarily ignored my bruised ego and said, "But if you want to go dance with someone else, go ahead."

"Why would I do that when I'm with you?"

No, not dancing. Sucking face in the dark—that was something else.

His bottle was empty. Mine was half full.

"Do you want another beer?"

He looked at his bottle as if he only perceived its emptiness when I called his attention to it.

"Sure."

His head was swiveling to the back corner and again toward me while I waited for his beer.

Ian Scott, an acquaintance from Cathedral Hill, stopped by. As usual, he was on the prowl for some blond college child he had followed from bar to bar and had so far evaded Ian's strategic stalking.

"I'll be right back," Jack said.

Ian continued to talk, but I had repositioned myself to catch a glimpse of Jack negotiating the bar and its patrons to return to the corner where he turned into the octopus that suctioned Minneapolis.

"Pardon me," I said to Ian, "but I have to get going. Good luck with your twinkie."

I walked toward the dark corner and standing behind Jack whispered in his ear, "I hope he has a car."

He jumped as if a seizure had overtaken him. "Wait," he yelled as I walked out. He tried to grab my arm, but I yanked it away and kept walking. "All this just because I was talking to some guy?"

"Piss off," I said without looking back, and once more breathed the fresher, carbon-monoxide laden air on Hennepin.

I walked past Wilhelmina and the rodents sometime after that. He asked me whether I had seen Jack.

"Not for weeks."

"I wonder who's driving him around now," Wilhelmina said.

He must have read the puzzlement on my face.

Jack was convicted twice of driving while intoxicated. His driving license had been suspended. That's why he needed someone to drive him to the bars. He walked to work and the grocery store, or otherwise took cabs.

I was beginning to believe that I really did not know anyone nice.

Perhaps Wilhelmina took it for granted that a prize like Jack would not hang out with me unless he was getting some mileage from it. He may have been right.

Lesson: All that glitters is often fool's gold.

Day 13:

I'm Wonderful, You're OK

I really was looking for an appointment book. Our office manager only purchased such supplies when Banks had one of its fire sales—meaning that Banks had bought merchandise salvaged from some disaster and was selling it at incredibly low prices. The pencils smelled like charcoal and the yellow pads were water damaged (watermarked, pretentious Greta used to say), but they did the job.

Banks never had appointment books. The quest for one late in January—I was hoping that Greta herself became tired of the mess of knock-off Postit notes—drove me to The St. Paul Stationery Company. Some were already discounted. None suited my needs and, since I was paying for it out of my own funds, I refused to settle for next-best.

Brian stood behind the counter staring at me. When he flashed his smile I swore I saw one of those glimmering effects from a screen parody of a serious literary work. It looked as authentic as polyester.

"I can't seem to find a suitable appointment book," I explained walking toward him.

Suddenly he reached out, grabbed the collar of my leather coat and while my head gave him enough operating room he turned the label out.

"Lakeland! Great taste."

"Thanks." I knew I was blushing. It didn't seem to stymie him.

"It's a gorgeous coat."

"Thanks. A former student of mine sold it to me."

The handsome student owned a tony leather good store in St. Anthony Falls. I had visited his store hoping he'd give me some sign that he was gay— I was cruising him unbeknownst to him. The cashier turned out to be his fiancée and I left the store with an overpriced garment I could ill afford.

"So you're a teacher?"

"Was. In college. At the U."

"What happened?"

"The usual. Business pulled me away. The money was better and the challenges didn't involve snotty frat boys."

He listened attentively. Too attentively. He had to reduce the Tom Cruise-on-speed perkiness. His carefully styled hair (the lacquer could repel bullets), his obviously shaped eyebrows and smooth skin, that carefully trimmed moustache screamed fag or model or both. He was strikingly handsome in a *GQ* way, which always threatened me. People like that could only want to be out with me to look even better than they already did. Maybe more plastic as well.

"I'm running out of time," I said. "I'll come back some other time."

"Leave me your card and I'll call you if I find other appointment books that you could want to look at."

Before I arrived back at my office on Fourth and Wacouta, three blocks east of the store, Brian had found several other appointment books and left a message with Beverly at the front desk.

"Let's make a deal. A win-win, okay?" he said. "I get you the book and you meet me for cocktails after work at The Buttery."

I accepted with the trepidation of a two-faced bastard who feared running into a female analyst from First Computer whom I had courted and bedded on a skiing trip earlier that year, when I felt I still had something to prove. She and her friend Carol often stopped at The Buttery for happy and pick-up-men hour.

Drinks turned to dinner, during which Brian did most of the talking. He emitted lots of "I'm not buying into that anymore," "We're both got to be okay," "I won't listen to his tapes, oh, no, not since I caught him."

His ex-wife was in charge of his burnishing. She worked for Horst in Minneapolis and was a top-notch, simply brilliant stylist.

"My congratulations to her," I managed to squeeze in between anecdotes and assertions plagiarized, I'm still certain, from *Psychology Today* and every imaginable tract under the general heading of "self-help."

He offered to drive me home. I knew where this was going and instead of refusing and taking the Grand Avenue bus took him up on the threat.

I shut the door, and like a performer who never misses his cue he jumped on me.

"Where have you been hiding?" he whispered in my ear as he bit into my neck. I thought he was going to ask where I was hiding the rest of my apartment. I felt like replying that evidently my hiding place was not effective. He made me feel as if I had FAGGOT etched on my forehead.

"I've been working and surviving this cave."

He didn't bother to look around, for which I was thankful. One look to the corner at the end of a diagonal line twelve feet away and his peripheral vision must have caught the claustrophobic boundaries of my living-bedroom. I didn't give him a tour, of course. I also decided it was not going to improve my image to tell him that for three months after I moved in I still had my mattress on the floor of mywalk-in closet, where every morning I woke up to the sight of my shirt tails.

Brian threw his coat on my piano bench. Even the old clunker embarrassed me. I was afraid he might ask me to play something and see that several of the plastic keys were irreparably depressed. I was beginning to relate to central E and A.

I had once gone home with someone in similar circumstances. When I looked around my surprise at the reduced space must have shown on my face. "My stuff is in storage," he had clarified. I believed him, though friends laughed at my gullibility.

He helped me undress. I thought the two mounds of clothes would take up so much room that we'd have to step out to the hall to entertain Mrs. Delaney with our athletic soixante-neufs.

My many hang-ups inhibited the flow of blood to the corpora cavernosa. Brian was not at all suffering from anxiety. He kicked off his bikini briefs, I closed my eyes and reached for a surprising amount of hardened flesh. I wasn't sure I'd ever get to the other end of that. Where did he think he was going to find room for it in me? Suddenly I felt I had become a reflection of my limited environs. My thing hung like an obese suicidal worm.

When he pushed me onto the twin mattress set on the corner and spread my legs, I knew where he thought that club would fit.

"This isn't going to work," I said as calmly and tactfully as I could, which probably sounded frantically hysterical to him. "I'm tired, I drank and ate too much, and I really need to go to bed."

"You are in bed," he said with a studied smirk.

"To sleep." I tried to smile and sound legitimately tired.

"Okay. I don't want to force a win-lose. Why don't we set up some time later? A win-win."

"What do you suggest?" He couldn't possibly mean later that night. At least I hoped not.

"Let's meet Saturday at my place. I'll cook for you, you'll stay over," he accompanied his staccato list with flips of the wrist that made his hand go left and right.

If that would get him out of my bed for the night, I was all for it. He picked up his handbag, one of those mock purses that lets men seek for the equivalents of lipstick and tissue in an annoyingly loud racket, and kissed me good-night at the door.

His apartment was in a complex off Portland Avenue, facing Interstate 494. I could hear the dull loudness of traffic from the instant I parked my car to the second I left the place. Low-flying airplanes made the buildings shake; I wondered if the landing gear ever left tracks on the roofs.

His was a one-bedroom apartment. Every inch of the living room and the tiny dining room, except for deliberately planned paths, was taken up by a jungle of chrome and glass. The heat was on too high, perhaps to compensate for the glacial impression the furniture caused, and my butt sweated until it stuck to the leatherette sofa. I started to worry that I would develop nasty smells around my genitalia and that my scrotum was glued to my thighs. Brian, on the other hand, was as fresh as the proverbial daisy, exuding self-assurance under a pesky win-win halo.

After dinner—it had all emerged from Kraft and Swanson containers—he got frisky. He led me to his bed, where I felt like the Titanic on the South Seas. The mattress wasn't firm enough, and the waves kept slapping me slightly. I kept bobbing uncomfortably and never along the same spot. I became stiff as a corpse, except for what I had hoped would react more hospitably this time.

After several attempts and my obvious discomfort Brian realized that he was not going up where he initially thought. He did climax anyway all over me and in moans and writhing probably learned from some porn flick.

Given my repeated failure to display my prowess, I thought it best to hide my shame and retreat.

"Sorry, Brian, I've had so many things on my mind lately—"

"No need to apologize." Sure, easy for him to say. He had just unloaded a pint of semen on my hairy chest, something that would stick there until I got back home to bathe. "We must accept things as they are. I do, don't you?"

Regardless of his sincere inauthenticity I was relieved to get out.

I only saw Brian again once after that, at the Old Chicago Bar, where La Casa Coronado had once stood. He was in Cinerama company—it captivated the sight of all patrons wall to wall—and made an obstreperous entrance. I hid behind a leatherclad man who had bought me a drink and had almost persuaded me to take a stroll to his van. I heard that Brian had been promoted to district manager. Must have been a win-win.

Lesson: Sometimes when you win-win, you lose-lose.

Day 14:

Public Service Closet

"Don't go away," the heavy man said in a nasal quiver of a voice. He had been leaning in the dark against a wall between the beer and hard-liquor counters. He held on to his sport coat, folded over his arm and close to him, as if fearing a thief would snatch it. His sweat beads glistened every time the dance floor lights strobed on.

I had been having a beer nearby with Craig Flash and Keith Hockert when the sight of the terrified patron caught my roving eye.

I walked over with the excuse of ordering another beer, and said hello.

His cracking voice greeted me back. Instantly I thought I recognized his dilemma. A closeted man, maybe married, on his first or so night at one of them queer bars.

I patted him lightly on the shoulder. "It's okay," I said with a smile.

I thought I saw tears welling in his eyes. Maybe it was just booze. I didn't know how long he'd been there, but he reeked of it.

I picked up my beer and as I turned around to return to Craig and Tom, he pulled my arm.

He pleaded in the same tremolo.

"My friends are waiting."

"Just for a while." The sweat beaded up on his brow to replace the droplets sliding down his face. That explained the wet shirt collar. His face reflected light like a sheet of polished glass.

He started hyperventilating. It was like the roar of a wave just before it breaks or the vaguely amusing deep breaths of anonymous callers before the telephone industry gave us Caller ID.

"Ohhhh. I love the feel of your skin." He was running his finger over my naked arm.

C'mon. Skin is skin. Sticky skin from hopping around on the dance floor is, well, sticky skin from.

"Would you like to meet my friends?" I offered.

"No!" He buried his fingernails on my skin that he loved. He reduced the pressure. "Just stay here." He ran his finger up and down my arm and grunted quietly.

Fear crept in. This could be one of those psychos, a self-loathing repressed fag with a wife and two point five kids out in White Bear Lake out to kill the twisted desire in him by stabbing me in the chest.

Keith and Craig had left or moved elsewhere or gone home. I needed to get Patty's attention away from the other guys he was handing beers to. In case I disappeared, the bartender could always describe this man to the police and help with the sketch.

"What's your name?" I asked the psycho, just to make some talk while I searched visually for someone who could provide detectives with pertinent data from the night of the murder.

"Why is that important?" he asked, surveying me from floor to head and then looking away.

"No reason. It's okay. I don't have to know. Really." I didn't want to drive him over the edge. He seemed ready to do that without assistance. I introduced myself, skipping the family name.

Through clenched teeth he asked me whether the place was always this crowded.

"It's Wednesday night."

He stared blankly at me.

"Wednesday night is cheapie night. A bottle of domestic beer for fifty cents, mixed drinks for one fifty."

He made some unintelligible sound and continued to pant and rub my arm.

"Do you dance?" I asked. I had run out of safe topics just by asking his name.

He looked at me as if I had asked him whether he spoke English. Was I stupid or what?

"Not here. I like slow music. I've never danced with another man."

No time like the present, I almost blurted out, used as I was to camping it out with fellow queens. His presence inhibited me from pursuing it.

"Well, I come here to dance, mostly, so if you don't mind I'd like to find someone to dance with."

He withdrew his hand from my arm. I felt as if someone had opened the prison gate and I was free to jump out. But the brusqueness of his gesture made me uneasy.

I decided to stay by him anyway.

"Can I buy you another beer?" he asked.

I thanked him and refused the offer. Actually, I tried not to have more than a couple of beers when I was out dancing. I'd go to the rest room and fill the empty bottle with tap water when I ran out, and that way I looked hip and still remained sober enough to continue to dance without making a fool of myself tripping all over the dance floor.

"I guess it's your first time here," I said idiotically.

He nodded.

"How did you find it?"

The music had become louder. He leaned closer to my ear to speak. His moustache brushed against my earlobe.

"My brother is a cop in St. Paul. He's always talking about the queer bar on University Avenue, so one day I asked him where the bar was."

"What's your brother's connection with this place?" I hollered in his ear. *The Best of My Love* was drowning my voice. I must have tickled his ear with my beard as well.

"Sometimes he has to stop by just to see what things are like."

"Are you afraid he might stop by tonight and see you here?"

"He's off duty tonight."

"Lucky you, then." I said and laughed nervously.

It was obvious that this man was going to spoil my fun that night, even without intending to do so.

"Look, I think I'm going home," I said. "Nice meeting you."

I moved away from him. On my way out I ran into some friends and kissed them good-night. When I stepped out of the hot smoky bar the late September breeze hit me with welcome relief. I needed to get home, shower and get the cigarette smoke off my hair.

"Can we talk a minute?"

The voice was somewhat muted, but still a shrill. It was also chilling, since I had not felt him follow me out.

"Oh, I don't think so. I have to get going." I wanted to run across the road and jump in my car, parked across the street at the Montgomery Ward lot, which seemed miles away now that this person was following me.

"I just have a question," he said, still following me in spite of my shuffling to get away from him.

"Ask it, then," I said standing on the median dividing University. Traffic was light, but I ran a better chance of surviving his attack if I stood in the middle of the road than if I stayed on the sidewalk.

"Do you kiss guys like that in public often?"

"Those are friends I've known for years. It's not unusual for us to kiss each other in a friendly way like that. It doesn't mean anything."

"It seems peculiar to me."

"I guess it's a matter of getting used to things," I replied and started out across the street when an approaching car was still far away enough for me to run and still intercept this guy. My knees were going to buckle under me.

"Wait," he yelled.

"Sorry," I yelled back and frantically ran toward my car. I thought I'd never unlock the door and get in before I'd be knocked unconscious or worse.

"I'm sorry," I heard him say after I was inside my car and locking my door. He was slowing down, but still speaking in that panting, whiny voice that reminded me of stories about perverts. One night in Chicago a man with a similar tone and timbre had stopped me to ask me whether I thought there was anything wrong with a foot fetish. I snapped back, "Not if you keep your feet clean," and ran as fast as I could. This was a lot more threatening.

"I bet I've come across as a real weirdo," he said, underestimating himself. He walked up to my car and spoke just loud enough so that I could hear him with my window rolled up. "I'm not."

I started the engine and his voice sounded more distant. He knew it and started to speak louder.

"I just wanted someone to talk to. Please don't run away."

I rolled the window halfway down. "I do have to go. I don't know what else I could say."

His was the face of an overgrown child. The pain was evident. He couldn't have been faking that grimace and the labored breathing.

I shut the engine and got out of the car.

"I warn you, though," I said, "if you want to talk you're going to have to cool down a bit. You're too tense and you're scaring me."

He took a deep breath. "Alright, I'll try. But you have to understand—"

"Uh-uh. No, I don't have to understand anything. Either you treat me like a human being instead of like a freak, or I'm getting back in my car and taking off."

"I'm just not used to this."

"Used to what?"

"Doing this sort of thing."

Did he think I was going down on him right there and then? He was one of those who assumed that a gay man would have sex with any penis-equipped creep regardless of what assholes they were. I was probably one of those gays out with an agenda to seduce married men. I started to understand even if I didn't have to.

"I have to warn you. If you think I'm going to pull down your pants and suck you off here, you're wasting your time. Someone in the bar may be interested in that, sure, but I'm not the one. And even if I were into casual sex in public places, you're not my type."

I opened my car door to get back in.

Behind me he said, "I didn't mean to offend you. I need some company tonight. Just someone to talk to."

And of all the queer bars in the world Wacky Waldo had to walk into mine.

He asked me whether we could go to my place if it wasn't too far.

"It's not too far, but I don't think that's a good idea. We can talk here."

"Okay." He lit a cigarette and filled the air with its stench. I thought I had been rude enough and, having just left a smoke ridden bar it would seem petty to ask him to put the damn thing out.

He actually was from White Bear Lake. I was expecting to hear about the rest of the average American tableaux, but he only had one son and was going through divorce. Not because he was queer, mind you, but because nothing remained of his relationship with his bitch of a fucking wife who was a thief, a cold fish who had ruined his life with her fucking pretentiousness and her airs. She had custody of their son, a ten-year old he loved dearly and would miss the most if his fucking wife got away with limiting his visitation rights when the divorce came through. If she found out he had been in a queer bar she'd make a mess of things, that fucking bitch, that thief who was living in their house, having full use of a house furnished with stuff he had bought and paid for, I mean, she had the twelve-chair table, the expensive china cabinet, the imported fixtures, the flower garden, the goddamned bitch had it all while he camped out at this brother's until he could find a place to live temporarily before she had to sell the house and give him his half for a house she hadn't paid one fucking red cent for, because he had made all the payments on that house and even made the down payment out of his pocket and he could buy a place of his own away from the fucking cunt.

I gathered this was not an amicable separation.

"Listen, could we go to your place?" he asked again.

I could see he was not joking when he said he needed someone to talk to, but it was getting late, I had to get up early the next day, and I was in no mood to sit quietly letting a total stranger vent about a situation and a female I knew nothing about.

"Sorry. I understand what you're going through, and you have my sympathy, but I want to go home.

"Do you think there's a chance we could get together again?"

I hesitated. My doctorate was in linguistics and speech, not in social work.

"Maybe we can get together for lunch sometime." I was hoping it would be one of those Hollywood lunches, where people just don't know what the heck to say to get away from each other and make a vacuous promise for a meal that's never going to take place.

"How can I contact you?" he asked.

"How would I know who's calling?"

He paused, looked down and put out his cigarette with his shoe. He exhaled.

"I'm Joshua. When we talk I'll tell you I'm the guy you talked with."

No, I was the guy he talked at.

I gave him my phone number and instructed him not to call me before five in the afternoon. We'd have to decide on a place for lunch, somewhere convenient to both of us.

He told me he worked downtown, and I told him I did also.

"Do you live around here?"

This was going to be another round of "Can I come over to talk now?"

"I live off Grand Avenue. On Lincoln."

"That's close by," he observed.

"Not that close." I got back in my car. "Call me tomorrow then."

The next day at five Joshua called. He was hyperventilating again, panting on the phone in a way halfway between perverse and stressed. He was wondering whether I was free for dinner.

"No, sorry. Lunch tomorrow would be a better possibility." I really didn't want to listen to any more of his pissing and moaning, but I had given him my word of a lunch, and if I ever ran into him again somewhere he would probably berate me for not keeping my promise. I could be a new bitch thief who had lied to him and kept him hanging on.

He suggested that we meet at The Little Apple, a deli only a block away from my apartment. I started to object. After all, if he worked downtown he would have to drive up to Grand and Dale, and I would probably take the bus, wasting at least half an hour each way or having to ride back to work with him.

"How about Horatio Hornblower's?"

"No, that wouldn't work."

"Where do you work?" I asked him, only to propose a more convenient restaurant downtown.

"Around city hall," he said.

Then Horatio's would be perfect for him, and I'd only have to walk up four or five blocks to meet him. The weather was going to be good for walking anyway.

"No, that won't do. I'd like to get away from here."

I gave up. The Little Apple it would be.

His name was Joshua Krakowski. I gave him my full name once I heard his.

When I arrived he was already sitting at a table, the red and white oilcloth deepening the color on his crimson face. He was dressed up and perspiring as if it were August. He was having one of those three-point-two beers that tasted like perfumed water.

He hardly ate his sandwich. Most of the conversation revolved around the same subject he had started two nights before. His imagination was limited when it came to insults against his soon to be ex-wife. The meal, the warmth of the room and the dull rumbling made me so drowsy I really wanted to go to bed, but not with him in it.

"Do you live far from here?" he asked.

"Not too far."

"Do you think we could continue this conversation in your apartment?"

I was so weary I really didn't care if he threw me on a bed and had his way with me. Anything to shut him up and get him to go.

When we came into my apartment he sat in a love seat that represented the only piece of non-sleeping furniture in my small place. I sat on my bed, made to look like a sort of sofa.

"Can't you sit by me?" he asked.

"That's not a comfortable seat for the two of us," I replied.

"Do you think I'm that fat?"

He was not anorexic, that was certain.

"No, I just want to have a little more room than that chair would give me."

He asked if he could smoke, and I said no. He put the cigarette back in its absurd gold case. When he stretched I noticed that his suit's vest had hidden the thin rope he was wearing for a belt.

"Do you mind if I sit by you?"

Why fight it. This guy was not going anywhere until we did something. I scooted over. He started the arm-rubbing business again.

I looked at him closer. He was well-groomed, his eyes were blue and his teeth were bright and even. But all that sweat made him look dirty.

"You know, you don't have to be so tense. I wish you could relax a bit," I said.

He didn't reply. Instead he attacked me with a voracious kiss that I thought was going to leave me both breathless and lipless. It was half exciting, half fearful.

"I had never kissed a man before," he said staring at the floor.

"Well, you sure seem to be in need of no training."

At the end of November I needed to start looking for another apartment or renew the lease on the one I had. During one of our almost daily conversations Joshua told me that he was going to rent a penthouse apartment on West Tenth Street, behind the Science Museum, a brand new building with a great view of the capitol mall across Interstate 94. It belonged to some guy who had to rent it because he worked in Minneapolis and, after a second conviction for driving under the influence, had had his driver's license suspended. If I wanted to, I could rent the other bedroom in that apartment for two and a quarter a month.

The apartment was convenient to both of us. He, as he finally admitted, worked in city hall as some kind of managerial staff honcho, and the building was within walking distance for him. My own office was a little farther east, but the building was connected to the maze of skyways that serpentined downtown St. Paul all the way to the Control Data Corporation building at the end of East Fourth Street.

I looked at the apartment and agreed that it would be a far cry from the studio apartment on Lincoln with the strange view of my coke-snorting neighbors' kitchen across the alley.

We agreed that we would only be roommates. He knew I had just broken up with a man I had been dating for six months and was not in immediate need of starting up something with anyone. Besides, I was clear that my feelings for that other man were still muddled. I was hoping he'd see things different from what he had once I walked out of his life, and then he would eventually come back looking for me again.

But the night I moved in after I went to bed in my own room Joshua knocked at my door.

"I'm sleeping all alone in a king-size bed. You're welcome to share it." His voice was trembling as much as the night we met.

Why the hell not. I was free and horny and as long as it was nothing but sex, why the hell not?

But we cavorted around in the nude too often, and I accepted the invitation to share Joshua's bed one too many times. By late January Joshua was making demands that sounded too much like a lover's, and a jealous one at that.

And one fine day in early February I received a note from my estranged boyfriend, who wanted to go to dinner. When I told Joshua I was going out he lost his color and started perspiring.

"I guess then you won't mind if I ask a friend over while you're out with that guy," he asked without looking at me.

Sure, a friend. And who could that be? He was trying to make me jealous with a nonexistent suitor.

"Who?"

"I guy I've known for a while," he said, puffing out smoke.

"Why hasn't he been over to visit?"

"To be honest with you, I didn't think it was appropriate. But if you're going to be fucking your boyfriend, I guess I can go out with him."

"You're free to do as you please, Joshua, but don't use the possibility of my sexual activity with my friend as an excuse to go do something you want to do."

The friend did exist. He was a local Army recruiter with an office on the state government mall, in one of the buildings within view of our apartment.

I left on my date and when I returned Joshua was sitting in the dark listening to one of his Lawrence Welk albums on my record player.

"Has your friend left?" I asked.

"He didn't come. Did you fuck your boyfriend?" Hostility made his voice shake again.

"No, I didn't, but if I had, I wouldn't tell you either. That's a private matter."

He put out his cigarette and drank from his glass of bourbon. The glass was one from my set of glasses that I had bought in sets of two until I had eight. I had only used two once; the rest still had the stickers on them. One day I came home and found Joshua scrubbing the gummed label off them with a Brillo pad. My heart sank. I ran to the sink and stopped his hand. He had only done one, luckily. When I put it up against the ceiling light I noticed the steel wool scratches he had left on the delicate crystal.

I stopped by Woolworth's and picked up a set of sixty-four glasses for nineteen dollars. It was a present, I told him, but it was really an effort to rescue my highball glasses that had cost me so far about my salary of one week.

"What does the N stand for?" I asked him one day after noticing that his mail was addressed to Joshua N. Krakowski.

"None," he replied unfazed.

It was true. His parents had registered him at birth responding to the "middle name" item with "None." His name was officially Joshua None Krakowski.

That same day of my enlightenment he informed me that he had invited his coworker Betty Lou and her husband to the apartment for dinner. I wasn't sure whether I was invited because I lived there or because impressing them required the use of my china. Chipped Corelle was not going to be good enough for Betty Lou and Mr. Betty Lou.

"She may look innocuous enough," he warned me about Betty Lou before she arrived, "but don't ever underestimate her." She was a seasoned veteran of local elections and could handle anyone.

I was not running for office against her boss at the county, so the warning seemed useless. Still I was curious about this MacArthur of St. Paul alley cat fights.

Betty Lou was too short for her weight; her prematurely bald husband seemed the one we could really underestimate. Next to the Walkiria he looked positively whipped, undernourished, hunched and kept in the dark, figuratively and literally.

Joshua cooked dinner in its entirety: dumplings, boiled rutabagas that had left a distinctively pungent stench in the air, pork roast that resisted all attempts at mastication, and some boiled new potatoes whose original shape became a mystery as mushy pieces of the tubers emerged from the boiling water. Betty Lou inhaled over half of the bottle of chilled Burgundy that Joshua had chosen and regaled her taciturn husband and me with war stories from her several campaigns in Ramsey county.

"How's the liquor license problem coming along?" Joshua asked.

Her snort rose from her diaphragm.

Betty Lou's son had just purchased a house a block away from a commercial zone. A bar was due to open soon around the corner. Betty Lou moved quickly to set up bogus hearings that would ineluctably lead to the revocation of the liquor license.

She appeared at the hearing, as if necessary, with testimonies of neighbors who opposed the location of the bar.

"The license is gone," she chuckled. Her husband smiled faintly. The rutabagas had not sufficed to help him regain his strength.

She flicked her cigarette precisely on the side of her empty plate.

"Nothing beats self-interest disguised as altruism," she said without addressing anyone in particular.

The only other guest Joshua had over when I was around, and only a few times, was Sylvia. She was a fellow county bureaucrat. Sylvia was an allegedly brilliant woman, single, middle-aged, attractive, who seemed to be going through life giving a flawless performance as a bimbo. Joshua's coziness with her led me to believe that the failed purpose of her presence was to elicit in me feelings of jealousy.

"I could fall for her, you know," he told me one day.

Looking at her elicited in me an emotional reaction, but not Joshua's intended effect. Sylvia was afflicted with FSP, fag sensory perception, whether or not Joshua knew it. I immediately recognized Sylvia as the constant companion of two old Lake Calhoun queens who were fixtures at The Gay 90s every weekend. Had Joshua spent more time in bars and less time rubbing elbows with Narcissists in altruistic clothing he wouldn't have made me so embarrassed for him that he believed Sylvia saw in him anything more than a sad closet queen in need of a girlfriend.

Resumption of my relationship with my lover, Randy (and yes, he was), was going slow; I purposely came up with excuses to avoid seeing him too often. I didn't want him to think that during our hiatus I had been sitting alone crying and waiting by the phone. As a matter of fact, I hadn't; I had even increased my involvement in the ski club so that I wasn't making anything up when I came up with a reason not to go see him in the middle of the week.

In view of the uncertainty of a renewed relationship, I saw nothing wrong with continuing to share Joshua's bed.

He, in turn, began to give me demonstrations of sexual habits and peculiarities of his that were probably meant to impress me in some bizarre way. For instance, he could ejaculate just by placing his thimble-size penis between my thighs. But the showstopper was his ability to lie in bed totally naked, moan and suck air between his teeth and, eyes shut while he held my waist, within minutes ejaculate without touching himself.

"My brother does it like that too," he confided. "We used to compete and I always won."

I had heard of pissing contests, but this? Well, this? Only in America.

He took me to his brother's for Easter. Joshua and his roommate, the guy with the Ph.D. who didn't say much.

We visited one of his aunts on Como Avenue, who being from the old country and having spent only forty of her seventy years in the United States, referred to me, ironically, as Joshua's boyfriend and asked him how his condom was working out in that new building down the town St. Paul.

The phone started to ring more often for him. The calls were no longer just from county pols and his son, but also from the Army recruiter. I noticed that shortly after Joshua came home the phone would ring and, invariably, he caller was the Army man.

It took a few days for me to figure out that the recruiter, in dereliction of more productive duties, was sitting in his office looking into our apartment with binoculars or, more likely, a telescope. The living room drapes were wide open and thus he could see when Joshua walked in. On a Friday afternoon when I felt particularly naughty I came home and shut the drapes. I stripped out of my clothes and opened the drapes again. When Joshua walked in I rose from the sofa, jumped all over him, kissed him savagely and practically tore his clothes off him. When he was totally naked I fell to my knees and took him into my mouth with my back to the balcony.

The phone rang.

"If you answer that I'll bite it off," I threatened. He remained where he was standing.

When the phone stopped ringing I stood up, shut the drapes and led Joshua to bed.

As my relationship with Randy heated up once again I started to spend increasingly more time away from the penthouse. Joshua was visibly disturbed by this.

I cut out all sexual activity with him and returned to my room, whose door I started locking.

One night in early May I wanted to invite Randy up to watch a movie. I asked Joshua whether he'd mind. He told me he'd go to his brother's and call before coming over.

The movie was a dud. Randy and I had started making out in the living room paying no attention to the TV screen.

Joshua called. He was in South St. Paul and would be home in an hour.

I figured Randy and I had about an hour to finish what we had started. Not ten minutes later, when it would have taken getting singed to realize that the apartment was on fire, that passionate had we become, I heard a whiny voice behind us, "That's disgusting."

How long had he been standing there? I had not heard the door.

The son of a bitch was downstairs when he called.

Randy, naturally shy and easily hurt, zipped up his pants after pulling himself out of my hands so fast he probably got rope burns, fixed himself up as well as he could, and stood up as Joshua walked into his bedroom and shut the door.

"Jesus Christ," Randy said. Shame burned his face. He started to walk out.

"Should I go with you?"

"Don't bother." The edge of his words could have drawn blood.

"Please don't leave like that," I pleaded.

He slipped into his coat, walked out and slammed the door. I ran after him asking him to please stop.

The damn elevator door opened shortly after he pressed the button.

"Je-sus-kuh-rist. What the hell have you too been doing in there?"

"Don't leave like that, please. Let's talk."

"Fuck you both," was his response, and the door closed as he pushed me out of the elevator.

When I walked in I stormed into Joshua's room and demanded that he tell me why he had done it.

"I didn't feel like letting you two get off where I eat," was his response.

"Fine. I'm giving you notice. I'm moving out next week." I went into my room.

A short while later I heard Joshua walk out and slam the door.

Eventually I fell asleep. I woke up at the sound of loud wailing coming from the coat closet in the hall on the other side of one of my bedroom's walls. A wounded coyote couldn't have sounded that awfully.

"No, no, no," Joshua cried and howled, "don't leave me, please, don't leave me."

I threw on my robe and walked out. He had actually fallen to his knees and was banging on the wall with his bare knuckles, crying like a very large baby.

"Please, don't leave. I'm sorry, I won't do it again." More howling.

I felt like laughing at the absurdity of the scene. But I was afraid that the pain might turn to violence at my derision, and I helped him up.

"Joshua, calm yourself. Get out of that closet, c'mon."

He continued to howl and sob and weep uncontrollably.

"Okay, Joshua, I won't leave."

I took him to his room, slipped him under the covers and lay by him until he fell asleep.

In the morning I repeated my warning as if no howling had ever reverberated in the apartment.

"Yes, I guess it's best for both if you do," he said, and walked out without finishing his coffee.

The day I moved out, with the help of five friends whose vans and station wagons proved invaluable in saving me the money I would have needed for a rental truck, he left early in the morning. Of course, my boyfriend found some excuse to avoid having to help me with the move he had actually demanded even before we were surprised by Joshua.

My landlord at the old apartment building had a vacancy, a corner one-bedroom that was perfect for me at only fifty dollars more a month than I had paid for the studio in the building next door.

Later that year Joshua was appointed to a director's job that required knowledge he had never even surmised existed, much less considered a requirement for the position. He had raked in political favors owed by county and city pols and got a job for which he lacked the most fundamental skills and for which dozens of qualified applicants without the right political connections had been turned down.

Since it was right in my line of work I asked him if it didn't scare him to know that he was going to be in charge of an important operation whose professionals knew much, much more than he could ever suspect about his work.

"I don't need to know. I have almost 200 workers under me who know their job. I just have to manage."

Well, I supposed, a manager can manage anything.

His wife gave him his divorce the following year. She evolved from bitch to "that woman." They shut out their attorneys and sat down to divide their belongings with a wisdom Salomon would have envied. He got six of the chairs, she got the other six and compensated him for his half of the table, their water bed and the rest of the Louis XIV furniture; likewise with the fine Mikasa crystal and everything else.

The Army man continued to court Joshua, but even Joshua realized that the recruiter was a dozen bullets short of a full round. Joshua reached his limit when he arrived at work one day to find five bouquets of two dozen roses each, their cards signed visibly by the same man. Joshua gave the Army man the boot, and it drove the intrepid soldier crazy. He attempted suicide by wrist slashing and was committed to the psychiatric ward of a military hospital. It was probably better than the prison we would have gone to if court martialed for sodomy.

With the divorce settlement money Joshua purchased a house in one of St. Paul's drabbest suburbs. And just as he had cried in the closet, Joshua would some day die in his closet.

I went back full-time to my boyfriend. By August we were again history, that time for good. For really good.

Lesson: When he walks into his dark closet, don't let the door hit *you* in the ass.

Day 15:

An Unhandy Man

For months I had been seeing Fred at The Happy Hour. He was cute in a masculine and yet boyish way. He was slender, not necessarily a point in his favor for me, but he was always smiling and seemed to enjoy himself in the company of others. But he never gave me a glance over, other than politely saying hello when I forced myself into his field of vision.

In my thoughts of him he always wore the same lumberjack flannel shirt, jeans, tennis shoes and a bottle of Bud that seemed glued to his hand.

Bars are never illuminated to let everyone see the many flaws we all have. Physical and otherwise.

That Saturday night I finally had to do more than just stand at a distance trying to find someone else to take home because that smiling guy with the appended bottle of beer wouldn't notice me. From the angle of his bottle when he took a swig I could tell he was close to the bottom. I had the bartender hand him another bottle.

Fred looked my way and raised the bottle in thanks. He excused himself from the other people in the circle and walked my way.

He introduced himself: Fred Gunderson. So bashful! He was self-conscious, it seemed to me. His eyes were squinty from all the smiling; he didn't seem to have a frown in his repertoire of emotions. He was charming. Of course, in the heat—yes, heat—of the moment I forgot that there is such a thing as shameless theatrics in the wonderful world of bar denizenry.

I drove him to his own car, a Nova no less than ten years old, rusted out and indelibly afflicted by that sign of overexposure to salt that represents road battle veteranship in Minnesota. He asked me to follow him to his apartment in a two-building complex on Lyndale Avenue.

"I'm the handyman here, so sometimes I get phone calls from tenants when I least want them. You'll have to understand that. Won't you? I'm sorry, but, you know, that's how it is," he said with the usual smile, brandishing his beer bottle high above his head as we spoke cozily in a sprung sofa.

He got the handyman job in exchange for free rent from the buildings' owner, who some years ago had expected sex from Fred. Fred didn't deliver, but strung him along until he got the job.

No, that was not his only job. He taught English in a Catholic elementary school. He got the job on the recommendation of a priest whose rectory he had shared for a few weeks. The teaching job didn't pay well enough. He couldn't afford rent and child support. The priest was demanding that he put out, but he really wasn't that interested in the priest, only in the warm bed. The priest got him the job to try to get him to settle somewhere else he could afford. The job helped, but he still couldn't afford housing. He lived out of his car trunk for months, until winter came. Then he met the buildings' owner, a married man who wanted to keep Fred on the side.

Often apartment repairs were beyond Fred's limited home maintenance skills. He'd call the building owner.

"Hey, you're the handyman, so fix it and leave me alone," the jilted lover wannabe would scream at him. "Or else you can get out and let me get someone who does know how to fix stuff."

Fred would frequently make problems worse than they were when he attempted to apply the logic of a dilettante to plumbing and carpentry projects. The owner would end up paying more to have a professional come in and take care of the mess Fred had made.

Fred found that funny.

It was getting late in the evening. Or early the following morning. I needed to know whether something was going to happen or whether I should just go home unfulfilled. He must have read my mind and took me to his bedroom, decorated by no one. It was a double-mattress set on an uncarpeted floor. An old stuffed chair sat on the corner. Above it someone had nailed a mirror framed in white plastic.

"How do you feel about…you know?" Fred asked with his squinty smile. I raised my eyebrows.

"You know."

"What?" I was becoming exasperated with the shorthand.

"You know. Doing it up there. In the back?"

"You want me to do that?"

I stopped trying to untie my belt. Somehow I was getting a feeling that this was going to be a waste of time with someone who didn't know what end was up. And I didn't run an employment agency, so I had only myself to offer; if that weren't enough, what then?

"I don't know," he replied sheepishly. "Do you like to do it?"

"You mean fuck you."

"Yeah."

"Is that what you want me to do?"

"I don't know."

"Then why do you ask?" Exasperation was fleeing through the cracks in my so far well-disguised mortification.

"I don't know. Some guys like that."

"Is that what you're afraid I'd like to force you to do?" Maybe he was into some rape scene kink or wanted to feel he had done it because I had forced him, not because he enjoyed it.

"Well…You know…I don't know." He had stripped and was lying in bed. I took that as encouragement and finished undressing.

I asked him the question I loathed the most. "What do you like to do?"

"Maybe I'd like to try that with you. But I'm afraid…You know…That you may find something dirty up there."

What had he been storing away up his rectum?

"There are hygienic ways of preventing that."

"I don't know. I feel uncomfortable thinking you could be grossed out."

"Then we won't do that. It's not a requirement." I really wanted this over. By then I didn't care whether we did anything or not. I wanted some kind of resolution to the idiocy.

And the worst was that he kept smiling throughout the annoying exchange.

"You worry too much," I said, and kissed him.

He seemed reticent. He confused me to no end: he took me home with him to what, sit around watching him drinking more beer?

I reached for him. Maybe if I accelerated things he would finally get into it, and I could go home to rest and forget I ever thought this man was worth spending time with.

Liquor does take its toll. Or maybe I wasn't attractive enough. Then why did he bring me home? It wasn't like he needed a ride. Was he just curious? Did he just want to look at me naked? Was he thanking me for buying him four beers back at the bar?

The phone rang. He got out of bed and picked it up.

"Sorry. I'll be right back. Don't leave, okay? Someone's toilet is clogged and I have to go take a look at it."

He left. I lay in bed wondering what to do. I didn't want to leave before he came back. If I ran into him again at the bar I'd be embarrassed that I had run out and left him behind, being inconsiderate of his maintenance duties. So all I wanted was sex and when it wasn't convenient I just picked up and left? That was true as far as this guy was concerned, but I didn't want to make it that obvious.

He came back about a half hour later. I was hoping he had washed his hands. I didn't want other people's feces on my dick.

He never did become erect. I lost interest.

"Maybe we should just go to sleep," he suggested.

I really had not thought of staying there. I wanted to go back to the cleanliness of my penthouse rental in St. Paul, even if I had to listen to my roommate with marital aspirations piss and moan about my lack of consideration.

I stayed.

Late Sunday morning I got out of bed before Fred woke up, but soon after that the phone was ringing again, some renter with a broken window that would have to wait until Monday, because fixing broken glass was not a handyman chore.

I asked him whether I could make coffee. He only had instant. I just wanted something warm and liquid that would wake me up before I got back on the road.

He kept his pot and pan (yes, *one* pot and *one* pan) in the oven, which he never used. The kitchen garbage pail looked as though he had stolen it from McDonald's: there was nothing there but Big Mac wrappers and beverage cups.

When the water boiled I reached for one of two mugs on a shelf above the stove.

"No, not that one!" Fred screamed as he ran toward me.

Too late. I looked in it. A partial denture featuring the blackest stains on the back of false upper front teeth sat at the bottom.

"Oh."

That explained why he looked so self-conscious when he smiled. It wasn't shyness.

He felt compelled to explain my finding after he removed the partial from the mug, put it on and told me I could use that mug for his coffee. I needed no prompting.

When he was fourteen Fred's stepfather had given him a beating so severe he had knocked Fred's upper teeth out. Fred went to a dentist who fixed him up and fitted him for partial dentures. While he waited for the permanent set, the dentist gave him a temporary partial. Fred had never returned for the permanent set. Fred was now thirty-nine. The partial still worked okay, so he didn't see any need to get another.

"This is none of my business," I said, "but your kitchen seems to be pretty sparsely equipped. Do you ever eat at home?" I already knew the answer to that.

"I'm not much of a cook."

When he took out a spoon to stir the Coffeemate in his coffee I also noticed the limited flatware set. Fred must have read my mind.

"When I divorced Cindy she gave me two of everything."

It was pretty Biblical. Maybe he was sailing in an ark.

"She gave me two knives, two forks, two tablespoons, two teaspoons, two plates, two cups and—"

"Two partridges in a pear tree."

"That's good," he chuckled.

"How long have you been divorced?"

"Eight and a half years."

"And in that time you haven't had a chance to get a couple more pieces of dinnerware?" I wasn't judging him, really. Yet I had been separated for a shorter period of time and had managed to buy a whole set of china and even a dozen glasses.

"I don't have people over. This is fine for me."

His children were seventeen and fifteen. The oldest, Monica, wanted to work and had lined up a job at a motel. Her mother was deadset against it. She didn't want her daughter to be handling other people's filthy sheets. Fred thought she should take the job. It meant less money for him to send back home to Bemidji.

The following Friday I called Fred to ask him out. We agreed to meet downtown at The Brass Rail that evening. I was right on schedule, but he had been taking beers from other patrons by the time I got there.

We went next door to The Happy Hour. He pointed to a middle-aged man who looked less than comfortable at the bar.

"I'm going to introduce you," he said playfully. "Wait a little and ask him what kind of work he does."

The man and I shook hands. I followed Fred's directions.

"A little white collar work out in Hudson," the man said, staring into his drink. On the other side Fred snickered.

Gay etiquette restrained me from asking anything else.

When we walked away Fred said, "He's a priest in Hudson. I spent a summer sleeping with him. He got tired of me. I didn't put out when he wanted me to."

Around midnight I followed Fred out of the bar. He asked me to follow him home, but the weight of a busy week made me opt for driving home instead. When I drove east on Washington Avenue I noticed Fred walking back into The Happy Hour.

When Sunday rolled around it was Fred who surprised me with a phone call. He wanted us to meet at the bar.

"On a Sunday night?"

"Why not? I'm usually there Sunday night," he replied undaunted. The picture was emerging clearly of why I had seen Fred whenever I was at the bar. He had relocated from his car trunk and the beds of Catholic priests to a bar stool.

"Tell you what. What do you say to dinner at your place," I suggested. I'll bring some groceries over and cook. How's that for a change."

He hesitated and finally agreed.

"I don't have any spices or stuff like that," he said. I already knew. His refrigerator had an echo when the door was open and he spoke into it while digging for beer in a twelve-pack box of Bud.

"That's alright. I'll bring some over."

I stopped at Byerly's and got a beef roast, potatoes, carrots, salt, pepper, mustard and ice cream. I also brought disposable plates and the ingredients for a salad. I returned that evening with a small roast, which I cooked for us. Fred did have a roasting pan; it came with the stove and was as clean as the previous tenants had left it. I dead roach had become fossilized under the rack.

He thanked me profusely. At the end of the meal we sat in the small living room. I drank coffee; Fred chucked his beer.

He gave me a look that I translated into his belief that he was going to have to pay for dinner with sex.

I had been hopeful that the other night was just a fluke and that given the right circumstances Fred would prove himself to be the charming lover I had fantasized him to be. But that look made me feel like a building owner and several Catholic priests.

"Do you want to lie down?"

"No, thanks," I replied. "I have to get going. Tomorrow is a work day."

A few days later Fred called me to ask whether I wanted to go to see Noel Coward's *Private Lives*, which was being performed at the College of St. Thomas. He shocked me. Perhaps the bars had closed for the night and he had no other place to go?

He actually wore a coat instead of the ragged Twins jacket that had become his most visible identifying feature. He also wore slacks and replaced the faded flannel shirt with a dress shirt. I felt bad for him that I had misjudged him, and appreciated the effort he was making to show me that he wasn't what he had already proved to be.

After the show he wanted to come up. My roommate Joshua was already home, and I wanted to avoid the strange confrontations that Joshua and I had been having.

"Thanks for the show, Fred. I do have to get to bed early tonight."

For weeks after that I stopped going to bars in Minneapolis. Months went by before I actually saw Fred again. When I did, I walked up to him and greeted him. He stared at me as if he had never seen my face.

"It's me. Remember? Roast beef at home? *Private Lives*?"

"Oh, sure. It's—don't tell me."

I told him anyway.

"Yeah, that's right. You're looking good. Thanks for saying hello," he said, and he meant it.

My heart shrunk.

Lesson: Don't look in other people's coffee mugs.

Day 16:

Having a Great Time—Glad You're Not Here

Before Tom Gandy's semifinal breakup with Ed Eishendeck, they rented a house neither of them could really afford on Valley View Road, an upper-class neighborhood in Edina. I was in the house several times, including the day when Ed came home early from a trip and found me having lunch with Tom in the kitchen. Had he arrived ten minutes later, he would have found us having dessert elsewhere. Ed pretended he didn't recognize me, and I pretended I was another real-estate agent out looking at houses with Tom.

During the crepuscular days of his doomed relationship, Tom had confided in Kris Swenson that he had been seeing me for nearly two years. A Saturday afternoon the fateful summer when later I finally told Tom that I was moving on with or without him, Tom invited Kris to stop over and meet me.

Kris stunned me. For someone who had grown up around and been surrounded mostly by dark complexioned people, the sight of this exotic Nordic god made my heart beat a lot faster. His deep blue eyes left me speechless.

"Nice," he told Tom, obviously referring to me without coming right out and saying it. "Actually, very nice." He went on talking about something else, and I never gave any indication of how flattered I was that this hunk of a man had found me very nice.

Kris was a human resources trainer for a local outfit that specialized in management development. Tom had wanted me to meet him, because

Kris had also been married and could have some words of wisdom for me about how to go about my own future dissolution. He was recently divorced from Marlene. When he finally revealed his sexuality to Marlene, she was livid, but not for the usual reasons. Marlene had successfully avoided her temptation to be unfaithful to Kris, because he was such a giant in her eyes that she was convinced he didn't deserve even the thought of betraying his trust.

Not with other men. With women.

Marlene was angry at how unfair it was that she had had to repress her feelings while Kris went around screwing men right and left.

But she meant to make up in spades for lost time, and she started leaving their two teenage boys with Kris every weekend at Kris' new quarters, a stately mansion on the St. Croix River bluffs in Bloomington that Tom had helped him restore—true to Tom's style, most of the renovation consisted of hanging paper over walls that should have been knocked down and rebuilt, with holes so big a small baby fit through them.

Kris had a reason for finally coming out. He was seriously involved with Terry McClaren, a popular caterer in the Twin Cities. However, things between them went sour when the two hyperactive boys started to join them for cozy Saturday evenings at home. The boys—well, with a gay father and a lesbian mother...Let's indulge in tasteful understatement and say that they were a tad confused. Which is equivalent to a fucked-up mess. Hyperactivity and confusion make a fine combination for junior hockey leagues, but they turned out to be an explosive combination at the Swenson-McClaren manor. A very special man was necessary to withstand them; Terry was not that man.

"It's really wonderful," Terry would say with a sneer when Kris was not around. "While Marlene spends weekends bumping pussy, I have to sit with Kris by the fire eating pop corn and watching action videos with those two misfits at our feet. They should be writing their own Teaching Tolerance ed book. *Daddy Has Two Mommies*."

They had other problems that were overshadowed by the future Stanley Cup winners. Terry was a top, and had made several attempts to get Kris to give it up for him. For whatever reason, Kris had not interest in being screwed. One day while they were having one of their heated arguments and the issue of sexual incompatibility surfaced, Kris told Terry, "If that's what you want to do, why don't you marry a woman and pretend she's a guy with a great chest?"

Soon Terry was out of the house, out of Kris' life and out of sight. Tom moved out from the room he got in exchange for cooking and cleaning house for the Swenson-McClarens and company, and drove back to San Francisco to once more attempt to live with Ed.

"This is Kris Swenson," he said one day when he called me at work. My heart skipped a beat. "I hope I haven't caught you at a bad time."

"Absolutely not." For Kris no time could be bad.

He had heard that I was no longer involved with George, and would I be interested in going out to a barbecued ribs place he knew down in Savage.

Would I? Was Cardinal O'Connor the biggest homophobe in the gay-ridden Catholic Church?

I drove out to his house and from there he drove us across the river to Savage. He was really a laid back man, a person who instilled tranquility and put me at ease. His humor enchanted me. Had I been looking for someone to seduce and at whose feet to grovel, Kris would be that man. No comparison was possible between him and the hell I had left behind on Como Avenue.

He had me in such awe that I felt totally, completely inferior to him—this man was really out of my league.

After dinner we drove to a straight country-western bar in town and after a beer went back to his house.

I meant to leave without coming in. Kris couldn't have had any further interest in me.

"You can't go back to the city tonight," he said, as if I were in the Hamptons and planned to drive back to Manhattan. "Come on in."

Was this really happening to me?

We sat in the den having a cordial, facing each other, and suddenly the warmth of his hand was on my face. He came closer and kissed me on the cheek, nibbled on my chin and sought my lips with his. It was a soft kiss followed by a harder one.

Maybe the cordial had me so hot I felt I was in flames, but I doubt it.

"Let's go up," he said, as if I needed direction.

In bed he started gently, caressing my body and kissing me everywhere. He never became wild. His lovemaking was in slow motion, as if Quaalude induced, and it was driving me crazy. When his turn came to have his tenderness reciprocated, he received it with surprising gratitude. He lay on his back, I sideways with my leg thrown over his, and the controlled intensity of our lovemaking had exhausted us as if we had been riding each other with insane abandon.

"I hope I didn't disappoint you," I murmured.

"God, no. You were plenty good. Pleeenty good."

I rose early the following morning to go home, shower and go to work. Later in the day Kris called me.

"That was nice. Very nice. I hope we do it again soon."

"Just say the word," I replied.

He never uttered the word. As days went by I became increasingly down on myself. I hadn't been sophisticated enough, I had been too chatty, not chatty enough, I had bored him, I was too ugly for him, a man who could have anything he wanted, what the hell did I think he would see in me, I wanted to dig myself into a hole and die.

One day I got a call from Tom, a surprising phone contact from his new quarters in San Francisco.

"I can't believe you were that low," he said. He was very unhappy and sounded ready to let me have it. "How could you fuck my best friend? I think that's the tackiest thing anyone ever did."

"Wait a second," I interrupted. "I don't think you have all the facts here." I had to explain that the initiative had not been mine.

"Regardless. You should have had a little more class than that. You had to know that it would get back to me. Kris and I are like brothers."

Like gossipy bitches, I was about to say.

"And that's what you did, you fucked my brother. I don't care if he took the first step. You could have always said no. I really expected more loyalty from you."

I couldn't think of what to reply. In a sense he was right. It didn't occur to me then that if we abstained from having sex with others who were friends of others who were friends of others we knew, who the hell were we going to have sex with? Did I have to limit myself to truckers and the kindness of strangers? Instead, the more Tom described his hurt at how I had taken advantage of a friendship he himself had initiated for me, the smaller I felt.

"I'm sorry, Tom. It was wrong of me to do it, but it's done."

After I hung up I left the office to take a walk around the block. Things looked a bit more in perspective.

Kris did it just because he could. And he grabbed the phone, reached out and touched someone where it was still sore, to let him know that he did it just because he could. With graphic details and some hyperbole, no doubt.

Lesson: If it looks too good to be true, it's not good enough for you.

Day 17:

A Lonely Hearts Club for One

When I saw Walt in the lobby, as we were both getting in the elevator of the building on West Tenth Street, I knew I had seen him before, and I knew exactly where.

"I saw you at The Brass Rail last Saturday night, didn't I?"

He chuckled and nodded. His face was like a beetroot, it was so red. His muffled laugh and his gaze were simultaneously impish and salacious; I must admit it was difficult to see his eyes behind the lenses thick as beer bottle bottoms, but his insistent stare led me to his blue eyes.

Although I had first seen him in the darkness of the back bar at The Brass Rail, I still would have recognized the red and black checkered flannel shirt and the jeans. They must have been the attraction. Otherwise, I remembered the frame and the bulk, not exactly his facial features.

I introduced myself before he walked out on the third floor. He told me his name and apartment number.

The next time I saw him, a Saturday night, he was sitting at the same place at The Brass Rail. I put my arm over his shoulder and asked him, "Do you pay rent on this stool?"

Again he chuckled. "I bring my own," he said.

He was a system developer with a major computer corporation in Minneapolis, a man with two degrees from the University of Michigan. He seemed reserved, but what he said was expressed articulately and with a slight drawl. When I pointed it out he explained that he was from Atlanta.

"Now, this is a much better match," someone said behind me. It was Pat O'Neill, my bartender friend. He squeezed Walt's chunky cheeks and pushed me closer to Walt. "You deserve someone like this," he told Walt, and then turned to me. "I knew sooner or later you'd find someone nice."

The following Monday evening Walt asked me to stop by his apartment. He came to the door in gym trunks and barefoot. Two black cats sneaked up around the hall. I tried to pet them, but they ran away.

"Those are Pest and Beast. They're not used to company." He chuckled again.

The apartment was not in extreme disarray, but it was visibly not clean. A scent I had smelled on Walt when I had stood by him at the bar on Saturday night pervaded the apartment, but I couldn't figure out what it was.

"You play the piano?" I asked. It was a blond spinet whose keyboard needed more than a little dusting.

"Occasionally," he chuckled again. "Do you?"

"Do you mind if I try it?" I had wanted to play a piano whose keys, unlike my old upright upstairs, actually worked when I pressed them.

"Please," he said.

The first couple of chords sounded horrible.

"Ach! Goodness, Walt, this piano is in severe need of tuning!"

He had moved it over the years from Atlanta to Lynchburg, Virginia, then to Minneapolis and finally to St. Paul, and had never had it tuned.

"Well, if you ever expect me to come back here, you're going to have that tuned!" I joked.

Late the following day Walt called me. "I had the tuner come in this afternoon. Now you have no excuse."

During the next few weeks we ran into each other often and met for lunch at The Buttery on a Saturday.

He wasn't a pretty boy, and it seemed to me that he knew it. He had occasional outbursts of arrogance, all related to stories he told me about how dumb some people could be. The subjects he chose for conversation revealed an exceptionally brilliant mind. He was unusually articulate, but his observations were laced with an acrid sarcasm that was often too dark and merciless for me, and I suspected for most other people. Walt was a lonely man. At the bar men would walk up to him, pat him on the back and say hello, but never stayed for too long. When he wasn't sitting at the stool he stood against a wall, always holding a drink in his hand.

"Are you staying here till the last dog goes home?" he asked me one night when he decided to leave the bar earlier than closing time, his usual point of departure. I was sitting with several acquaintances and next to my roommate, who that night had braved the world beyond the closet door and driven with me to Minneapolis.

"Hell, no," I replied. "I'm afraid if I wait till then I'll be the last dog."

When he left one of the friends closest to me asked, "Who's the nerd?"

"Careful," my roommate and occasional bed partner said. "He and this one are like this." He crossed two fingers.

"He's alright," I said.

A Sunday afternoon as I was walking up to Dayton's at Rosedale Shopping Center I caught a glimpse of him and called him out. He started walking in my direction and, when he realized that I had my children with me, turned around and walked away.

"I would have liked to introduce you," I told him that evening.

He chuckled.

A few days later he asked me to lunch at La Fonda de Acebo, a Mexican restaurant on Highway 13. I drove out from downtown and met him there. We had three or four giant Margaritas before and during lunch. Outside the restaurant, where I had decided that I really couldn't go back to work and had to go home to sleep it off instead, Walt grabbed me from behind, pulled me up to him and kissed me hard on the lips.

It so took me by surprise that I couldn't think of anything to say, so I came back with the first thing that sprung to mind.

"Are you collecting for lunch?"

His face melted. A vague semblance of the shadow of a smile remained on his face, and he muted a chuckle.

"I'm only joking, Walt," I said. "Don't be mad at me."

"I'm not," he said, and walked toward his car without saying anything else.

Once in a while I'd stop by in the evening to watch TV with him. The smell was driving me crazy: what in hell was that? It certainly wasn't a deodorizer, but it smelled chemical; it wasn't a clean smell, either: a sour lining made it repugnant. I subtly tried to track it down. It wasn't the bathroom, though it needed a good scrub, especially the sink on which sat the remains of a dry set of contact lenses. It wasn't the kitchen, which Walt seemed to use infrequently. The smell seemed to come from the second bedroom, where I had not been yet.

A few days later Walt had to travel to Germany, where he often went on business. He was the troubleshooting star of his company's computers' operating system, and was in great demand every time a software release revealed that the new and upgraded system had more bugs than my old apartment on Lincoln Avenue.

He came up to our twenty-first story apartment. "Would you be able to look after my cats?" he asked me. He usually drove them out to a friend's house, but she was going to be traveling as well and, if I didn't mind, it probably would be the best solution for him.

"Of course," I said. "I can always take care of pussy."

He chuckled absently and handed me his door key.

That evening I went into his apartment, wondering what taking care of cats entailed. He had left a note on the kitchen counter telling me where the cat litter and food were. I was to take the litter box to the garbage chute in the hall and dump it there, then put fresh litter in it.

It troubled me that the cats were not visible. I figured they were hiding, as they usually did when I first came into the apartment, only to appear later with their intriguingly annoying antics.

The litter box was nowhere I could easily see. I looked in his bedroom and then under the bed in the second bedroom, where the smell that had bothered me so often before became stronger. One of the cats—Pest? Beast?—dashed out when I lifted the bedspread; the other one must have been hiding elsewhere. The stench threw me back. The litter box had not been changed for some time, and the cats had taken to leaving their potty anywhere they could around it. I thought my stomach was going to unload right there.

Clutching my nose I managed to clean out the floor, change the litter, put out dry food and water in the dishes on the floor, and sped out of the apartment after cracking the sliding door that led to the balcony. The smell was a mystery no more.

Early the following morning Walt called to remind me to pick up his mail; he had forgotten to give me the mailbox key, but I would find it in the first drawer of the dresser in a corner of his bedroom. When I returned to the apartment that evening it smelled better, but not much. I headed for the dresser, opened the drawer, and found many things other than the key, which I never did find. Instead, in it Walt had stored several reels of eight-millimeter male porn films, over a dozen half-empty bottles of amyl nitrate, and a rubber replica of a male organ so disproportionate to the real object, that it must have been labeled "Sold only as a novelty item." Nonetheless, it was obvious that the toy had served ambitious intentions.

Whenever my mother asked me to get something from her purse, I would bring the bag to her and let her open it. Privacy had always been an obsession of mine: I found out about anyone was to be strictly what the person wanted to let me know. Even when gossip was meant to save me misery, I resented the breach of decency implied in someone else's misguided belief that he had the authority and right to divulge what was none of his business.

Although I was not snooping when I discovered the items, I felt like a heel for knowing a part of Walt that he had not freely shown me.

But, my lands, that dildo! He must have been fearless.

I wasn't offended. Instead I felt great sadness at what the props represented. Walt had to replace human contact with these approximations. I also felt ashamed of myself and others who had only focused on his physical attributes and found them lacking.

Some days after my unwitting find, in late January, I made up with my partner, from whom I had been separated since Thanksgiving. I told Walt in passing.

The following day I walked out of the building and looked at my car, parked on the other side of the street. An envelope was held down by the windshield wipers.

It was from Walt. He was hurt by my news that I was going back to Randy, a man who didn't deserve me, a man who had treated me like a second-rate trick who had stayed around too long, leaving me behind and failing to nurture our relationship while he went out with his female beard to parties where he could pass for straight.

In all this Walt was right.

Walt wrote that perhaps I should look closer to see who was more willing to spend time with me and give me the respect I deserved. He quoted from *Desperado*. Why wouldn't I come to my senses?

I thought it was sweet of Walt to be so concerned with my emotional well-being. And then I realized what he was really saying. I called him at work; he was silent during most of our conversation. I thanked him for his words about me; however, I felt that my partner and I had spent some good times together and wanted to know whether we should still give our relationship another try.

"Well, you know what you're doing," he replied. Again he chuckled, but not because any of it was funny.

The following morning again I pulled another envelope out from under the wiper. Walt was in pain. He didn't know whether he loved me, because he had never loved anyone; but if it hurt like this, he couldn't see why anyone wanted it so bad. What was I going to do? Waste my life with someone like that other guy, or give him a chance to let his feelings grow into something he had not experienced before, if I could benefit from it as well?

I didn't know what to say to that, but I stopped by his apartment that evening. His face turned from red to purple as I spoke. I was very thankful, but I saw him as a good friend, a soulmate almost—we could have been brothers, I joked: we had been born two weeks apart.

Sadness clouded his eyes, but he accepted my proposal for friendship.

Soon after my partner and I reestablished our relationship, he demanded that I move elsewhere. He didn't trust my roommate, Joshua Krakowski, and, besides, he couldn't stand him.

Moving day approached, and I had not found anyone to help me. Eventually I got Walt to help together with Tim Ritchie, Karl Steffenhagen and Carlos Rodriguez, a Colombian drug counselor whose house's aromas helped you get high without ever putting a joint to your lips. Carlos had made several attempts to get me in bed. He had finally succeeded one evening when he invited me to his house under the pretense of cooking a large meal for several people, the main dish of which would be *ajiaco*, a spicy Colombian soup I had tasted in Bogotá and wanted to have again. When I got to his house he had made the ajiaco, but I was the only guest. He asked me to sit at the table, then crawled underneath, unzipped me and blew me while his head bobbed up and down under the tablecloth. Carlos had not given up his notion that sooner or later a common language would make us the perfect couple; his lingual abilities were outstanding, but linguistics alone was no basis for a relationship. Besides, junkies scared me.

When we were done with the move I treated everyone to pizza at The Green Mill, off Grand Avenue. It was early April and, although it was still cold, we were overheated from the day-long job. When I sat down my muscular system started to unwind from head to toe; I didn't know whether I would be able to get up after dinner. Tim and Steve sat on the opposite side of the booth; Carlos sat to my left and Walt to my right.

During dinner Carlos slipped his hand under the table and lay it on my crotch. I was too tired to bother to slap it off.

Suddenly I felt Walt's hand slithering on my thigh toward my crotch from the other side.

Then both hands had an unexpected encounter. They both looked at my hand, I suppose wondering whether the other hand was one of mine, but mine were both on the table. The two hands jerked their way back to their respective owners, and I started to laugh uncontrollably.

Neither Carlos nor Walt found it as funny as I.

Some months later I went to work for the same company as Walt. I saw him every day and often consulted him on technical issues about which he was the undisputed expert. He was also a gifted writer whose prose made even the most arcane computer lingo clear to the dullest mind. His interest in me had cooled off, and I felt guilty about it. To ease his discomfort I made the incredible mistake of asking him to dinner at my partner's, where he sat watching us close together and cuddle.

At work the next day I found another envelope. He could not believe my insensitivity and the additional pain I had caused him when he was beginning to heal. Never was I to ask him to come along on anything that included that miserable son of a bitch. I still had his respect and affection, but he thought it would be best if I stayed away from him except for professional reasons.

The truth was that I would have given Walt more than just a little time and attention. I admired him for his intelligence, and I found his reticence endearing. The feeling he could not name, out of something more than just lack of habit, was obvious in his eyes, on his entire countenance, whenever I was around. Even knowing that his physical needs were met through extraordinary facsimiles made me feel he deserved more than just my condescension.

Walt had a very stubborn streak running through him that I only saw him relent on with me. That alone should have drastically changed my aloofness. Even his hygiene had improved while he tried to court me. I don't think he would have ever given his cats away for me, but I would have learned to ignore them.

I'm going around this to avoid saying that I loved Walt, but he scared me: his uncommon intelligence, his obdurateness, the intense passion he tried so hard to quell and that tortured his soul, all of it made me fear that he would overwhelm me and crush my low sense of self-worth. His domestic hygiene we could work on; my self-esteem was a completely different matter.

Two months after Walt warned me about my partner's unworthiness I was again by myself. We ran into each other at work now and then, but nothing was ever the same between us. Walt bought a huge and impractical house in Highland Park: its only valuable feature was an enclosed exterior hall that provided a great deal more room for Pest and Beast than the two-bedroom condo on West Tenth Street. Danny Teeter, a mutual friend, told me that he was seeing someone, and Walt was hoping that the new boyfriend moved in with him. I felt an unexplainable rush of jealousy. The idea that he was with someone else pissed me off.

Walt had not finished unpacking in the new house some four or five months after moving in. He went to the hospital with pneumonia on a Wednesday and had died by Saturday. I had been living for about a month in Pittsburgh by then and was unable to attend his memorial service.

I miss Walt. Most of all, my guilt is still as fresh as if I had last had lunch with him the day before yesterday.

Lesson: Don't let irrational fear make you spend the rest of your life wondering what it could have all been like.

Day 18:

The '60s Were Not Good to Him

Someone with whom I was cruising around The Happy Hour introduced me to Lars Bongard in 1983. He was a compact man of obvious Nordic ascent: his moustache was almost white, as were his eyebrows and abundant hair. His eyes were a translucent blue that could be seen even in the misleading semidarkness of a cruise bar. His face screamed out, "I'm on the far side of fifty."

His eyes lit up when we met. They also fixed their gaze on me. The beautifully straight teeth was an added plus to his smile. He inched his way away from the bar and closer to me.

Lars was gushing, no doubt about it.

I drove him home to St. Louis Park. Along the way he told me that he was a typesetter for a magazine. When we pulled into his house I wondered why I was wasting my time as the vice president of a software company. If typesetters could make enough money to buy mansions in St. Louis Park, I was ready to learn the trade.

He caught me looking at the motorcyclist cap hanging from the mirror above his dresser.

"Relics from the past," he giggled. I tried to imagine this minute Loki in leather gear, but the pink sweater created a bit of cognitive dissonance.

"I was one of the first bartenders at the Ramrod in San Francisco."

"You're from the Bay Area?"

"No, silly. I moved there from here."

He anticipated my next dumb question. "I came back because it was time to get away and rescue myself," he said enigmatically.

Infused with the libertinage of South of Market and the Tenderloin, Lars had shed his Midwestern bashfulness and jumped right into the thick of things. He tried everything at least ten times.

"I became trisexual," he said mischievously. "If I hadn't tried it, I wanted to."

No drug made its way to the dance floors and chain-link fences inside every leather bar and disco in San Francisco that Lars had not tried.

One night before work he replaced dinner with two black capsules, a red pill and a yellow tablet, and donned his bovine apparel down to the Castro to catch a bus to work.

As he descended, around Hill Street, he saw the Pacific slowly crawling down Divisadero. It came up to him, surrounded Lars, reached up to his neck and, no matter how hard he tried to remain afloat, it reached his chin, his nose, his eyes, and covered his entire head. He was drowning, and not until someone shoved a hose down his throat and into his stomach did he feel relief. Actually, he regained consciousness some days later in an intensive care unit at the University of California Medical Center.

That made him want to go back to the simpler things in life—a beer or vodka gimlet once in a while and just a couple of joints a day.

Seeing everyone he knew or had waited on drop dead by the six pack in less than a year may have also contributed to his decision to return to what an acquaintance of mine from New York called boredom with a Swedish flavor.

He wanted to prolong the thirty-eight years he now was. In the morning he offered me a toothbrush. It wasn't new.

"It's alright," he assured me. "I sterilized it." He was serious.

I took it, but used my finger and some toothpaste instead.

We only had time for some coffee. I drove him to the Foshay Tower. He smiled broadly.

"Call me later?"

"Okay," I said, and squeezed his hand.

"Later today?" He smiled.

"Uh-huh, sure."

During subsequent conversations I realized that Lars' charm was his smile. I couldn't see that over the phone, and the awkward silence that followed my remarks put the burden of continuing the conversation on me.

He asked me over for spaghetti the following Saturday night. He was just as obsequious, but a bit more talkative, perhaps because we were joined by Gary, a saturnine though handsome man in his thirties who sat in the living room rolling joints. He offered me one before, during and after dinner, all of which I declined. Lars and Gary, however, smoked them the way other people eat bread sticks. Gary barely said three words all night. At the end of the meal he retired to a bedroom and gave Lars and me the privacy we needed.

The following Saturday Lars was hosting a party to which he invited me. Over and over again. One of my employees lived in St. Louis Park; the party came up in conversation.

"You're going to a party where?" John asked surprised.

I told him again.

"Those guys are a patrol car magnet. Their parties tend to get pretty rowdy."

John knew, since he lived two blocks over and claimed to hear the racket as if it were in his own backyard.

I decided not to go.

Friday of that week I had my wisdom teeth removed, and I had the perfect excuse to skip the party.

Oh, but at what price, I thought. I got dry sockets, a common problem with wisdom teeth extractions: the gum surface starts to heal sooner than the inner pocket where the tooth is removed. The pain was so severe that by mid-afternoon Saturday no amount of acetaminophen manufactured anywhere was enough to soothe the throbbing ache. Any man who's ever had his balls squeezed in a vise grip can relate to the experience. The difference was the pain's location.

I walked up to Ramaley's on Grand Avenue and availed myself of the largest bottle of Jack Daniels they had. My plan was to drink myself into a stupor and pass out until the pain had subsided. It was a plan fraught with sound and fury and solving nothing. Alcohol was the worst for the problem, I found out Monday when I went back to have the sore sockets packed. Then I was drunk and in excruciating pain that lasted all weekend.

Monday morning's paper carried the news that made my bed-confining agony all worth it. The house on Cedar Lake Road had been under surveillance. Our quiet Gary—as my granny used to say, God deliver me from still waters—owned a marijuana farm in Iowa, and brought his crop across the state line to Lars', where it was packaged and distributed. Saturday night the police raided the party and the cavalcade of paddy wagons outdid Wringling Brothers parades.

Thus was the mystery unraveled of the typesetter with the impressive house.

Lesson: Stay out of mansions whose owners couldn't possibly afford unless they have suddenly become grand heirs to the remaining Rockefellers—even if the sex belies myths of Nordic coldness and takes you into hitherto unknown out-of-body experiences.

Day 19:

The Banality of Evil Personals

An acquaintance of mine by the name of Tom Ryan used to advertise in the personals of the *City Pages* in Minneapolis. He had dozens of stories about failed attempts to meet Mr. Perfect, Mr. Right or even Mr. Right Now through his ads. The last one was his lover, a young candidate for some twelve-step program whom he surprised in bed with someone he met at Lund's on Lake Street—it was inevitable: that particular supermarket had been voted best all-around cruising place in the Twin Cities the previous year. The worst case before that one was the physician who had sent Tom a picture from freshman year in college, when he was 200 pounds lighter and still had some hair on his head. He spent the night asking Tom when they were going to make whoopee—asking Tom, of all people, who had a deep-seated phobia against anything over 1 percent of body fat. His other phobia, he had discovered, was to grown men who were still asking for whoopee in 1983.

Tom and his friend Floyd Hill shared letters. Whenever Tom got a letter from a would-be homo Romeo that he felt was more suitable for Floyd, he would take it over to Floyd, and Floyd, in turn, reciprocated.

Floyd was a short-order cook in a diner on University Avenue. He claimed he was a chef, which I believe he was, but was cursed by fire. He had worked at three major restaurants that, for accidental reasons, had all burned down to the ground.

From a distance of a mile away anyone could tell that this man was very much in touch with his feminine side. At least his wrists so indicated. He had a loud, high-pitched voice that he often rose beyond what was necessary.

One morning when I was just stepping out of the shower to go to work, the phone rang. I thought my wife might be calling me with an emergency: no one else called at seven in the morning.

"This is Floyd," he said. "Floyd Hill. I'm a friend of Tom's. Tom Ryan's?"

Was Tom dead?

"He gave me your phone number so that I could call you."

Right there I developed a profound dislike for both Floyd and Tom. Handing out my phone number was not something I appreciated, and I would call Tom to let him know in ways that he would never forget.

Then Floyd went on to tell me that Tom and he exchanged letters, replies they had received to their ads.

"I didn't meet Tom through the personals," I said in my iciest tone.

"Oh, I know, but I just wanted you to know that he wouldn't be referring me to you if you weren't alright."

Yes—but how about you? He was not reassuring me that he didn't have a loose screw.

"I was wondering if you'd like to stop by sometime? Or maybe we could go out to eat or something?"

"I'm sorry—what was your name? Boyd? Floyd. Pardon me. I don't know you, and until I talk to Tom I don't think I should say anything one way or another." I told him I had to run.

I called Tom Ryan, who was still in bed. What in the fucking world ever possessed him to think that I would appreciate him giving my number to some burger turner?

Tom didn't think it would bother me so much, but added that he had known Floyd for a few years and he was perfectly safe. I had nothing to worry about.

Later that evening, when I came home from visiting my children, the phone rang. It was Floyd again. Had I called Tom? What had he said? Well?

I was too tired to argue or offend someone I had never met. That he was pressuring me, however, did not bode well.

I suggested that we meet for breakfast downtown St. Paul the following Saturday. He protested: it was getting cold to stand out waiting for the bus and, although he lived just below St. Paul's Cathedral, it was too far to walk in the cold either. He would go, however, if I'd pick him up.

He was in the two-story building's lobby waiting for me when I drove up. He brushed the sidewalk with fast shuffling of his feet until he got to my car. His dyed hair was styled into a hairsprayed helmet. The eyeliner was obvious around the blue eyes. His lips had never fully developed into more than a thin pink line. I couldn't see his torso: the fringed turquoise suede jacket covered it.

"Oh, this stuff is aaaaawful," he kept saying during breakfast. He could have prepared something a lot better, and we would have never had to leave his apartment.

Floyd had been involved in a very serious relationship with a very, very, veeeeh-ry abusive man who lived up in Roseville. Ah! Whenever his lover was ill and confined to his bed, Floyd would make him a very, very, veeeh-ry fancy meal and take two bus changes—two!—to get it up to him. And did he appreciate it? Uh-uh, never. Never! As soon as he got a chance, bam, he'd have his fists in Floyd's eyes. He had been very, very, veeeh-ry unlucky in love, no one appreciated anything he did, everyone took advantage of him.

For food that was so aaaaawful, he sure ate it slowly and completely.

"I'm sorry," I said, "but it's getting late, and I have to go pick up my children."

"You have children?" I could not read his expression. I didn't know whether it was disappointment or interest popping out on the lump on the side of his full mouth.

"Yes, two. They live with their mother down the street here, so I have drop you off and drive back."

His expression was more legible then. It was acute disappointment, evinced by his rolling eyes and his twisted mouth. It was a tacky consideration, but if my children could help me out of this, I'd need all the help I could get.

I paid the bill and we left. I drove up to the curb, but instead of opening the door he remained immobile.

"So you don't have time to stop in for a little while?"

Oh, Lord, this was beginning to look like a hideous mistake.

"No, I don't."

"How about later today?"

"I don't think so. Tonight I have to go to the library to do some research."

"The library? Down there?" He pointed downtown toward the public library.

"No, back there," I said, pointing west. He was completely lost. "Wilson Library. The University of Minnesota. The West Bank."

"Why? Aren't you too old to be in school?" His tone was beginning to grate on the stub of my last nerve.

"I'm writing my disser—a book I have to write to get my doctorate."

"Oh. A brainy one." He paused, mouth agape. "Can I call you later?"

Oh, geez, what the hell for?

"If you wish."

During the next few days Floyd kept my phone line busy, if not with me at the other end, at least with repeated attempts to reach me.

On a Thursday he called to ask me to go dancing that night at The Grand Finale.

"I have work to do," I explained.

"Well! That's very, very, veeehry interesting. But you know, all work and no play, you know what they say."

"This is not regular work. I need to check some references at the library, and I have time to do it tonight. Plus I have to check out some books."

"I could go with you," he said, "and then we can go dancing."

How many ways were there to tell his guy I had no interest in him?

"Okay, if you want. I'll pick you up around seven."

"Come on in and we'll have a little dinner before we go," he offered.

"No. Tonight I'm eating with my children. Thank you, though."

"Hmmm. If you'd rather have dinner with brats," he said, surely without a clue of how he had ruined every chance he never had of getting past a few phone calls with me. My children were, still are untouchable. No man ever got anywhere near my heart who said a word I interpreted as even slightly negative about my children. The burger turner had served me the last greasy hockey puck.

"No, tonight is when I have dinner with my children, not with brats."

He caught it—so he wasn't that stupid after all.

"My offer is on the table," I said.

"What table?"

"I mean my offer is open. You can accept it or turn it down," I said.

"Oh. Sure, I'll go."

He came down the steps and stormed out of his building in knee-high fringed suede boots to match the jacket's material. His pants were yellow denim. Not until we arrived at the library and he took off the jacket did I realize that the yellow shirt's sleeves were puffed.

I walked ahead of him, hoping I wouldn't run into anyone I knew. I felt him bouncing along trying to catch up with me.

"Oh, dear, all these books!"

I found two books I wanted to check out, and pulled out one to look through the index, in case I could use it also. Floyd sat at the other side of the table looking around and tapping his fingers. I realized several other people were glaring our way, and I stood up to leave.

When we got to the club the clientele was thin. It was before nine, and the crowd that usually filled The Grand Finale was yet to arrive. The music started to blare, and, as if under its spell, Floyd grabbed my hand and migrated to the dance floor.

"Let's dance!" he said with an unabashed flair.

"I'd rather wait until there are more people on the floor," I said.

"Oh, don't be shy. We're wasting great music," he protested. It was *The Dancing Queen*, on the speakers and on the dance floor.

He continued to pull me by the hand, and rather than make a scene by knocking his brains out as he tried to drag me onto the dance floor, I went along.

The lights were strobing, the music deafened us until neither of us would have heard the fire truck alarms that Floyd was so familiar with. He let go me and started to spin in the middle of the dance floor. Soon he was flexing his knees and whirling around like a plumed thespian doing the Mexican bird dance.

I shut my eyes, hoping that everyone I already knew or could have ever met was home watching some brain-dead sitcom. Eventually the damn song ended, something else less linguistically exotic blended in with the "only seventeen" coda of ABBA's masterpiece, and Floyd was warm enough to want to get off the floor.

Around midnight I told him that we had to leave, since I had to work early the following day. I stopped in front of his apartment building, and again he tried the pressure-sell approach from some days before.

"Floyd, I'm tired. I've had a long day, and I need to get home. I really don't want to sit here to discuss it. Please get out."

He pouted. "Well, that's very, very, veeehry nice. I accompanied you to that boring library, then you hardly danced all night, didn't talk much, and now you don't even want to come up for a little while."

"That's right, I don't. I really have to go home."

I was beginning to understand why his serious lover had become seriously irritated enough with him to give him serious shiners.

Saturday he called to invite me to lunch at his place on Sunday. He was going to have several other people there. Tom Ryan was going to be there. Tom's friend too. And some other people he didn't know if I knew. I was to be there by noon.

I knocked at his door at five after twelve. He came to the door and yelled at my face, "Well, it's about time you showed up!" I looked behind him at the rest of his guests, most of them people I had seen in bars and wondered what starship they had fallen out of.

Floyd moved out of the way to let me in. He turned around and screamed, "I hope the grapefruit is not dry! If it is, it's your fault!" Everyone in the room was staring at me. They had taken time out from their inspection of back issues of *Blueboy*, all of which apparently Floyd had provided for his guests in lieu of hors d'oeuvres.

"I hope you know everyone here, because I don't have time to introduce anyone. I have to take the grapefruit out of the oven!" He left me in the middle of the living room and disappeared into the kitchen.

What can anyone say after the host has berated him at the door for causing Southern Comfort to evaporate from pink grapefruit halves?

Conversation was much less amusing than I had anticipated. I had anticipated that it would be as sharp as a ten-year old syringe needle. Most of it had to do with recent disappointments and exquisite joys with tricks obtained through personal ads. The guests were all graduates of Floyd's School of Charm, with the exception of some who had gone on to finishing school. Tom Ryan was even more worthy of the name Joshua Krakowski had given both him and his gay brother, the Lee sisters, Home and Ug; Tom had earned his own nickname, Delia. Delia Dull.

Other than the grapefruit I dried up with my unforgivable tardiness, by the following morning I could not remember what else we ate. As soon as several other guests started to get up to leave, I figured I should be out of there before I was the only one left with Floyd.

"What, you're the last one to arrive and the first one to leave?" he yelled.

"Sorry, you know I have other responsibilities." Before he could inject another barb, I raised my voice and added, "Thank you for a wonderful lunch."

Some weeks later I was being courted in a bar by a stunning man, a waiter in a Chinese restaurant downtown St. Paul. He had given me his undivided attention all evening long at The Town House. He excused himself to go to the restroom, and without a warning I saw Floyd six inches away from my face.

"I can't believe this!" he whined. "You've been standing there with that trash all night, that—that man, I mean, didn't you see that disgusting scar on his forehead?" He came even closer to my face and pinched my waist. "You wouldn't give me the time of day, and instead you spend all this time with that? I was willing to let you make love to me, and you refused me. For that? Oh!" he said in dismay.

"Floyd, get the fuck away from me right now and get out of my face before you end up on your ass," I said, noticing the approach of my attentive waiter. I didn't want him to think I was being tacky with someone else while he was voiding his bladder.

Floyd turned away with his nose in the air. Whenever I ran into him again after that he made the same gesture after first making sure that I had seen him.

Some eight years later, after I had moved away to Pittsburgh, I stopped at The Town House with a group of friends during a visit. An old friend, Patrick Donohoe, stopped by to say hello. Standing behind him, and holding his hand, was a bleached blond with no lips and obvious eyeliner. When Patrick tried to let him come through to meet me, the blond said, "I think I know you from somewhere. The name escapes me. It's—wait, let me think," he said, feigning temporary amnesia.

When my name finally reached the thin lines of his lips, I simply replied, "Yes," and proceeded to ignore him until he walked away with his nose in the horizontal position. But at least this time he did walk away.

Lesson: True friends seldom pass your name, address, telephone and Social Security number around to people they would rather have for themselves. If someone is passing your telephone number around to like-minded losers, make sure you slap him good five or six dozen times. Then move to Pittsburgh.

Day 20:

Black Holes and Other Cosmic Cavities

Greg Miller was that way. I don't know why I bothered, but I did. During that brief interval we spent together he carried out all of those stereotypical acts that we don't want to admit to when heterosexuals point their judgmental fingers. Trouble is, heteros are sometimes, lamentably right—not that we have cornered the market on disloyalty and duplicity.

He stood on the side of a queer road contained by the four walls of the Y'All Come Back Saloon as I traveled one night through the Minneapolitan drunken universe. He held a homo equivalent of a Reaganomical sign: will fuck for a chance to scar you for life. I must have been intrigued; it's the best explanation I can give for applying my brakes. I did roll down the window. Nothing was very clear except the sign, but I let him hop in anyway.

That memorable first time, when the bar closed he took me to a loft in Abe Rosenberg's downtown store, which during business hours Greg managed while mismanaging himself. Abe's was a few steps away from the bar where we met. Greg disabled the burglar alarm, we entered and climbed the precarious steps to the loft. Amidst the squalor of the underdesigned second floor and the threatening noises of marauding rats, I exploded into his ample bottom.

He was full of crap. Figuratively, that is. He told me he had broken up with Arnold Kaplan, and my willing naiveté believed it. Until, that is, one night when we stood at the bar at the Happy Hour on Hennepin. Everything seemed as usual, but suddenly Greg threw my arm off his shoulder and pushed me away from him. This Arnold who had reportedly passed on to that limbo where extended one-night stands are supposed to go? There he was, alive and well. Greg walked toward him. I slipped around the bar into the Gay 90s side of the complex, and went home.

The phone rang later that morning. Greg wanted to know why I had disappeared. It sounded like a completely different person on the other end of the line, totally baffled by my departure. I felt embarrassed for him, as is usually the case when I run into these characters who think they really have taken me for a fool. Often I refuse to go my own way, perhaps attempting to confirm that I misjudged such people, believing that no such scum can inhabit the earth, and I'm just paranoid. Just as often I simply end up stressed out and angry, accused of pathological Latino jealousy, cursed with an overactive imagination.

On a trip to Key West the previous week, Greg had pushed my head down toward the bottom shelf of a showcase in a department store.

"Check if there's a better pair of those glasses down there."

He had not realized that the trifold mirror on the counter afforded me a complete view of the lustful faces he was making at the clerk behind the case while I supposedly looked for eyeglasses. I felt no jealousy. I was only embarrassed for him.

"We call him the Black Hole of Calcutta," this total stranger told me an evening at The Brass Rail while Greg excused himself to go to the bathroom. "One night I took him home and me and my four roommates fucked him on the dining room table. I think he could have taken five or six more in and still lay there fresh as a tuna truck."

And that was the person with whom I had spent what now seemed a pretty significant chunk of my life. I was embarrassed for myself. Being fooled is not so bad if we know we are being fooled and go along for the ride, fully aware of the game, and knowing that we have the power that the betrayer mistakenly believes to hold himself. But to realize that beyond the ruse the person is also something everyone else perceives as a specimen of the filthiest, most worthless human tripe—that's quite different. Mother used to say you can't dig your bare fingers in mud and expect to remain spotless. Greg helped me understand the wisdom of her neurosis.

The last time I saw Greg a couple of years later I was walking down Marquette and happened to look into Abe's. Greg looked like a caricature of himself: his skin was stuck to his bones and a portent of impending death lurked behind his eyes. He didn't seem to recognize me. Maybe my terror contorted my countenance into the image of someone he had not yet had.

Lesson: Be leery of men who have recently broken up with a lover— their ex may be surprised to know.

Day 21:

Back to Poodle Skirts and Bobby Sox

On the evening of my thirty-seventh birthday I kept an appointment with Laverne to have my hair cut at Philip Pelusi's Salon in Ross Park Mall, in Pittsburgh's North Hills. It was my gift to myself. I had lived in the area for about three months; Laverne was the only stylist who could handle my crewcut without making me look like a fool.

When I walked out of the fancy barber shop my eyes noticed the cutest tight butt on the cutest buffed body, not large, but compact and definitely complete in all important ways. I waited until he turned around: he was just as good-looking from the front. He noticed me as well. I pretended to window-shop, he pretended to be just as interested in ladies' shoes at 9 West.

Nonchalantly I continued to look into store windows, but I was actually looking for a reflection to tell me, without having to turn around, that he was still following me. He was.

At the end of the wide hallway I saw that set of letters, Sears, which together with "Rest Area Ahead," all practicing gays know well, is the universal symbol for quick restroom sex.

I walked in first and stood at the urinal. He followed me in and washed his hands until the only other person in there left. He walked up to the urinal next to mine, started massaging himself and looked over the modesty panel.

"I'm sorry," I said. "These places make me nervous."

"Me too," he whispered.

I zipped up and walked out. Within seconds he was out also. I approached him and asked him whether he wanted to go to my car.

He nodded.

On the way there he introduced himself as Luigi Mannina.

"Ah, Italian," I observed.

"Yeah. From Bloomfield." He was thirty-one. "You shopping."

"I'm celebrating my birthday with an overpriced haircut," I joked.

"Hmmm. Happy birthday. Let's see what I can do to help you celebrate."

From the looks of it, plenty. But the promise of pleasure and its delivery are often at odds, and so they were that night. We were both worried that we might be caught in a parked car. Though, he pointed out, Pennsylvania doesn't have antisodomy laws, they can still get you for indecent exposure.

I asked him how I could contact him. He asked me where I worked.

"That's a spooky place," he laughed nervously when I told him. "That's where they're making nuclear shit."

"It's not true, but you're right. It's a creepy place full of creepy people."

He gave me his phone number, but warned me that he worked nights and was seldom up before noon. He was a lab technician at West Penn Hospital on the Avenue, as locals referred to Liberty Avenue. Not to be confused with the artery that ran through the black neighborhood north of Bloomfield, East Liberty—'Sliberty.

We talked on the phone several times before finally getting together for dinner at Ritter's Diner, a funky eatery known for the blend of human types—weekends past midnight it's a haven for revelers and drag queens. From there we went to Schenley Park's Wedding Ring. This is a part of Schenly Park known to about 10 percent of Pittsburghers as the Queer Ring. Once you enter the dead-end street, you can't be going anywhere except the ring, which is a wide cul-de-sac lined up with cars day and night, year round. Some cars are empty; its occupants are probably behind the bushes and on the perilous hillside—one wrong step, and you end up on the Penn-Lincoln Parkway below, just down from the Squirrel Hill tunnel. Some cars have one or two, perhaps three people in them. One or two of the temporary occupants may be the drivers of the cars with no one in them.

It's not the safest place on earth. Fraternity boys from nearby Carnegie Mellon University and the University of Pittsburgh have been known to find great pleasure in assaulting park denizens and their vehicles. As soon as I stopped my car on the side of the road, I knew it was not going to work. The threat of attack or peepers made an otherwise exciting opportunity very undesirable.

He suggested we go to his house. However, this was not going to be an easy proposition.

I drove into the alley behind his house, at the end of one of Bloomfield's narrow streets, overlooking the railroad tracks in the ravine. He got out of the car while I stayed behind. He first had to check whether someone was in the house. He came out a while later and got in the car. His sister and her boyfriend were in the living room, but if I didn't make any noise I'd be able to go up to the converted attic that was his bedroom without his sister noticing me. The stairway was separated from the living room by a floor-to-ceiling wall.

I entered the kitchen behind him. He signaled me when to stop before he'd walk ahead, listening out for any indication that his sister might be coming toward the kitchen or the adjoining dining room. I walked on. When he got to the threshold of the living room, he signaled for me to stop as he kept walking. He stopped to say something to his sister, and while standing by the wall he signaled for me to go ahead upstairs.

I climbed the stairway as quietly as I could and continued until I arrived at the attic door. He came up behind me and unlocked it. The room was dark; he walked ahead and turned a lamp on. The view overwhelmed me, but I tried to conceal it. A room could not look like that unless a tornado had hit it repeatedly over a decade. Mounds of dirty clothes littered the floor. I suddenly realized why his clothes always looked as if he had pulled them out of a dirty laundry basket. Here and there were

sheets of paper made into balls that have obviously been attempts at writing something or, from the heading visible on a few of them, someone's
attempts to get payment on Visa and MasterCard accounts. The bed had
not been made, maybe in years. The bed sheet on it must have been used
to mop the kitchen floor, maybe the dirt backyard, and put back on the
bed immediately afterwards. In a compartment separated from the rest of
the room by a folding door he had a half-bathroom, a sink and a toilet.
The toilet had not benefited from a scrub perhaps since it was installed.
The soap scum on the sink was iridescent: maybe the water that flowed
through it came from Neville Island, a toxic dump on the Ohio River.
Next to his bed lay a pile of *Blueboy, Inches, Playgirl* and other nude male
magazines, and next to the pile a kicked over, half-empty giant-size jar of
Vaseline petroleum jelly, no lid. The two-tone brown and vanilla carpet
most likely hid untold filth.

"We have to be very quiet," he warned me. That meant that we could
not both walk simultaneously around the room, and when *that* moment
came, I had to be quiet as a mouse. I'd ask how quiet that was from one
of the many I was sure lived under the piles of rubbish and dirt.

I feared lying on his bed. Something had to be growing on it, something he was used to that would have a feast devouring my skin. I had
lived in South America, where mosquitoes never bothered the locals, but
left me welts the size of half-dollars. It was deja-vu all over again.

I conquered my fears and stripped, but before getting in his bed I
slipped my hand under the sheet and, while he kissed me, I pushed it off
the bed. It was a gamble: God knows what organism thrived on the bare
mattress, but at least the light was out and I had not seen it, whereas the
sheet posed a certain health hazard. Out of sight...

When we were finished he handed me a towel stiff with dry substances,
which I cast aside slowly, not wanting to betray my revulsion. I wiped my
hands instead on the bare mattress.

He had to go to work, as it was close to eleven. I dressed up as quickly as I could, and he repeated the entrance routine in reverse to make sure that I left undetected by his sister.

During the next few months I learned more about Luigi, and it was not all great news. As a young man he had done drugs of all kinds. This explained why sometimes while we talked over dinner or parked somewhere he would go into a deep trance. I was beginning to think that I had a soporific effect on him, but I was no hypnotist. His brain was—how to say it? Burned out. I pitied those poor patients at the hospital, whose blood samples were being handled by a man who should have hung a sign on the side of his head: "Vacancy."

But I also felt sorry for Luigi. His mother had been laid off from her job as a secretary when she refused to work on a computer and forget the typewriter, and was reduced to sweeping floors at Shadyside Hospital six days a week at minimum wage. While his father was alive things had been more comfortable; he was a plumber, and his income provided for the family. Now his sister was enrolled at Allegheny County Community College getting a degree in developmental studies, but she was deep in credit card debt and drove a car that was, quite literally, falling apart. Luigi felt he was called upon to support his mother and his sister; that he couldn't be the provider his father had been hurt his pride and made his life a constant mortification.

His mother and sister had no inkling of this. His mother's idea of scolding him was to belittle his hygiene. His sister took more direct shots at him: "Hey, faggot, someone's on the phone for you." It didn't matter who was calling or for what reason.

Unfortunately, he searched for quick fixes and get-rich-quick schemes that always backfired. He started a service to provide printed advertising for neighborhood businesses using my computer and design software. He miscalculated how much materials would cost and ended up making up the difference out of his own pocket. He purchased cheap jewelry in a warehouse on the Strip District, that he planned to sell in a kiosk at

Northway Mall. But when the Christmas shopping season ended, and he had to pay the mall for the spot, he was hundreds of dollars short. He bought a pickup truck from his older sister's husband, who was a car sales-man, to carry firewood that he was going to sell on the side of the road. He spent four days under freezing rain without a single person stopping by to get any of the firewood he had paid for with cash withdrawals against a MasterCard account. In a month he had to turn the pickup truck in and lost the money he had invested in it as a business venture.

He was such a Sad Sack that his mere appearance made him a chump before his lowered tone of voice made it clear that he was over his head.

He hated going to bars, which was alright with me, except that his reac-tion when we did go to one made me realize how much he hated himself. People who were standing around with their arms around each other were disgusting; anyone kissing anyone else, as a friendly gesture or as a way to demonstrate affection, was nauseating to him.

"Ugh" was his favorite expression whenever an obvious gay man was around. Slowly I began to see myself in those terms: after all, I, too, was one of those ughy people. It told me how little Luigi respected me and our relationship. I had survived several years earlier in my life with a person who felt the same way, and didn't want to go back into a closet of low self-esteem that someone else had built for himself. When it came to that, I needed no architect other than myself.

We continued to sneak into his house. Close calls started to scare me. His sister came up the steps one night and almost caught me stark naked and with something in my mouth. One night several people were milling through the house downstairs, and for a while it seemed as if I would never be able to leave. Finally, just before he had to be at work, everyone moved to the kitchen, and I was able to slip out through the front door—the only time I used that way of getting into his house.

Eventually the feeling that I was back in junior high school, getting ushered into some school slut's house while her parents were away, got to be too much for me. When he started saying that he needed a little coke to snort to get him out of the gutter, I knew that his was not a gutter, but a deep sewer that was about to drag me with its waste into a tightly shut cesspool. No cocaine has ever been refined enough to pull him out of that.

"I'm sorry, Luigi. I need to be with a man. No, I don't mean that you aren't masculine, far from it, you're very, very masculine, very straight acting and straight looking, really you are. I mean that I need to be with someone who's evolved into full maturity."

What I needed was someone who had evolved into full humanity, but why rub his nose in it?

Lesson: The mess they live in is exactly the mess you're getting into.

Day 22:

Blanche DuBois Does Pittsburgh

Have you ever known someone who is plumful of stories of sleaze, acts he has witnessed but never performed, all involving his best friend? In Louis Molinaro's case, that would be Ray, who according to the narratives was evil incarnate, the whore that ate Pittsburgh and several cruise ship crews, and never was above any perversion. It never dawned on me: What was Louis doing while Ray did all of these things, if they went everywhere together? But who wants to admit that his boyfriend is a common tramp? No sooner did Louis and I walk into a bar, followed by the pink horde of friends *cum* old tricks, he'd start to point out all the men he had had. This Jezebel had more playtime than Capablanca. Back in the '70s that would have made him popular; in the late '80s it raised a flag of fear that he might be a carrier of unknown bugs.

Never mind the peculiar way we met.

Well, okay, if you insist.

On a Sunday afternoon in late June, I was shopping at Ross Park Mall, looking for a computer book at Waldenbooks. This hunky guy in shorts kept walking by. I looked up, smiled, and the next time he walked past me he grabbed my crotch. I didn't kick him; instead, I gave him my phone number. His name was Tom.

But, alas, Tom was involved with a very possessive man, Greg, an electrical engineer who had ways of tracking incoming and outgoing phone calls when he wasn't home. So Tom called me from work at St. Francis Medical Center, where he was a medical technologist. We tried to come up with a convenient way to meet, but Greg's shadow weighed heavy on Tom's fears, and he came up with a scheme that involved a friend of his.

He would call this friend, Louis Molinaro, and give him my phone number. Louis Molinaro would then call me, and we would agree to meet at his house later in the week. During the weekend Tom and Greg would come to visit Louis, and I would be there as well. I would thus meet Greg, and subsequently when Tom and I met for lunch, let's say, Greg would know who I was and wouldn't be as suspicious. I would be Louis' friend— "You know, you met him."

When Tom called me Saturday morning after talking to Louis, he was very unhappy. He had not expected Louis and I to become sexually involved so quickly. Louis and I were supposed to go to a movie, then each should have gone home. We were both to blame: Louis should have known better than to have a taste before Tom got to it. After all, he had trusted Louis. Was there no decency left?

How could I not like Louis? At least I had to be grateful. He was pleasant to look at, especially the bubble behind him, if you could focus on him long enough without becoming sea sick: he had a habit of biting his nails as he swung from side to side when he was standing. He quickly started smothering me with praise: if flattery were slime, I'd be putrid. He needed me, he wanted me, he couldn't live without me, he couldn't count his blessings, what a catch, what a find.

"If you hadn't wanted to do it that first night I would have been crushed," he'd say, and enthralled by his sticky eloquence I did not realize that what he meant was, "If I hadn't seduced you that first night, I'd have one less notch on my ship mast."

He introduced me to his friends—how could he not, they were always around—all of whom had female nicknames—Louis' was Emily, and when they attempted to call me Consuela, well, that's where I drew the line. His was a whole troupe of viciously gossipy queens, all except Daniel, who had been a lover and on whom I often wanted to try the old mirror trick: if steam formed on the mirror, he must have been breathing. To say he was boring in speech and demeanor was just not enough. He was stultifying. His mere appearance had the same effect as Xanax.

Louis was a travel agent with a company that specialized in travel arrangements for corporate clients. He had an office close to the GNC building downtown Pittsburgh. At noon when he went to lunch he must have had nothing better to do than get me greeting cards. During the three months we saw each other he sent me a greeting card every day. I assumed he cared for me more than just for a passing fancy. I did feel grateful; no one had ever shown such an interest in keeping me around. Or at least in mailing me daily affirmations of love in Hallmark verse.

When August rolled around he made me join the gay bowling league, whose past president he had been: "It's never been as good as when I was in charge." The marriage of bowling and me was not made in heaven. But every Sunday afternoon, when the second-floor bowling alley made a concession to let the fag league bowl before the real bowlers came in, there I was, riding with Louis to Oakland to bowl with the rest of the beer guzzling queens. You couldn't miss Louis. He didn't roll the ball down the lane: he dropped it when his arm arched up and gravity took care of the rest.

He had been to many bowling championships, the most memorable to him in Columbus, Ohio, when his team, all in drag, was left stranded at the hotel lobby waiting for a bus that then broke down on the freeway. When a state trooper walked into the bus to inquire whether he could help, one of the team members screamed from the back, "Look, a man in uniform!" The trooper stepped out and got back in his patrol car.

When he wasn't bowling or entertaining the troops, he was starching and ironing his clothes. He was very particular about this chore. It was the only time when Louis did not answer the phone, which seemed to hold a spell on his otherwise uncluttered consciousness: the phone rang and Pavlov was once again vindicated.

I had planned a trip to St. Paul in late August. Louis was broke and couldn't go. I told him I'd miss him.

He started to sob uncontrollably. "I'll be miserable every day you're gone."

It didn't cross Louis' mind that a week earlier he and Ray had gone to Los Angeles to visit an old friend, and Ray came back full of nasty hints that they had done more than visit the friend with some new acquaintances they had met at Oil Can Harry's. I had already been accused of being pathologically jealous, so I bit my lip and tried to ignore the obvious allusions to activity I was not supposed to know about. "Ray, Ray!" Louis kept yelling as I drove them back to Louis' from the airport. I needed Ambesol and an ice pack for my lip by the time I got home.

So when my turn came to visit old friends in the Twin Cities, I had not thought it was necessary to bring Louis along. He felt differently. He got the free airline ticket from the agency, and I picked up the tab for everything else.

When we got on the USAir plane, the female flight attendant came around to ask whether we wanted a beverage when we took off.

"Whatever you have to give," I said jokingly.

"You guys want everything, don't you?" she said flirtatiously.

When she turned around, Louis yelled, "She wants your cock!"

During the rest of the flight we had no smiles and even less service.

At the Alamo Car Rental counter I checked out a car. Louis grabbed the keys, and that was the last time I saw them until we left again two days later. Louis had this vertigo problem that only affected him in cars, not when he was sailing on his feet. He couldn't ride cars, he said, unless he was driving. So it didn't matter that I was paying for the car, and it mattered even less that I knew my way around a place that had been my home for most of my adult life. I had to serve as navigator.

He made ugly, disdainful faces whenever I suggested walking or driving somewhere in the Twin Cities. The only time he enjoyed going anywhere was when he drove me downtown, and at Suncoast Pictures he bought a copy of *Good Morning, Vietnam*.

The weather had been so great that weekend—the first weekend of sunny days all summer long, locals said—that it was a shame to spend it indoors vegetating in front of a television set. I told him I was walking up to Victoria Crossing, and he made one of the faces.

"You sure like to walk," he muttered through his contorted mouth.

"I didn't come halfway across the country to watch TV. If you don't want to come along, you can stay here." Our host and I were glad to have some time to ourselves to catch up on each other's lives over the previous three years anyway.

He came along and the five blocks between the house and Victoria Crossing became his Lewis and Clark expedition.

"I spent a week in Rome when I went to Italy with my father and never left my hotel room," Louis said proudly.

Our host and I simply made subvocal noises that translated to him as "Oh, really," but were actually closer to, "Jesus Harold Christ, you unabashed boor!"

The extent of Louis's educational and cultural interests were evinced by two revelations he made to me in both moments of total honesty.

One involved the reason he moved to Pittsburgh from DuBois. "My friends and me came to Pittsburgh to a concert by The Village People at the Pittsburgh Arena. Right there I knew I had to quit my job managing the Burger King and move here. Everything was in Pittsburgh. Then Dad bought me the house." He had neglected to tell me that his father, who facilitated his relocation to Village People country, was a combination dry-cleaning mogul and loan shark in Clearfield County, both feared and loathed for his loud vulgarity and joie de mafiosi vivre.

The other was the reason he had hated the new high school built in DuBois during the last year he attended it, before going on to Burger U and airline ticketing school. "It was so different from the old one. It had no places to hide for me to give blowjobs. It was a difficult year for me."

Soon after returning from the exhausting hikes in urban Minnesota he planned a fun trip to the Clearfield County Fair. It had been one of the highlights of Louis's younger days, why, with all the rides, the elephant ears and the snake-pit competition, it was the place to be Labor Day weekend.

We arrived Saturday afternoon and stayed at his friend Ron's house. Ron was a worker in a bottle-making plant who lived in the outskirts of Brockway in northwest Pennsylvania with his blind sister, Barbara. Apparently traffic was heavy at Ron's. Many were the truckers and other doorbell trade who found comfort and joy at Ron's. Whenever he had a guest, he would send Barbara off on a long walk down the country road.

The weekend I joined Louis and several other friends on the pilgrimage to the county fair Ron had sent Barbara off to stay with some relatives.

"God," said Jim, one of the members of Louis' entourage, when we were driving back to Pittsburgh, "I wonder what it must be like to be the village fag."

I was not in a light mood. While Ray and another one of the fellow travelers rushed upstairs and monopolized Barbara's bed, the rest of us had to sleep on the floor in the den. We were joined by Jim and his lover, Herbert, a strapping redhead in the style of Paul Bunyan who seemed capable of sleeping on a bed of nails. My back had not been made to withstand those trials, and I was in pain.

To make our visit more enjoyable, Louis had hooked up with some other belles of the county, one of whom had returned to DuBois after several years working for a circus and was then the bartender at the local country club. He opened the club for us once we got to the place through back roads somewhere in DuBois. The bartender offered us some drinks; I sat at the bar trying to ignore the colorful reminiscing going on around me of days of yore when a group of local queens used to gather at someone's apartment and have drag contests. And so forth. Louis's name continually came up as the host or protagonist of the many dramas.

I realized I should have listened to Ray when he'd tell the out-of-school stories about Louis' past lives, but the closest I ever got to Ray was that night, when irritated by his constant allusions to Louis' sluttishness I almost put his head in the toilet at the country club. Luckily for Ray I was able to control myself and rejoin the others at the main room of the country club, where tables were decorated with yellow and white checkered oilcloths, and every record in the jukebox had some kind of connection with Nashville.

Louis spent the following weekend with his parents. When he came back Sunday—the two-hour trip mysteriously took him almost five hours, and his hands had vestiges of dry seminal fluid, I suspected not of his own manufacture—he had to take a shower before sitting down to talk. He told me that he no longer felt about me the way he had when he left Friday.

"You fight too much," he said in tears.

It was right, I did, perhaps unwarrantedly. I argued with him the time he told me that he always ordered his prints nonglossy at the film developing shop, because it made pictures nasty to lick. I asked him why he had to lick pictures—I was hopeful for an explanation that made him a vanilla obsessive compulsive type—and he replied that he had pictures of men that he liked to lick, especially pictures of some Australian guys he had met on a cruise. Louis and Ray had redefined the concept *cruise ship*.

We argued when he returned from his sojourn to Oil Can Harry's and who knew what West Hollywood alleys.

I also argued heatedly during a birthday party he hosted for one of the minionettes. He wanted to take a picture of his friends, and I turned my back to the camera. He yelled at me to look at him. I got up and left the table, one of two set up for the birthday bunch. I didn't want to appear in a picture he was going to send to the Australian tricks.

When I returned to the table Herbert told me they had been talking about me. I got up again and left the house.

"When Daniel and I lived together we never raised our voice. We never had an argument," he said, earnestly and still weeping.

"You never argued? They never did. "You never became angry?" Never.

What kind of a relationship was that? It lasted five years, and never a cross word, an argument, nothing ever said in anger?

"Anger is a normal human feeling, Louis. I admit that during our time together I felt more uncomfortable than many other times in my life, but I'm not going to apologize for a natural emotion."

He continued to cry. He was dumping me, and he was the one crying.

"Tell me something, just out of curiosity. When something Daniel did bothered you, what did you do?"

"I just pointed it out courteously, and that was the end of it."

Yes, but I had the disadvantage of being equipped to respond to a stab of a steel nail through my hand, whereas Daniel was always in character for a cattle call for *Night of the Living Dead*.

Could it perchance be that Louis was used to getting away with murder without any repercussions?

"Perhaps all that pent up aggression was what made you drift apart."

"We just…Well, we remained friends, and that's all that matters."

"I guess you're right. We're not compatible," I said, reaching for his hands. I was beginning to feel guilty for his tears. I kissed him and, as if in the throes of sex that could bring tears to your eyes, he continued to cry even as we copulated. I felt perverse: his tears made me horny, but it was unclear for which of us this was a pity fuck. The only faux pas that could have ruined this was if he had stopped and, as he had done several times before, asked me whether I had changed my mind about the Hershey's kisses thing.

The next day I thought about the breakup. It puzzled me more than Louis' account of how he had baked with a 25-watt bulb in the Easy Bake oven his parents had given him for Christmas when he was five.

I called him at work and offered to pick him up. We had to talk.

On the way to his house on Kathy Drive (I couldn't make this up if I tried), I tried, cap in hand, to make amends for my transgressions, apologized for letting my anger flow freely, lowered myself to accept his conditions, whichever they were (within unreasonable reason) and suggested that we renegotiate the terms of our relationship.

He remained silent on the passenger side of my Bronco.

"So what do you say?" I asked, finally.

"I just don't feel the way I used to. Things have changed," he shrugged.

Suddenly it became so stupidly clear, everything that great sex had obscured the night before.

"Oh, dear God, I feel so stupid."

"Don't beat yourself up. You said what you needed to say. I think that was really nice," he replied.

"Sure, you would. I have just made a fool of myself. You dumped me, chrissakes, you dumped me, and like a jerk I'm here, driving you home and hoping that we can build on our relationship, when you were telling me to go fuck myself."

We had arrived at his red-carpeted house of ill repute on Kathy Drive. He didn't budge.

"You need to get out," I said. I was more embarrassed than the time I suffered from stool incontinence after eating a panful of bread pudding.

"I think we can be friends," he said, so derivatively and annoyingly.

"I don't see how."

"You can stay in touch. When we have parties you can come over, stop by to watch a movie—"

"And be another Daniel, sitting there in the corner of your tacky sectional while you make out with your current boyfriend? You seem to forget that I am not Daniel. I prefer to think that I can preserve my dignity even after having touched you. You and I can't be friends. We have nothing in common, you spoiled mafia queen. Now get out before I kick you out."

"See," he said, "this is exactly why—"

"Get out!" I was beginning to reach for the softball bat on the back seat, so he must have felt it was healthy to follow my pressing advice.

What I hadn't realized was that Louis's capricious affairettes only lasted for quarters of a year at a time. He saw something he liked, he took it and, when tired of it, he'd put it on a shelf with the rest of the Lobotomy Barbie collection. My quarter was up.

Several years later, when I was dating Jeremy Beaman, I ran into Louis at the Crossover Bar in Pittsburgh's North Side. I said hello, he said hello back.

And after Jeremy Beaman and I were history, Bernie Janosco told me that the two were becoming an item during line-dancing lessons at Donny's Place on Polish Hill.

Pittsburgh was a small place, but, oh, my, such a class act, doncha know?

Lesson: Some people have more than one way to bust your balls and then blame you for leaving them where they could be hurt.

Day 23:

Yuns Got Elegance

"No one I could have had in a classroom were I still teaching." That was my unwritten law for dates. It was full of logical holes. One of my college composition students was a state trooper two years older than I—about three months after school was out he forced me to amend my law.

My legal requirement actually had more to do with age than with the possibility of magisterial conflicts. I did have a bias against becoming physically involved with anyone who could have been my son. Boys in search of daddies abound, but that's a different category of paternal oversight altogether and sometimes is totally unrelated to chronological sequencing.

Others, I have learned, impose far less stringent requirements of a mate. Some just don't want to get tangled in the possibility of jail terms by violating state or federal law regarding minors. A few only demand, from a potential partner for life or for the night, that the candidate be able to spell. His own name is a satisfactory condition for the literacy standard.

I wasn't sure what Bernie Janosco, 60, had in mind when he introduced me, 38, to Greg Howard, 23, at The Crossover Bar. It's true that his corpulence was that of a thirty-year old. A very well fed thirty-year old with an ass as wide as the seat on his aunt's tractor and those thighs that rub against each other like Russian cows'. He was taller than I and certainly bigger in several other areas—not in *that* one, where he was a preschooler. The University of Pittsburgh had just awarded him a degree in electrical engineering; when he was told I worked for a rival school whose international reputation was infinitely superior to the one he attended, he became entranced.

Greg was impressed with credentials, lineage and sophistication. Not because he related, but because he was an active aspirant to the middle class. His mother was a secretary in a small town close to State College in central Pennsylvania; his father was a state trooper—no, not the same one—who could trace his ancestry back to Troy Hill, a community isolated by its own will atop a promontory that overlooked the rest of Pittsburgh. Its inhabitants still referred to blacks as spooks and claimed they would rather burn their houses to the ground than sell them to anyone whose skin was not white.

Greg lived with his grandmother on a hillside facing McKnight Road in Bellevue, a neighborhood just north of Pittsburgh's very black North Side whose erstwhile mansions had given way to multiplex housing and run-down Victorians. In the morning he rode the bus downtown to Fifth Avenue, where he worked as an engineering technician for a computer service bureau.

We had to sneak up the squeaky steps to the second floor of the ragtag building, perched on the edge of the ravine. It was conceivable that if Greg shook around too much the house would slide down and we'd find ourselves fighting traffic on McKnight Road down below. I was quiet for that reason more than for the possibility that we might wake up his granny, retired from Sally's Beauty Shop on West View Road.

Quiet sex laced with interdental implorations to be quieter when I'm already so quiet that I can hear my own breathing is not my idea of excitement, but somehow I managed.

The next day I was summoned by the guard at the front desk of the secured building where I worked to pick up a parcel that had been delivered for me: a teddy bear and a box of chocolates.

"Who left this here?" I asked the surly guard.

He did not lift his eyes from the newspaper. "A tall guy who asked me to wait until he had left to call you."

Greg called later to confirm my receipt of his gift.

During the next couple of weeks Greg and I went to some bars around town, to a late movie in North Park where he tried to unzip my pants to play with my genitals, and to a symphony concert at Heinz Hall. It was pouring when we left the concert hall. Greg had made the mistake of wearing a navy jacket and white pants—it was mid-October, so much for sophistication. I asked him to wait for me in front of Heinz Hall while I went for my car. When I drove around the corner, he had been standing too close to the pouring rain, and his pants had soaked through, revealing from the dark spot on his crotch that he had not worn briefs. I wished no one had seen, but several people had been standing on the other side of Fifth Street pointing at him. I did believe he enjoyed the attention his minuscule appendage attracted, as he giggled like a school girl when he got in the car.

"I'm going on my annual pilgrimage," I told him a few days later when we talked at The Crossover. He didn't understand. "For the past ten or so years I've flown out to Los Angeles, then driven up Highway 1 to San Francisco. I call it my annual pilgrimage to cleanse my mind and recharge my creative battery."

"Oh?" He was enigmatic. "Would you like a traveling companion?"

I had not expected this. My pilgrimage was mine, to be shared with no one else. In the past I had made that trip with someone who had meant a great deal to me, but other than that I didn't want to be held accountable for time schedules within the framework of the ten days I allotted myself to travel. If I wanted to spend a couple of days in San Luis Obispo, tasting the mouth-watering goodies of The Apple Orchard, I wanted to be able to do that. If I wanted to take three more tours at the Hearst Castle in San Simeon, I could stay in a nearby motel and return the following day. If I wanted to gaze into the Pacific for hours from one of the lookout points around Carmel, or sit quietly in the woods in Big

Sur, without anyone to rush me or ask me when we were leaving, that was alright also. If I wanted to plant my ass for three days on a stool at the Twin Peaks on the Castro, or if I wanted to go wait for a whale to deem me worthy of the sight at Point Reyes, it was my time to do so.

But like the proverbial sheep to the slaughterhouse, or the martyrs to the furnace, I told Greg he could come along.

He brought along a video camera as big as his ass, which was already the eighth wonder of the modern world. And he insisted on hanging out of the passenger side of the rental car, filming every filthy corner downtown L.A.

"This is not a safe area to do that in," I warned him. "Get yourself back into the car. One of those gang boys over there is going to steal that camera from you."

"They'd have to chop my hands off before they could do that," he whined.

"Trust me, they will."

Two days after our arrival in L.A. and after visiting all the touristy places I was so tired of seeing, we headed north on the Coastal Highway.

"I want to drive," he whined. "I mean, after all, I'm paying for half the car." The truth was that so far he had paid for nothing. The agreement had been that I would take care of all bills, and then hand him the invoice for his half of expenses when we arrived back in Pittsburgh.

We had barely left Santa Monica behind when he sped up to fifty-five on the leftmost of the two lanes. Behind us an angry blond in a Mercedes convertible blew her horn at us.

"Let her pass," I said. "She won't pass you on the left."

"Why not?"

"We're in California. They drive crazy here, but not that crazy. Move over and let her through."

"Well, I'm doing the max, so I don't need to go any faster."

"Here you're slow traffic. Move over and let her pass us."

"I'm doing the max," he whined again.

"Will you get out of the fucking way and let that woman pass us? You're not a cop, that's her problem. This is California."

Thus was set the tone for the balance of the trip, which had not had a promising start.

We arrived late that evening at a motel in Morro Bay. The only eatery open was at the Arco gas station. I missed the scrumptious flautas I had enjoyed the night before in Long Beach. The closest pseudoedible reminder of the chicken flautas of my dreams was a long dog colored in an unnatural red, rotating in a heated box by the soda counter.

Back at the motel I was tired from the day's drive, but not so tired that I had forgotten the purpose of bringing along a gay traveling companion who had demonstrated great interest in pursuing the physical aspects of our acquaintanceship. It might be difficult to pursue my expectations considering the twin-bed arrangement in the room, but tighter spots had been known to provide sufficient space for a quick romp. Greg was munching on the chips he had picked up at the gasoline gourmet shop and washing them down with a can of soda while watching some TV show.

I went to the bathroom, and when I came out in my underwear Greg had set aside the crinkly bag of chips and the soda can. "You want to wrestle?"

What?

"What was that?"

"Do you want to wrestle?" He almost spelled out each syllable in his whiny nasal voice that always sounded as if he were doing impressions of someone with a speech impediment.

"No, I don't." For a moment I thought he was joking, but now I could tell he was serious.

"Oh, come on," he said. He left his bed, jumped on me and tried to tackle me to the floor, not a Herculean task for a man who was almost as wide as he was tall on the body of a six-foot man who weighed all of 180 pounds.

"Hey, get off me!" I was afraid we might be thrown out of the cheap motel in the middle of the night and have to sleep in the Corsica. "I don't want to do this!"

"You know you want to," he insisted, grabbing my sweater and pulling it until it tore.

"No, I don't," I yelled in his ear and smacked him across the side of his head.

"Okay," he said in a tone that was closer to saying, "Okay, if that's how you want it, but let's see if you're gettin' any from me the next time you're horny."

The following morning we drove up the road to gawk at Hearst's vulgarity. Greg was in awe, except that every other object in the buildings was just like the one his aunt Lucy had seen, bought, brought back or shown him following one of her many trips to so many exotic places. It was too bad that his aunt Lucy had not invited him to go on a trip that coincided with my vacation.

"Most of it stolen from European ruins after World War I," I said when we took the bus ride back down to sea level.

"Did you have to ruin it for me?" he said in dismay.

Eventually we arrived in the city that my ruby-red slippers had led me. I wanted to go to the Cliff House and watch the ocean change from blue to lead in the span of a few minutes, to Muir Woods, Exposition Hall, the Palace of Fine Arts, the top of the Hyatt; I craved for walks around North Beach, Chinatown and Nob Hill, I had longed for a year to sit outside Ghirardelli Square and do all of the silly things that tourists do around Fisherman's Wharf, to take the ferry to Sausalito and take in the night view from Twin Peaks and, of course, the even better sights of Castro Street from Castro Station to Twentieth Street. My feet itched to trek down to Union Square and do a little reckless shopping at Nieman-Marcus, I. Magnin and Gump's. Before all that could happen we had to register at the Holiday Inn on Van Ness.

"My aunt Lucy has several pieces just like these," Greg said when we visited one of the museums. "My aunt Lucy has a watch just like this one," he exclaimed in his customary tone as we walked around one of the many jewelry stores in Chinatown. "My aunt Lucy brought back one of these same screens from one of her trips to Japan." "My aunt Lucy bought." "My aunt Lucy always shops." My aunt Lucy was giving me a pain in the nouveau riche ass.

He didn't like the bloody Marys at The Cliff House. The seals at Seal Rocks made too much noise. The ruins of the Sutro Baths looked tacky. Muir Woods was too damp. The houses across Alamo Park on Steiner Street were clichés. The Transamerica pyramid was weird. The fish in the tank at the Aquarium looked neurotic. The Oriental Garden at Golden Gate Park was just like one aunt Lucy had seen somewhere in the Pacific.

I just wanted to get the hell away from Little Lotta and hide in Hamburger Mary's, where I knew he wouldn't go, because aunt Lucy would have never gone to a place like that. Sure, she would have never gone to the San Francisco Eagle or The Lone Star Saloon either, where he insisted we had to go before returning to Pittsburgh, but I suppose that was different.

"Tonight I'm going to dinner at Leticia's," I told him. "It's my favorite Mexican restaurant in all of San Francisco. If you feel you'd rather do something else, feel free to choose."

"No, I don't think that would work," he whined again. "After all, we're traveling together."

But not joined at the funny bone.

"Afterwards I have tickets for Beach Blanket Babylon. If you wish, feel perfectly welcome to go eat elsewhere—I know, I know, but let me finish. You have that option. You can go elsewhere and then take a cab to North Beach. But if you come along to Leticia's, I don't want to hear any disparaging remarks about the food, or the color of the walls, or the men at the bar, you understand?"

I knew I was treating him like a spoiled brat. Yes, I was. He controlled himself during most of the night, although he was not a bit amused with the show at Club Fugazzi. Tough shit.

The following day would be our last—hooray—in the city, and I drove us to Bay Street for Irish coffee and to sightsee the only tourist traps we had not yet fallen into. In the evening I had been invited to the Oakland marina by an old friend to have a drink at the bar where he worked. I wanted to be on time, and I planned my day accordingly—by then I was hoping that Greg had caught the drift and started planning his own day whichever way he wanted, but he wasn't that perceptive.

"You know, for the money I've spent on this trip I could have gone to Paris and had a much better time," he said over lunch across the cable car turnstile at the end of Powell.

He could have also gone to hell. One not of his own making.

I had parked uphill on Powell. I figured that when we were within safe driving time, past rush hour, we would drive up to Broadway, go right and then take a left on Van Ness, which would take us to the parking lot at the Holiday Inn.

"I'd like to drive. Do you mind?"

I minded, but I was in no mood to explain why he was not the best person for the job, especially given my time constraints. I handed him the keys.

I pushed my seat back and shut my eyes. By the number of stops Greg made I could tell we were two blocks away when he turned right—we were not on Broadway. A few more blocks ahead he took a left turn. It could not be Van Ness. I held my peace. The trip back was taking longer than necessary. I had had enough. I pushed my seat's back forward and looked around. We were on Folsom, which meant that he had probably taken a turn on Jones somewhere and crossed Market Street.

I was afraid he'd want to stop for a drink at one of the leather bars on Folsom, so I didn't say where we were. He probably could not put S&M and Folsom together anyway, so it didn't make any difference.

"Where are we?" I asked, faking innocence.

"I think I'm lost."

"That's a mouthful."

I made him pull over to a phone booth to call my friend in Oakland and tell him I'd be about an hour late.

"If you hadn't gone to sleep there and told me where to go, I wouldn't have made a mess of it."

He had no idea how I wanted to tell him exactly where to go.

The next day I dropped him off at San Francisco International while I returned the car at Alamo somewhere in Burlingame. I was secretly hoping I'd miss my flight and would be able to come home later without little Greg.

He remained silent during most of the flight, his ears plugged with earphones so that he could listen to his portable compact disc player. I drove him home from the airport in Pittsburgh, and when we said good-night I knew that whatever had existed before the trip had fizzled, and that was alright with me.

The next day I called him to tell him I'd be sending him a detailed breakdown of expenses, and I expected his check as soon as he received it.

Some days later I ran into Bernie Janosco at The Crossover. I was looking for Greg, who had made himself scarce that week every time I called him at work and at Granny Howard's.

I gave Bernie an abridged version of the vacation I had suffered through. Half-jokingly I told him, "You're to blame. Don't do me such favors again, dear."

"Well, it's over, anyway," Bernie joked.

"Not quite. The check he sent me to cover his share of expenses? It bounced."

Lesson: If you already have children, raise your own, not someone else's. If you don't, stay away from cribs.

Day 24:

A Leech by Any Other Name Sucks
Just as Much Blood

Under the shelter of a barren cliff overlooking McKnight Road in the North Hills of Pittsburgh sits a small building whose neon signs identify it as Newsstand. On one of the panels next to the doors another neon sign alerts drivers that it provides twenty-five cent private viewing booths. Adults only. These signs are in the same category as the letters "Sears" and a road sign that reads "Rest Area Ahead."

The alleged newsstand is divided into three distinct areas. The first is the well-lit newspaper and magazine section, separated from the second by barroom doors that state, very clearly, that only adults are allowed in it. That's where the customer can find all the alleged marital aids—such as cheap sheer lingerie and the Jeff Stryker sized live-like rubber penis—as well as cellophane bagged magazines for every possible sexual orientation and preference within that orientation. That's only on one side of the section. The opposite displays VHS tapes for purchase and rental. No, *Little Red Riding Hood* is not one of the tapes. But *Little Red Riding Slut* may be. And on the same side, behind a display counter that features bottles of amyl nitrate, playing cards that depict sexual positions involving all possible gender combinations, and several other specialty items of indeterminate applicability to sexual activity, stands an obese, foul-mouthed woman who is deprived of makeup temperance and the news that hair is no longer ratted anywhere in the world except in her household.

She dispenses the tokens that patrons need to access the farthest section of the newsstand, the darkened room that houses some sixteen video booths and several stalkers from the land of the living dead, pretending to be walking around for the exercise and not interested in walking into one of the private booths with some other patron who strategically leaves his door unlocked to allow access to him who, when it seems that no one else is looking, disappears behind the booth door. And *click!* goes the lock.

Traffic around the narrow halls of the video booth section is heaviest late in the afternoon, when suburbanites on their way home to the little woman and the kiddies have other things to take care of first. Some are accountants, some construction workers, some Baptist deacons and pillars of the family-values focused community, some are bums, and most just want to get off so that they can hurry home to prestigious Wexford and McCandless.

Late one evening in late August I found myself drawn to the mysteries of Pittsburgh's video booths. I saw an attractive enough man standing outside one of the booths, and joined him inside to not watch the movie on the television screen.

In mid-December I once more beckoned the call of prurience, paid the female Cerberus behind the counter and crossed to the other side. In the shadows stood the same man I had last seen there in August, all smiles and practically shaking his tail.

He followed me outside afterwards. His name was Jeremy Beaman, and he had been going there several times a week for months hoping to find me there again. I told him he had been wasting his time.

He was a bus driver with the Pittsburgh Port Authority, forty-one, divorced and recently separated from his lover of fifteen years, himself a married bus driver.

It was too cold to stand out there talking. He gave me his telephone number and asked me to call him.

Before I got in my car he yelled out, "You're going to call me, aren't you?" I assured him I would.

He lived in an apartment in Wilkinsburg. I got directions and the following week I too was enjoying the view of the city from his bedroom window.

His was a sad story. After five years of marriage he divorced his wife. Well, they hadn't really divorced. He moved in with his parents, and she retained custody of their little boy. Then she found out that he was seeing another bus driver for more than occupational reasons, and took him to court to impose supervised visits: he could only see his son in the living room of his parents' house, with his parents present. He retaliated by withholding child support, for which she had him in court every other week.

Eventually Marco Esposito, his male lover, moved in with him, but he had not divorced his wife, who stayed back in Penn Hills with the four children. While Jeremy's wife was taking him to court for not supporting his son, he was working double shifts to support Marco's children: Marco refused to work overtime, and his wife was a stay-home mom. Jeremy taught her to drive so that she could get herself around, but then she needed a car.

Jeremy took out a loan and bought her one. Marco was supposed to pay for it, but he never got around to it.

Marco used to bring his youngest child to sleep over, and thus the child overheard Jeremy and Marco talking about their forthcoming vacation to Naples, Florida, to visit a friend. The boy wanted to come along; Marco said it was alright if he did. They would be comfortable enough in Jeremy's Honda.

The boy went home and told everyone else he was going to Florida with his dad and Jeremy. The phone rang at Jeremy and Marco's. The other three children also wanted to come along on their vacation. Marco said they, too, could come along. Then his wife got on the phone, upset that everyone was going to Florida while she stayed back at home, and it wasn't fair.

By the time they headed south, Jeremy was driving Marco and Marco's entire family to a Neapolitan holiday.

The floodgates were open. The family came along on all vacations. Jeremy bought a Coleman camper to accommodate the entourage.

But the children had grown and they didn't fit in Jeremy's car, so he traded it in for a converted van that sat everyone comfortably. Marco slept all the way to their destination, his wife napped on the back seat, and the children screamed and complained from the moment they left until the moment they arrived.

While Jeremy worked double shifts and weekends to make sure they had enough to pay rent and buy groceries for both their household and Marco's, Marco started driving out to Schenley Park to hang out behind the bushes facing the Penn-Lincoln Parkway. Otherwise he sat at home downing bottle after bottle of whiskey—Marco had a bit of a drinking problem and the emotional and sexual sense of loyalty of a flea.

But on their relationship continued until the summer before I met Jeremy, when Marco decided to move back in with his family to be freer to pursue an interest in a couple of guys he had picked up at Schenley Park.

And before I knew it, there I was, spending more and more time with Jeremy Beaman, where the memory of Marco's ingratitude had not exactly faded. Jeremy's best friends, Josephine and Sheryl, who had accompanied Jeremy and Marco when they needed female beards and on several road trips to Provincetown, were often visiting for dinner and bringing up the good times all over again.

Sometimes Jeremy and I would drive down to Moon Township to Josephine and Sheryl's trailer home, where I would hear the many wondrous stories all over again. It tickled me not to hear the stories retold as if they had been the rosiest times in the world for all concerned. But I kept silent.

I was determined to eradicate the presence of leeches from Jeremy's memory. I'd leave work in the afternoon, drive up to Ross Township on the other side of town to take care of whatever I needed to do at home, and then I'd drive out to Wilkinsburg to cook for Jeremy the groceries I had stopped to buy along the way at the Giant Eagle.

Whenever a good show was on at the Benedum Center or Heinz Hall, I'd buy tickets for the two of us. Before showtime we'd stop at a nice restaurant in Shadyside or downtown for dinner. Late that winter he and I drove to Rock Hill, South Carolina, where we helped his brother move to a new house.

When the echo in the refrigerator alerted me that he was running out of groceries, I'd stop at the store and buy enough meat to freeze for the week, vegetables and whatever else he needed. Jeremy had just been adjudicated bankruptcy in federal court and, although that loosened the financial noose a little, he still was strapped for money: Marco had dug a deep hole in Jeremy's pocket, and Jeremy owed money to people who were not exactly exempt from payment in court.

"I'm not used to this," he said one day when we were shopping in Monroeville and I took out my checkbook to pay for the groceries.

"Then get used to it," I said.

His friend Michael had just purchased a duplex in the Pittsburgh neighborhood of Oakland, each of whose two apartments was a single-bedroom unit. Michael offered to rent one to Jeremy, and because of the savings it represented, Jeremy took it.

Jeremy made constant references to his many friends, most of whom I had not seen, but when the time came to move, the two of us had to do it all alone. The day before the move I noticed that he had not packed anything.

"When I was a kid we used to move every three or four months," he said. "I'm used to it."

"Hmm. But if you start packing as you move, it's going to take forever, and it's only the two of us."

"Oh, I don't pack," he said. "I throw everything in garbage bags and put them on Josephine's truck's bed.

I convinced him that it was not an effective way to move. "I bet your parents had a lot of things break."

"Yeah. We replaced them."

That night I went out to buy boxes at U Haul and we stayed up most of the night packing. The move took four days anyway—there's just so much a small pickup truck and two people can handle under the pouring rain.

The new apartment had been refurbished with new appliances and carpeting, but it still needed work. Jeremy wanted to hang paper in his bedroom, but didn't have the money. I drove us out to Sears and bought wallpaper and supplies; I also came back the next Saturday to spend the day hanging the paper. Then he complained that the closet was tall, but it lacked shelves. I went out to Hechinger's and purchased wire shelving and other closet organizers. I spent one Sunday drilling cement walls and hanging shelves in the closet. The bathroom had a tub, but no shower; Jeremy wanted a panel to separate the tub from the wall and an extension on the spout for a shower. I drove to Builders' Square and bought all of it, plus a cabinet to put under the sink.

And every day after work I'd run back to Jeremy's, unless I had to stop by the grocery store first, to fix dinner before he came home from work.

He waited for me one day to show me an ad in the newspaper: a large furniture store was offering an interest-free sale. If I bought him the bedroom set he had been planning to get for a while, when the debt came due twelve months after the purchase, he would pay it off. It wouldn't cost me anything, because by that time he would have the money and would pay the whole thing himself.

We ran out to Monroeville, where I signed off on a promissory note for a $2,000 bedroom set.

One of several times that we had Josephine and Sheryl for a dinner of roast and vegetables, homemade bread and dessert I had prepared, we sat around the table all meal long talking about Marco's new friend, the trips Josephine and Sheryl had taken with Marco and Jeremy to Erie, to Virginia and elsewhere, the many parties they had attended together.

"I don't want to sound jealous or petty, but, you know, I have been here for several months now, and I really don't want to spend my time talking about ghosts. Perhaps we could better spend time now developing new memories that we can talk about when we all grow older, instead of bringing Marco up again and again."

Josephine and Sheryl were apologetic, but Jeremy had not liked my remarks. When they left he was sullen and silent.

"What's wrong?" I asked.

"You didn't have to be so rude to my friends."

I told him it was just as rude of them to continue to talk about Marco as if he were such a presence in their lives. I was beginning to feel that they thought I was not enough for him, and they missed the good old days when he supported Marco and his family, his drinking habit, and also put up with his screwing around.

"You're going to have to realize that Marco was part of my life for a long time, and you have no right to judge him. I'm always going to remember Marco."

"I realize that," I replied, becoming increasingly angry. "I'm not trying to deprive you of your memories, but if things were so memorable between you, why is he back with his wife and screwing around with every drunk he meets, according to Josephine and Sheryl, and you're stuck here with me?"

He didn't answer. I went home.

The following day, as I usually did Monday through Friday, I waited for him at the bus stop on Negley, two blocks from where I worked, with his lunch. I'd get on the bus and he'd drive to the end of the line, where he would have the soup and sandwich I'd get him. Then he would drive me back and drop me off where he had picked me up. Usually that was not the first time I had seen him that day: I had also waited for him outside the Forbes Avenue McDonald's in Oakland with a cup of coffee for him to drive off with.

I got on the bus and he gave me a cold greeting. At the end of the line I tried to make small talk, waiting for his apology, which never came. But lunch had perked him up and at least when he drove me back to Negley Avenue he wasn't as grouchy.

We started taking road trips; we rode the Honda for which he had traded the van, and I did the driving. We drove to New York one weekend to see *The Phantom of the Opera*, and he was upset with me because I was unfriendly with some older woman who sat by us on the first row telling us everything about this her first visit to New York, where she was staying and where she had gone.

"That's how out-of-towners get mugged and held up here. Because they think they're still in Loose Fart, Idaho," I said.

Besides, I had paid for the theater tickets and didn't feel I was under any obligation to also go out of my way to be amiable with total strangers.

He took a week off work and we drove to St. Paul at the end of August. On the way there we stopped for dinner at TGIF in Chicago, where he complained so much about the slow service and his hunger that a drunk woman threw him a roll from her basket and yelled, "Here, pipe down, Fido."

He thought it was hilarious.

My time came up for my annual pilgrimage to San Francisco late in October. Jeremy took a week off to join me on my trip. We stayed at The Apple Inn in Oakland, a modest motel that was reasonable enough to leave me enough funds to spend on more interesting pursuits across the bay.

He didn't seem to enjoy the trip as much as I had hoped he would. It was a cross country trip, one I had already made with a very undesirable traveling companion the previous year with disastrous results, and since I was paying for everything except Jeremy's airline ticket, I had wished that he would enjoy himself more.

We drove out to Point Reyes. He seemed withdrawn, but not necessarily upset, so I decided to avoid confrontations and ignored it. Driving back through San Rafael he suddenly turned to me and asked, "You're lost, aren't you?"

I resented the question. For one thing, no, I wasn't. More important yet, because whenever he traveled with Marco, he had to drive, because Marco, who otherwise knew his bus routes around Pittsburgh, had no sense of direction and once, on the way to Philadelphia, had ended up on the Pennsylvania Turnpike heading toward Ohio.

"I know my way very well."

"Oh, yeah? You're not from around here. You're lost, admit it."

"I'm not Marco, Jeremy. And even if I were lost, all I have to do is look at where the sun is, and follow a southerly direction. I learned that with the Boy Scouts."

On one of our last days in the city I drove to Columbus Avenue to have dinner in a delightful Italian restaurant where several of the waiters were Argentine Italians. I ordered in Italian and Spanish, and held unimportant conversations with the waiters, who were probably used to speaking their native language with patrons in that area.

"You're such a showoff," he said to me.

"Why, because I ordered in Spanish?"

"No, because you want to make me jealous with your cute little chats with the help."

"In the fifteen years you lived with that Italian parasite, what's his name, oh, yeah, Marco? Didn't he ever teach you an Italian word or two?"

He looked away and tears started streaming down his cheeks.

"I'm sorry. That was uncalled for," I said. But I also noticed that the mention of his ex-lover made him unhappy in a way different from just the memory of bad times.

At the airport in Pittsburgh Josephine picked us up. She wanted to know how the trip had gone.

"Oh, it was cold—unbearably cold," he said. "I might as well have stayed in Pittsburgh. I guess this is really the time to head down to Florida, not California," he added from the front seat, and I figured the comment was meant for me in the back.

Some weeks later he put in a bid to change stations, from the East Liberty terminal to the South Hills. I surmised that the reason was a comment I had made to Josephine during a recent night out with her and Sheryl to see *A Little Night Music* at the Benedum Center.

"Jeremy sees Marco every day at the terminal. Isn't that enough? Do you think it's really necessary for you to continue to bring him up?" I had said, visibly bothered by the two lesbians' bad habit and insensitivity. Marco was never there, but he always was. I couldn't be jealous of that drunk who had called Jeremy in the middle of the night the week before to ask him to come and get him from the spot where he had crashed his car, so that Jeremy would crack the steering column and he could claim that someone had stolen his car when he called he police the following day to report the theft. I couldn't consider myself inferior to a man who had begged Jeremy that night, while I lay by his side in bed, "Please, Jeremy, I need you now more than I ever needed you."

Jeremy told him he couldn't do that.

When he hung up I asked, "Would you have gone out to help him if I hadn't been here?"

Jeremy paused for an uncomfortable while, then said, "No, I'm done with that crap."

I was also beginning to feel that I couldn't be jealous of the man who encouraged the two women to continue to bring Marco up in my presence. How could the invisible man feel such an emotion as jealousy?

But I noticed that the mention of a Mr. Sorell, Jeremy's new supervisor at the South Hills terminal, became more frequent. Mr. Sorell said, Mr. Sorell was saying, Mr. Sorell has a cabin up in the mountains, Mr. Sorell had told me this joke, Mr. Sorell brought me lunch. One day Jeremy and I had gone to a movie in Dormont, in the South Hills, and had run into Mr. Sorell, a middle-aged husky man with as unrefined an edge as I could expect from most other bus drivers.

The second week in January Jeremy went to Rock Hill to visit his brother and his family. He returned on a Sunday night when I was ironing my shirts.

Hearing his voice on the phone surprised me.

"I thought you'd be here when I got home," he said.

"I didn't know when you were coming back," I replied. The previous year, when he had driven to South Carolina to visit his brother, he had called me every night to whisper sweet nothings and, I figured, to make sure I knew he was thinking of me so that I wouldn't go roaming around. He had even cut his visit short by a day because he was so eager to see me again.

This time he hadn't called once. He really had not told me when he was coming back. I didn't see the point in spending evenings by myself in an apartment much smaller than my two-story house, wondering whether that would be the night he'd return.

"But I'll drive over now that you're home," I said lukewarmly.

"You don't have to bother," he said.

"No bother. Just let me finish this one shirt, and I'll be on my way."

When I arrived he was watching television from his recliner. I asked him how the trip had been. Okay. How had the drive been through the mountains, with all the snow. Okay. How long did it take him to drive back. He wasn't sure.

I sat on the sofa feeling increasingly unwelcome. Suddenly he stood up, got dressed and said, "I'm going down the street to pick up a pizza."

He returned half an hour later with a large box. He went back to the recliner and started to eat his pizza. I wasn't offered any.

He lay the box on the floor. A short while later he stood up again and said, "I'm going to bed."

I didn't know what to do. Was I being invited to bed? Did he care whether I joined him there? Should I just leave?

I chose to get out before I was thrown out.

The next week was quiet. Jeremy seemed bothered by something, but I ignored it. Then Friday night I addressed the current tension. Jeremy said that he felt I was inconsiderate with his friends and didn't seem as interested as I had been before.

"Is this all because I wasn't here the night you came back home?"

"Not just that. You seem distant," he said.

"I'm distant? I've been waiting for you to tell me what's going on."

"Well, it's other things too. I don't know. I can't put my finger on it. Damn it, anyway, you're upsetting me."

"I'm sorry. Aren't you going to eat dinner. I fixed—"

"I don't want dinner now," he said, which really told me something was definitely wrong. This man had not turned down food since the first two hours of conception.

"I need some time by myself," he said. "I want you to stay home and give me space."

Actually, I agreed with him. I really needed time away from him. I couldn't see that this relationship was headed anywhere but to disaster, and time away from each other would give us both the chance to find a way to break it off.

"Okay," I said. "Do you have any idea when you might want to get in touch with me again?"

"Damn it, don't rush me. There you go, being inconsiderate again. I'll call you."

Yeah, don't call us.

The next day I stayed home organizing a lot of paperwork that had been piling up for months while I was cooking at Jeremy's.

By Monday morning I had decided that I wanted to leave Jeremy a note at home while he was at work, apologizing for my immature behavior. At noon I drove out to his apartment and parked outside. I unlocked the front door and the first object I saw was our picture, the one of him and me that usually sat on an end table by the sofa, turned down.

That in itself made me angry. It felt like a direct hit at my heart, an unwarranted rejection, an act of incipient unlove.

I head noises coming out of the bedroom and walked down the short hall toward the dresser whose mirrors I had spent so much time mounting after my signature allowed the furniture store to deliver it at Jeremy's. And in front of the dresser, oblivious to anything else in the world, right on the same bed where I had done the same thing with him so many times before, Mr. Sorell was mounted on Jeremy, who lay on his back with his legs up in the air.

"So this is the space you needed, you fucking bastard?" I yelled. I was angry, but frozen to the threshold.

Mr. Sorell pulled out and rolled to the other side of the king-size bed. While he tried to cover himself with a sheet that would not give because Jeremy was lying on it, Jeremy was trying to jump out of bed to put his trousers back on.

"What the hell are you doing here?" he asked in an annoyed tone.

"I was here to drop you a note to apologize for being a jerk, but I see now what the drama was all about, you son of a bitch!"

I could have sworn he was about to say that it wasn't what it seemed.

I turned around and walked toward the door. On my way there I stopped and pushed to the floor the curio cabinet, full of figurines I had bought Jeremy to commemorate special events during the year I had spent with him. Somehow the clash, the cracking and the shattering made me feel a lot better as I walked out.

"What the hell..." were the last words I heard before I slammed the door.

A few months later I called Jeremy to remind him that he had to pay me for the bedroom set, since it was either paid in full or I had to make payments on it. And a year with Jeremy had almost put me financially in the exact same place where Marco had left him.

"You're passing out bills now?" he asked. "Because if you are, I'm going to have to pass you a bill for room and board for all the time you spent here, and for the dinners I paid for when we went out, and the movies we went to, and for all the figurines you busted, and for changing the oil in your car, and everything else."

He was serious. I knew it was time to take out the savings passbook and pay off the furniture.

The following year I moved away from Pittsburgh. Jeremy had moved into an apartment building in the South Hills with Mr. Sorell, according to mutual acquaintances.

Lesson: Parasites are not only the ones you see through a microscope, but they are all equally pernicious.

Day 25:

Confessions in a Video Booth

"Take me to see Father Wilfred," my mother requested one Sunday afternoon in winter when she was visiting from Puerto Rico. "He's in a place called Millvale."

"Millvale?" I knew Millvale well. The bell towers of its Catholic church presided over the valley where the small blue-collar town was located, between the Ohio River and the more affluent suburbs to its north. Its run-down buildings were a testament to the demise of the steel industry. Its potholes could swallow an eighteen-wheeler.

Father Wilfred had been assigned to a parish in Philadelphia after a long stint in Puerto Rico. He had been in our parish for as long as I could remember. He wasn't there when I was baptized, which meant that he arrived sometime after 1950, but he administered my first Holy Communion, he stood by the bishop during my Confirmation, and had been our church's Boy Scout leader; he had also officiated at my sister's wedding, and had administered the sacraments to her and my brother when their time had come to receive them. I remembered him as a hulking man whose ruddy cheeks turned crimson whenever he was angry, which was often.

He spoke Spanish with a heavy Philly accent, but he had a relatively strong command of his operating language. Until I saw him again in Pittsburgh I had never heard him speak English. It's true that not all of his usage was correct. He often stumbled when he was preaching, and instead of saying he was stupefied he declared to be stupid. Everything sounded heavy-handed when he spoke: his baritone voice had to struggle to make it through a mouthful of pebbles.

Parishioners feared Father Wilfred, his thunderous voice and his frequent bouts of anger. However, he was friendly to several families with whom he visited and whose children he was in charge of as a Boy Scouts leader.

I took my mother to the rectory in Millvale and waited for her in the car. From a distance Father Wilfred looked as if he had shrunk. I must have been about his height the last time I saw him, but he must have been some four inches shorter than I. His hair seemed the same, and his pants, always belted under his pouch, just as unnecessarily long.

Sometime in the summer of the following year I was shocked to see Father Wilfred again. Of all the sleazy places in the world, the last one I would have expected to find him, quietly whistling while standing against a wall and bumping together two small piles of tokens, was at the McKnight Road newsstand's video-booth parlor.

I turned around and walked in the opposite direction. I wanted to give him time to get out before he embarrassed himself; I wanted to give myself time to erase the hallucinatory vision from my brain. A little while later I walked back into the hall, and there he was, standing like before.

His brazenness surprised me: Millvale was only four or five miles away, and it was certainly possible that one of his parishioners could drive up the road and see him walking out of the newsstand.

He couldn't have been there for *that*. Maybe he was doing some research for a sermon. He couldn't be there looking for sex. Not Father Wilfred, my leader, my priest and confessor.

I kept my distance. I wanted to leave, but I couldn't. Would he recognize me? What would he think of me if he did? What would he do if I walked into the booth in front of him and left the door unlocked? Would he come in? And if he didn't, would I feel humiliated that he had not considered me worthy of him? What was I thinking? He wasn't there for *that*.

But what if he was? And if I didn't hurry into the booth, would one of the other indoor pedestrians in the parlor snatch him?

I slipped into the booth, dropped a token in the slot and turned the knob to a male video. I stood to the back of the booth so that I could see Father Wilfred standing against the wall and he could see that someone was in the booth waiting for him to make his move.

It didn't take long. Still whistling, he pushed my booth door just far enough to slip in and locked the door behind me.

Not only was he there for *that*, but he was very adept at it. He knew what to touch, how to touch and squeeze, what to unzip, what to take in his hands and what to put in his mouth. This was definitely not his first time at *that*.

Don't you know who I am, I wanted to ask him after pushing his head away from my groin. My mind was split between the sensations I was receiving from his expert manipulation and the sleazy knowledge that this holy man of the cloth was converting his every sanctifying word into a profanity that defied my most extreme fantasies.

He didn't ask for reciprocation. Instead he continued to bite, grab, twist and apply suction as he deemed necessary. I was a schizophrenic bundle of raw nerves that could not decide whether to feel betrayed or thankful. Happy, however, I was not.

When I felt that I was close to responding blissfully to his creativity, I pulled away. He tried to stay on it, but I jerked away from him.

As silently as the transaction had been carried out I pulled up my trousers, buttoned my shirt and prepared to open the door by holding him back, signaling that he could stay in the booth until I was gone.

But he stopped me and whispered in my ear, "I would have swallowed your juice."

My heart pounded with the anxiety of someone who has heard a ghost tell him that he will soon see him in hell.

I hesitated, but I didn't know what to say.

"Do you think we could meet here again sometime?" he asked.

I felt at my most perverse. Shame was a powerful weight on my soul, but a devilish playfulness took over me.

"Sure. What do you have in mind?"

He said the next time he wanted me to enter him. This was Father Wilfred, who had held up the host during consecration and held it in his hand to administer it to the faithful every Sunday when I was a youngster.

Revulsion can be an overwhelming deterrent to action, but it's much less powerful when it's mixed with a vile curiosity that begs you to find out how a fellow human being can vilify himself when driven by a passion stronger than any biblical passage or belief cancelled out by a weakness that knows no bounds.

"I can only get away on Sunday," I said. "How would that work for you?"

"Depends on the time," he replied with the same emotional detachment that produced his statement of desire to ingest my seminal discharge.

I did not sleep that night. Father Wilfred's words resonated in the chambers of my darkened brain. I remembered religious ceremonies, Boy Scout camps, trips to his religious order's mother house to spend the day in the swimming pool, the times he shared our table for a meal, his closeness to my father, my mother's admiration of his energy and dedication to the parish, his parishioners' consternation when he was reassigned to another parish in northern Puerto Rico a few years before his superiors ordered him to take over a school in Philadelphia.

He was there the following Sunday afternoon, as he said he would be. I waited in my car until he drove into the parking lot and walked in. Then I drove away, sad and confused.

Lesson: Pillars can crumble and crush you under their weight.

Day 26:

Someone Died and Made Him Czarina

On the third Thursday of every month, a group of gay Pittsburgh professionals meets for cocktails, dinner and a guest speaker in one of the dining rooms of a well-known and highly priced restaurant. The second time I attended one of the soirees I met Dick Zanka.

It was difficult to ignore him. His exuberant voice, always at the center of one of the subgroups that assembled in the room, drowned out every other conversation. Once his voice had captured your attention, his gestures mesmerized you. It was difficult, however, to follow his reasoning, full of items of misinformation ("Zachary Taylor is suspected of being gay—he was our only unmarried president, you know!") and non-sequiturs.

His looks were not as fascinating as his defective discourse. He was pretty bald for a thirty-five year old, and his teeth arrived everywhere one step ahead of his pigeon-toed feet. When he got carried away talking, saliva accumulated progressively on the sides of his mouth and eventually he had to stop to suck his upper lip into his mouth to prevent spit from drooling down the sides of his chin. Sometimes his preventive measure wasn't successful.

Dick was in charge of putting positive spins on negative decisions and actions by the president of one of the local institutions of higher learning. He carried sarcasm to new levels, yet he could charm his way around a roomful of snakes from the local media looking for dirt. And he would never give up.

Before leaving the meeting that evening, he had secured a ride home from me; his roommate could have driven him home, but somehow I ended up taking over the chore—Dick did not know how to drive.

As so many other times in my life, the opportunity to at least meet other gay people, and the fact that I had nothing better to reserve my social time for, led me by inertia to get dragged into encouraging Dick's friendship.

Over the next few weeks we went out to a few movies. Although I was not particularly looking for it, I was surprised that his ebullience had not made him reach across the car seat yet. But the moment came; I think I jumped a bit when I felt his hand on my thigh, because he immediately withdrew it. It was an involuntary reaction, just the way my face contorted at the sight of his naked feet the day he caught me looking at his pigeon toes. He immediately slipped them back into his shoes.

He started calling me at work to ask me to lunch—our buildings were just a block apart. Then came dinners at home, which we shared with Dave, his roommate and actual owner of the house where Dick had the upstairs plus the use of the kitchen and living area downstairs.

Gourmet is not the word anyone would use to describe his culinary talents, but he managed to defrost and boil as well as the next gay guy. One of the dinners included Dave and his current boyfriend; apparently Dave's education in typesetting had not prepared him for kitchen works either. We had a breaded deep-fried fish of indeterminate genus, and some vegetables that had been microwaved into elasticity.

Dick was an amateur Egyptologist of refined tastes, or so he preferred to be categorized, although he was a bred-in-the-bone son of the blue-collar neighborhood of Lawrenceville, where sophistication couldn't even be spelled, much less recognized. His musical taste that summer line-danced toward *Achy Breaky Heart*.

And soon enough my availability for friendship became a promise of a relationship that I was not pursuing. I couldn't find a way to dissuade

Dick: he seemed to be lurking around the corner every time I left work; I'd run into him everywhere on Fifth and Forbes avenues, where previously I had never seen him. His face was constantly immersed in books at Jay's Bookstall, where the owner knew him well, but I had never run into Dick before.

I must explain that my life had become somewhat more complicated by the time Dick and I met. Just before leaving St. Paul for the Slavic Riviera on the Monongahela my wife and I decided to move together and share a house in Pittsburgh. She and I were sharing child-rearing responsibilities, and I needed to be home more often to help my children with homework, help with house chores, do grocery shopping and take care of whatever else my wife was not able to handle. Therefore, my dating time was limited. Besides, after the Jeremy Beaman disaster, I had become even more reluctant to an involvement with anyone who made what I considered unreasonable demands on my time. The Beaman circus, driving back and forth three times a day between the North Hills and Oakland, where I worked and Jeremy lived, was not to be repeated. Money was not a problem with Dick, since he seemed frugal and responsible enough in that regard, but other resources were at a premium in my life: time, availability and interest.

My daughter was going through a difficult period in her life: to the usual agonies of adolescence, she had the added burden of suicidal tendencies induced by a bipolar disorder. Naturally, I was not going to make myself scarce at a time when she needed support and supervision. Her mother was not a mainlander, and American cultural preferences regarding dating habits and personal freedom were alien to her. Clashes between mother and daughter were frequent, some due to overprotection and others to instances of cultural shock. I tried to become the demilitarized zone, with varying degrees of success.

Dick found all this puzzling.

"Oh, children do those things," he'd say patronizingly. "You worry too much."

I didn't know whether I had presented an accurate picture of my home life and he still didn't understand, or whether he just preferred to downplay the importance of my domestic life for his benefit.

The inevitable conflict finally erupted.

One afternoon my wife called me at work to tell me that our daughter had run away in a car whose occupants were two of the area's most troubled teenagers. She had been sitting on the stoop outside our front door with her brother, and he had walked in the house to tell his mother that his sister had jumped in a car and ridden off with John something and Kathy whatever, both satanic poster spawn for sociopathy in the otherwise affluent and snobbish suburb where we made our home.

"I'll be there as quickly as I can," I told my wife, hung up and, under the despair of the circumstances, failed to call Dick to let him know that our date that evening was off.

I came home, called the police to report my daughter's disappearance and, like most other hysterical parents these officers had dealt with, demanded from them information about how soon they would be hanging Clyde by the balls, putting Bonnie in solitary confinement, and returning my darling, misguided, confused fifteen-year old daughter home.

"Oh, no," the officer said when I told him in whose company my daughter was. "Not nice people." However, they had a pretty good idea of where they hung out: it was not the first time they had been in trouble with suburban law.

My private telephone line rang shortly after the officers had left. Dick, whose presence on this planet had escaped my awareness for the previous three hours, wanted to know whether I had forgotten our date.

"I'm sorry, Dick. I'm having some problems at home tonight," I said. "My daughter has run away from home, she's probably in Ohio or who knows where by now, and I need to stay home in case the police call with any news." I wanted to say that she could have been sold into white slavery or traded for crack cocaine by then, but I wanted to sound less frantic than I was.

"Oh, you're overreacting," he said coolly. "All children run away from home."

Yes, but not my children. My children should know better. Besides, they were my children, not Dick's.

All of my biases against the limited understanding gays have of family life—fostered by my refusal to remember that most of us came from traditional, sometimes dysfunctional, granted, but traditional nonetheless, families, and that gay men did know what family life is all about. At that particular moment, I wanted to choke Dick for being so unaware, self-centered, for turning into a nonbreeder cliché.

"Yes, I'm sure everyone runs away from home," I said, without adding that I had done that, but my parents never figured out, because they had to pay for my four years of boarding school, a subtle and effective way to escape their infernal household without being chased down by the law. "But this is my daughter, not anyone else's, and I want to be here in case something comes up. I also need to keep the telephone lines open, so let me call you when things have simmered down, Dick." He didn't know that we were on my private line, which no officer was going to call me on.

The following day my daughter was apprehended after I made calls to our congresswoman and she put the squeeze on our township officers of the law. My daughter came home, we went through the usual Latino family yelling, recrimination and threats, and a few days later we were back to normal. Whatever that was.

My need to share time with Dick, already at a very low point, evaporated. I started eating lunch early in the afternoon, when I knew he had already had his and was probably back at his office, or skipping it altogether to avoid running into him anywhere in Oakland.

"Hello, stranger," he said one morning over the phone. He sounded subdued and easygoing. I let my guard down. "I was wondering if you'd be free for lunch today," he asked.

I didn't see any danger in that. "Where and when do you suggest?" I asked.

We would meet at a restaurant half a block away from the building where I worked. The restaurant was popular among people with whom I worked.

He was already sitting when I walked in. He seemed his usual self, which meant that at least the six tables around us could hear him clearly, and the cooks could hear the din without making out what he was saying.

The waiter had brought us our drinks when, without previous warning, Dick's voice hitched up a couple of notches.

"So how is your troubled family?" This was not the bubbly Dick who had greeted me when I sat down. This was a budding demon.

"Is your virginal daughter back home? Was she scratched in any way when she got home? I mean, for you to break our date for something as trivial as that—she did show up twenty-four hours later, didn't she?—and then to ignore all the messages I've been leaving you, it must have been quite a little drama you must have had there in the North Hills."

I was looking directly at him, frozen to my seat, but I could tell that the other patrons around us were either glancing over in faked lack of interest or staring.

Dick took advantage of my silence to continue.

"I mean," he said, eyes opening as wide as his eyelids would stretch and shaking his hands in front of my face, "you think that you're the only one who has problems, I mean, you really must think that your life is singled out for complications, I mean," and he'd continue to mean, rolling his popping eyes and occasionally turning his head, like a student in a public speech class making sure the entire audience feels that his oration is addressed at each member of the group, "all of these Byzantine turns that read like a baroque novel!"

The uniqueness of the situation dumbfounded me. Should I stand up and in a grand gesture throw water at his face, thus risking the possibility that some of those people at the corner table, the ones who worked down the hall from he, would get to confirm it was me being berated by this creep? Or should I ask him to quiet down and stop calling attention to himself—to me, actually—knowing that this gay ham would not relent in his effort to let me have it?

I remained silent. A static, muted, red-faced bag slumped on the restaurant chair.

"Calling off dates and canceling engagements just because some teenager is acting the way all teenagers do? What's that? I mean, your life has more plots—you're the Puerto Rican Dostoevsky!" He was smiling, as if congratulating himself for the novelty of his imagery.

"Now, you need to know that there are people like me who care for you and feel you shouldn't be stressing yourself out like that. Do you understand? If we are going to further this relationship, you have to let me help you, you have to give me access into your heart, you have to trust me. I mean, do you understand?" Spit had collected on the sides of his mouth, and he had to pause. *Slurp*. "Are you okay with that?"

No, Dick, I'm not okay with that. I'd rather continue to kiss frogs at the risk of getting even more emotional warts. I'd rather eat dirt, worms and apples grown on Neville Island's toxic waste dumps, than ever give you an inch of access into my life, you self-important sack of shit!

"Yes, Dick. I appreciate your concern."

"So we can continue where we left off? I mean, I want you to be happy and comfortable. Be cool, you know, I mean, really. Really."

We never started out, you dumb prick.

"It seems that way. But right now," I replied, looking at my watch, "I have to go back to work. I ran out of time. That's okay, you can stay here and have lunch, don't bother to walk up with me, it's okay, it's okay."

Dick had fed me enough; unfortunately for him, I was not about to digest any of it. Not even a judicial order would get me to go anywhere with Dr. Dreadful again.

During the next few months I declined to take his calls and thanked heaven that ours was a secured building. I started missing lunch or bringing a bag from home.

Two months later I was relocating to South Carolina and bringing my family along; leaving Dick back on Penn Avenue comparing me to angst-ridden Russian realists was an added bonus to my departure.

I spent the last month before leaving Pittsburgh at home packing and traveling south to look for a place to live. I had my private telephone line disconnected; the other one was unlisted and unpublished, as he must have found out when he called information for the number. My former secretary, who did have my home number, called me one day.

"There's this guy? Dick Zanka? Claims he's a friend of yours? He's been calling two and three times a day to try to convince me that he can have your number?"

Ah, the would-be Czar of Lawrenceville.

"He says it's okay, because he's a friend of yours? Well, I told him that all of my friends have my telephone number, and if he didn't have yours, he couldn't be such a close friend. He won't give up. I need a little peace of mind, you know? Like I really don't need the aggravation?"

"I'm sorry, Beth. I wish I could tell you to give him the number, but I'm not going to do that."

"No, that's okay," she said. "I told him I would call you and ask you whether I could give him your number?"

"No, you can't. When he calls again tell him that I will get in touch with him. He has to wait until I do that."

I did get in touch with Dick. I sent him a note: "I understand you're trying to get in touch with me. I can't see why. You know how difficult Dostoevsky's plots are to follow, so save yourself the trouble. Please don't bother my secretary again."

Some years later I returned to Pittsburgh for a visit. I stopped at Jay's Bookstall and out of twisted curiosity asked the owner whether he had seen Dick again. Dick was working for a small college somewhere else in Pennsylvania and was living in the country.

Ah, the country! How pastoral and uncomplicated!

Lesson: Stand up and throw water at his face. Otherwise he may think it's okay to continue to interpret your life and edit it to fit his reading needs.

Day 27:

Ah Jez Wanna Be Alone—
After You Pick Up the Tab, Sugah

James Scottsman was an unemployed phlebotomist. He had just returned to his home state, South Carolina, after three years in Baltimore, where he had maintained copying machines and, I gathered from his accounts, spent most of his free time at the Baltimore Eagle. After he finished his six-week phlebotomist training program, that is.

I had been living in South Carolina for about a year, working as a software and communication. We met through a mutual friend who was misled into believing that I had a hair fetish. James had hair growing on his hair. It was conceivable that some of his body hair—I never did get to see what hid under the mat on his back—had bifurcated. I have seen area rugs thinner than the coat on his arms.

Luckily for him hair doesn't grow out of human eyes, and he had the most beautiful blue eyes I had seen in a long time. They exuded an innocence that he was far from being blessed with.

We first went out to The Olive Garden on a Good Friday, after I picked him up at our friend's apartment. Later that night he sent me an email message: "I'm thinking of a very nice man I met tonight, who took me to *diner* and then didn't *preshure* me into having sex. Don't get me wrong, I enjoy sex very much, but it's so *annoing* to go out on a date with someone who just uses *diner* as an excuse to get in my pants. I hope we stay in touch."

Spelling aside, I was hoping to stay in touch. The only disadvantage I saw to him then was his age, fifteen years less than mine. But at first sight he seemed balanced enough to make the age difference unimportant.

I asked him to go to the movies that weekend before he returned home to Pamplico, in South Carolina's Pee Dee. He told me that he was looking for employment in Columbia—did I know anyone who might be looking for a phlebotomist? I didn't, but I'd keep a vein open.

The following Saturday night I was having a beer at a bar on Huger Street in Columbia, when James walked in with a friend of his, Joe. I waited until he saw me.

He walked over and kissed me on the lips. It was as surprising as it was pleasant and encouraging.

"I didn't tell you I was coming to town this weekend, because I wasn't sure what Joe's schedule would be, and I didn't want you to cancel any plans you had made already," he said.

And who was this Joe person?

We were introduced. Joe was an old friend who worked for an accounting firm in town.

Although I appreciated the attention, I had arrived at the bar by myself and didn't think James had to stay by my side all night. He did stay, however, and when Joe and he were ready to leave to head for another bar on Assembly Street, he asked me to come along. Before we left the bar he pulled me aside, hugged me and kissed me again. I was in pilose hog heaven.

At the other bar he stayed by me; Joe and I bought whatever beers each of us had that night.

Emboldened by his unusual receptivity, I put my arm over his shoulder, and he put his around my waist as I stood by his side. I had not noticed that most of the entertainment at the bar consisted of scrawny go-go boys laying their jockstrapped balls on the heads of geriatric patrons at the bar.

At that moment, with James' arm around me, they could have been staging mass executions against the back walls, and I wouldn't have cared one bit.

During the following weeks we spoke on the phone frequently. I was beginning to feel the urge to put an end to the absence of pressure he had been so grateful for before, but whenever he came to town he'd stay at his friend's apartment, where we could not be intimate.

"When are you coming out here again?" I asked one Friday night during a phone conversation.

"I don't know. I've been helping my father with his buildings and doing some work for my cousin," he said, "and since I'm still unemployed, I need every penny I can make. I'm so tarred." It was the equivalent of the Northern *tired*.

"I'd like to see you again," I begged with poorly veiled subtlety.

"I don't know how, unless you—"

"Unless I what?"

"It's a long way to come, though. I meant, unless you wanted to come out here tomorrow."

Finally.

"I'd love to."

We met in the parking lot at Roses in Florence early the following afternoon. He wanted to stop at the department store before I was to follow him home: he lived about twenty miles from there.

I had never seen so many tattooed people under one roof, especially strange because tattooing is against the law in South Carolina. Most adults wore cowboy hats, although the area is known for tobacco, not cattle ranching. James was looking for an antacid. We stood in line to pay, behind a man holding too small children by the hand and, in front of him, a woman with a baby on her arms—his wife, I assume.

"Did you notice that this box is open, ma'am?" asked the cashier of the woman ahead of us. She was referring to a box of Kotex sanitary napkins.

"Yeah, sure. I opened it myself. I took it to the ladies' room back there and used one."

We started out toward Pamplico through country roads lined by swamps. Eventually we left the paved road and drove onto a dirt road, James leading ahead of me. He turned into the driveway at his parents' house and continued to the end of the pebble path. The buildings he had told me he was helping maintain were two open sheds housing two lawn mowers and several garden tools. Next to it, to the back, were James' quarters, his deceased grandmother's one-bedroom trailer. A small rainbow flag flew on the corner of a metal carport structure that protected the trailer's front door and a ceiling swing.

I never did see a town about which I could say, "Here's Pamplico." It was more like a mismatched collection of houses scattered here and there wherever humans had claimed land from the swamps. Vast tobacco fields flanked the lots.

We went to Florence for dinner, where once the waitress asked, "One check or two," James quickly replied, "One." Of course, he being unemployed n'all, the one check was going to be mine, yeh know what ahm sayin'? It was the pattern we had established, but I preferred to be the one to decide what my money was going to pay for.

We came back to the trailer and sat down to watch the static-ridden television set. Sometime past midnight I started to wonder when this handsome man sitting in a rocking chair across the narrow width of the trailer's living room was going to suggest that we retire for the evening.

Around one I took the initiative to ask whether I could go to bed.

"Oh, go ahead," he said. "I'll be there in a little bit."

I undressed. Sitting for so long watching television my arms had become cramped. I stretched them and my hands got caught in the ceiling fan's blades.

"Are you ahraght in there?" he asked from the living room, some ten feet away.

I grunted my answer. He didn't reply.

It was four before he came to bed, and lay on his side with his back to me, a wide chasm open between us.

The next day before I left we sat in the swing. Under the effect of my nocturnal disappointment, I asked James whether something about me had repelled him.

"Not at awl. Ahm jez not feelin' too happy. Ah've been back for almost a month now, and ah still don't have a job." He had applied for jobs with several area hospitals and doctors' offices, but had not received encouraging news from anyone. He had taken his résumé to every shop on the Grand Strand in Myrtle Beach, but no calls yet.

He paused and looked down to the ground, then lifted his gaze to the distance and spoke as if possessed by a need to tell his most painful story to no one in particular. I just happened to be the ear du jour.

The man who paid for his phlebotomy training had been his lover of over a year back in Baltimore. "He was fifty-two, but he was built," James said clenching his teeth, as if offended by the fact and simultaneously aroused by the image, "like a brick shithouse."

It was a difficult mental treasure for me to compete against. I felt I was built more like a padded broom closet.

"He had a hair salon," James added.

I could see where he got his musculature. All those heavy hair dryers, lifting gallons of conditioner—they'll do it every time.

They met twice a week, when the hair dresser would come over to James' for dinner and other accoutrements. The rest of the week they would talk on the phone; the hair dresser was too busy with his business, continuing education courses in hair dye and related concepts, and other stuff he needed to take care of. He felt that James needed to get some more education, something that would guarantee him a job almost instantly and provide him more stability. The two associate degrees in management and arts that James had from a defunct proprietary junior college in Winston-Salem were simply not enough.

"Ah resisted the idear. Ah already had 'nuff edjekayshun," James told me. "But he offered to pay for it, and it was only a few weeks, so."

Shortly after James received his certificate in phlebotomy and venipuncture, the stylist started coming up with excuses to stay away on their assigned days.

One night James borrowed his roommate's car and went out to the Baltimore Eagle. When he walked in he saw the hair dresser with some other guy at the pool table. He walked over and demanded to know what the hair dresser was doing there when he was supposed to be studying hair roots.

"I was done early and came out to relax."

James wouldn't go away. The hair dresser told the other man to go out and wait for him by his car. He turned around and told James that he had no right to be following him around as if something unusual were going on.

When he left the bar, James followed him out to the parking lot. The hair dresser and his companion took off, and James followed them. They went to some other bar, and James walked into it as well. Then they left, but James couldn't catch up with him and ended up returning to the Eagle to get drunk.

The next day James called the hair salon to demand an explanation, but the hair dresser wouldn't come to the phone. James showed up at the shop, but the hair dresser had taken flight.

One of the women at the shop called him to a room in the back. "Hon, you're wasting your time with him," she said cryptically. James couldn't understand what she knew of his affairs. Or more appropriately, affair. "He's had a lover for about twenty years. I bet you've never been to his house, have you? There's a reason. He probably talks to you on his own phone line, locked up in his study. You'd be better off finding someone else—this man's a jerk and he has been yanking your chain for a while."

The realization of the betrayal depressed James deeply. It was the most powerful reason for his return to the swamp. He said Pamplico, but for me the two had become one and the same.

It mystified me how someone had been involved with someone else for such a reasonably significant period of time and not even been in the other person's house.

"Didn't you—"

"What?" James asked.

"No, nothing."

During the next week we spoke on the phone. James' sadness had made an impression on me. I started asking around for information about who might be hiring phlebotomists. During one of my appointments with the ophthalmologist I stopped by the human resources office of the hospital where my doctor had his office and noticed two different positions open for second-shift phlebotomists. I tried to call James right away, but he had just started a job that day doing third-shift stock work for Wal-Mart in Florence, and had taken the phone off the hook.

When I finally got through, he told me he was not going back to Wal-Mart. It was grueling work in the oppressive heat. He thought he was going to pass *aht* twice the night before. It was July in South Carolina, when even the devil returns to hell, where it's cooler.

I told him about the jobs. It was a Thursday. If he wanted to apply for the positions, he'd have to drive to Columbia the following day; it didn't seem the positions would remain open for long.

"I don't know how I would be able to do it. I'm leaving with my parents tomorrow to spend the weekend at Lyle's parents' in Winston-Salem." Lyle had been James' lover when he was attending junior college in North Carolina. "Unless I took a detour and went into Columbia on my way there, but I doubt it."

Who the hell was doing whom a favor here?

"You're going to wait until Tuesday to go apply for the job? That might be too late."

"Well, I guess that's a risk I'll have to take."

"Let me do something for you, then. I'll go pick up the application forms, and I'll take them out to you tomorrow morning. Then I'll bring it back and turn them in at the hospital late tomorrow afternoon. I mean, if that's okay with you."

"Oh, if you want to do that. That would be nice," he replied.

When I took the applications over, he told me he had worked before in a hospital in Columbia, working with medical records. I asked him why he hadn't gone around there to inquire about a position.

The reason was as simple as it was somewhat unusual. James had held a second-shift position at the hospital. He claimed that he had been very clear when he was employed that he could not work a third shift. His sleeping cycle was such that working from close to midnight until early the following morning was too much. The hospital's administrator changed, and James was switched to the graveyard shift. He protested and reminded his supervisor of his limitation. They gave him no choice, or at least an unpalatable one: the third shift or no job.

On the night when James was to start his new schedule, he walked into the records area in full leather gear—harness, jockstrap, chaps, boots, leather cap—and submitted his resignation. That incident had put a damper on his hopes of ever working there again. He had gone from that display to his copier job in Baltimore.

The Wednesday after he returned from Lyle's I went out to the swamp to visit him in the evening. We went out to a barbecue place in Florence. I had never had this Southern delicacy that bears no resemblance to barbecued anything in the North, a pile of shredded, greasy pork that looks like dry cole slaw. It alone must account for the high incidence of heart disease and obesity in South Carolina.

Then we returned to the trailer to watch television. He had gone into his bedroom to change, and returned to the living room in a tank top and gym shorts. He sat next to me in the love seat by the window, where we were lit up frequently by constant lightning.

He raised his leg closest to me and rested his foot on the edge of the love seat. His leg's hair brushed ever so slightly against my arm's bare skin. The hair on my neck was standing on end.

So much time had elapsed since my initial interest in James and this obvious offer of a carnal gift, that I wasn't sure what to do. More hesitantly and timidly than I could ever remember being, I placed my hand on his thigh. He didn't slap it off, so I assumed it was alright.

The tentativeness of the situation had dried my mouth as if I had been on antihistamines. I stood up and had two glasses of water from the tap. Outside the storm raged on. I was hoping for an invitation to spend the night. Not only did I desire to consummate my designs, but driving back through those back roads I had hardly negotiated before, in the midst of such a storm, was beginning to scare me.

When I returned to the love seat James seemed less wanton than he had been earlier. I wasn't sure what the next step would be, but I felt I understood what Jerome, the obsessed voyeur, had experienced in *Claire's Knee*. I wanted to make out with James, to lead him to bed and end the suspense once and for all, even if I never saw him again.

"I think this might get worse," he said.

"I can't imagine how," I replied.

"If we get more wind like this, trees will be down on the road. I expect we could even get funnel clouds."

I was glad I had not followed his observation with my own line of thinking.

"What do you think I should do?" I was hoping for a suggestion to share more than dinners and movies I had been paying for, in deference to his joblessness, and casual chitchat while watching a blurred television screen.

"You shouldn't wait much longer to get going."

I hesitated, but I had reached a point of no return, and I needed to know what James intended to do with my fate, now pretty much in his hands.

"I understand that you have been under a lot of strain. I can't imagine what I would be going through if I were in your shoes right now," I said, although I had begun to realize that James was more interested in carrying on about his hopeless job situation than in doing something about it. "But we have been skirting—I have been skirting an issue since the first few times we went out, and I need to tell you something. I have fallen in love with you."

"I've known for a while," was his reply.

What could I say to that, "Let's toast to your sensitivity"?

"Oh, good. I was afraid you hadn't noticed."

"I've noticed." He paused. "Do you want a drink of water before you leave?"

We parted without fanfare, without a good-night kiss, without further comment. I drove back wishing there would have been a motel of some sort between the Scottsman house and Florence. The storm had been severe. Although the rain had stopped, fallen trees made the roads dangerous to drive in their total darkness. Steam rose from the swamps and hovered over the road, making it even more strenuous on my eyes.

A week or so later I had not heard from James, so I called him to find out how he was doing. He had a job at McLeod Hospital and was commuting every day. The only distressing news was that during the storm the week before the wells had run over and become contaminated. His water came from a well on his parents' property, and when they became contaminated water had to be boiled for drinking.

"I have to get going," he said. "But I'll call you in a little bit."

Some weeks later I realized that "a little bit" in his jargon meant "one of these days," but the implication of the phrase was more along the lines of "Let's do lunch" when two people meet in passing on Rodeo Drive.

A short week after our last conversation I started to suffer the ill intestinal effects of drinking contaminated water from rural wells. The drainage continued uncontainably for over two weeks.

Some three years later my partner and I had returned to Columbia late on a Saturday afternoon from a shopping spree at a gigantic flea market in Charlotte. We were both two tired to cook and headed for a Greek restaurant in northeast Columbia. As we entered the dining room, I noticed a handsome man clad in black sitting at a table in a somewhat odd arrangement. The older person with whom he shared the four-seat table was sitting diagonally from him, as if they had been dining with two other people who had left their respective seats already. My partner and I sat at a table behind them. From their interactions it was obvious that they were together.

Of course, it should be obvious by now that the handsome man in black was James, whom I did not greet. The expression on his face when he recognized me was unreadable to me: I believe that the pleasant look preceded the awareness of who the man wallking toward him was. We had no further exchanges.

When the waitress brought their check, I noticed that his dining part-ner took it, then left a tip on the table. They both stood up and walked out, but not before the other person stopped by the cash register to pay. I could almost swear the bills had been coated in sugar.

Lesson: Don't bother to try to quench your thirst in a dry well, but stay even farther away from poisoned reservoirs.

Day 28:

The Meat Menagerie

Internet resources provide access to information, services and other lives. As with the rest of humanity, Internet surfers are not all gorgeous, highly educated and successful people. Nonetheless, many Net users would have the rest of us believe that they are not only all that, but honest and sincere as well.

Time was when the exchange of love letters between two people who had never met face to face took long enough to kindle passions and increase the suspense, to trade information and opinions that made each party sufficiently cognizant of each other in most aspects other than the physical by the time they met. Today electronic resources accelerate that process, and the result is that most relationships established through computer media last no longer than the first encounter. At the risk of demonizing current technology and glorifying the unprogressive past, I might venture that we all shared a higher sense of decency back then. Maybe we were simply so uninformed in the dark ages B.M. (before Microsoft) that we assumed a level of ethical conduct that survives only in William J. Bennett's mind.

Be that as it may, it's true that we were starved for information back then. Hauling a thirty-volume encyclopedia around was too impractical. Today an electronic notebook the size of the smallest yearbook tome of the *World Book Encyclopedia* affords us an excess of information we would not be able to digest in seven lifetimes. And any yahoo with a few hundred dollars and a telephone jack can force-feed his lies, bigotry and narrow-minded misinformation down the throats of yokels even more ignorant than they.

Among us lives a man such as those, by the name of Gary Winmore. He subscribes to an Internet Service Provider that gives him the opportunity to profile his many attributes. Apparently his alias alone should be indicative of the depth and span of his soul: Fuzzyonchest. His occupation was unlisted, but not so his hobby, "fucking bears"—he meant the two-legged beast of the chubby, hairy variety. His age was something vague—fiftyish—but his penis size was specifically stated: eight inches. As a forward sales clerk had once told me at Sears while referring to car speakers, eight inches is a lot of inches.

Starved for the company of a gay man who, at the very least, could introduce me to his friends and thus end my feeling of isolation in a cultural environment so alien to me, I sent him an email message. After all, he claimed he was on the lookout for "friendship and more." It sounded no different from most personal ads in free-distribution rags. We were all in search of friendship. Or more.

"We must meet for a drink," he wrote back.

Where? My first encounter with Southern gay culture in South Carolina had been in less than hospitable bars. With a Damron guide in tow I walked on a Friday night into an establishment identified in the guide as gay, the Capitol Club. It had earned a certain degree of notoriety during a national political campaign when Phil Gramm of Texas opened his headquarters in office space next to it. I looked around the familiar darkness, took a breath of the stale brew and nicotine mix and walked up to the bar.

"Bourbon and water," I asked the bartender. The six or seven geriatric cases at the bar turned toward me.

"Are you a member?" the unfriendly bartender asked.

"A member? Of what?" Of the Friends of Dorothy Club?

"This is a private club."

My face burned, but in the darkness none of the myopic patrons would see. "Oh, I'm sorry. I thought it was a gay bar."

"It is. It's a private club," he repeated.

"How does one join it?"

He pointed to a small table by the door. An open book sat on it.

"Take an application form from the drawer," he said and turned away.

The open book was a register of patrons, all of whom had to sign in at the door. The membership application form asked for name, address, telephone number and the names of two club members in good standing who would recommend the applicant for admission to the club.

I had no friends in Columbia—hence the desire to join the club—much less two who belonged to the club. What was I to do, stand by the door, introduce myself and ask incoming members to vouch for me to the admission committee?

When I was out on Gervais Street I rolled up the application form and put it in a trash bin. I drove up to Metropolis, a disco on Barnwell Street on the other side of downtown. There I needed to pay a membership fee, and show my driver's license and a membership card from another gay club. I left Metropolis and went to Affairs on Huger Street, little more than a quick pick-up hole where membership required a sponsor—I was back to square one and reduced to scanning electronic bulletin boards and searching for friends among men who were interested in nothing more than a quick lay. After all, in the rest of the world people sometimes take years to become what can be called friends. Among gay men a friend is the previous night's trick if he recognizes us at the bar the following night. If again we leave the bar together that night, we're family. Semen is thicker than water, after all.

Today's friend, close, good or nominal, is thus yesterday's Mr. Right Now. Friends made through email are seldom any different from those acquired in video booths or at Sears urinals. They just require some keyboard action to precede them.

"We must meet for a drink" turned out to be dinner at Diane's, an above-average restaurant where Gary evidently often had dinner.

Had his looks been what interested me most, he would have been out of luck that night. His full head of very abundant gray hair made me suspect he was wearing a rug. His broad shoulders sat atop a hunched back that spoke loudly of hobbies and an occupation—interior decorator, except that he said designer—that required no physical activity. Nothing memorable was spoken that night over dinner. At the end I knew as little about him as I knew before. He wouldn't let me pay for dinner. I feared he expected reciprocity in flesh, so I shook his hand and took off toward my car.

The next day I sent him email to thank him for dinner.

"We must get together again soon," he replied.

Days went by. My feeling of alienation continued to grow: it was already at an ever-climbing peak when I resorted to keyboarding contacts. It went beyond a physical need, so I was unwilling to go for relief to a nearby video booth shop. I had stopped there for a sort of inspection visit once, and perhaps if I had been in one of those modes—any port in the storm, say—maybe the place would have done.

It was an unusually sleazy store that rented adult videotapes and provided "preview booths." In front of the shop several insomniacs hit buttons on video poker machines. The cashier, on a platform overlooking the entire store, was a pre-operative transgendered being who was going to waste her money miserably if anyone had promised her post-op beauty. The booths were littered with soiled tissue; some included pools of urine. The zombies who stood by booth doors the way whores sell their wares in Amsterdam were overwhelmingly creepy and unattractive. I walked into my assigned booth and locked the door determined to get at least an ejaculation from the five dollars I had paid for the preview, but porn has never led me there. The awareness of the mechanical detachment with which performers carry out their tasks, the patently phony sounds, the cheapness of the sets and the horrible delivery when the living machines attempt even worse dialog—it all combines to fascinate me for all the nonsexual reasons.

And besides, once you've seen one erect penis attempting to impale a butt, do you really need to see so many others? Momentum builds with the sight of the first half dozen you seen in your life. After that, their visual appeal would have to be due to some teratological feature that would provoke more shock than sexual arousal.

I needed the company of a man. If sex was the portal to friendship and a social life, then, by golly, so be it. Gary was available.

His condominium apartment, somewhere near a local Army base, was decorated in whorehouse reds and gold trims. Had my interest been his furniture, I would have left as untouched as a leper in Calcutta. The sectional reminded me of the '60s; the chrome and glass—well, reminiscent of Brian Richards' warmth and sincerity. For an interior decorator—pardon me, designer—he sure knew how to crowd a space.

"I'm glad I soundproofed the walls," he said in what I interpreted more as a warning than a statement of fact. I hoped he meant it kept outside noise from penetrating the apartment more than the opposite.

He had greeted me at the door wearing nothing more than an unbuttoned white long-sleeved shirt. He had not lied about his chest: it was covered by a mat of graying hair.

The hair on his head was his, I found out a little later.

His claim of extraordinary length was duly substantiated. He had not even implied that the yardage ever became erect, so I had no reason to complain about false advertising.

After sex his demeanor indicated that it was time for me to leave, so I did.

The following week we met again under the same circumstances, with the exception of his total nudity when he opened the door. Apparently he wanted to get into it right away unencumbered by the effort required to remove an unbuttoned shirt.

After several weeks my visits became predictably mechanical. A greeting in the nude, a drink, a jump in the bed, an orgasm, a cleanup, a dressup and a bye at the door.

"I have two tickets to a performance of F. Scott Fitzgerald's *Fie! Fie! Fi-Fi!* next Thursday at the University of South Carolina," I told Gary over the phone. "Would you like to join me?"

I was trying to diversify the range of activities in which we could both participate, from one to two. His availability was welcomed.

The performance was superior to most USC theatrical productions, although that was no feat, and I was content that Gary and I had found something to do outside of his bedroom.

A few days later I called Gary late one afternoon. It wasn't good to keep blossoming friendships uncultivated. When he answered the phone he sounded out of breath.

"How are you doing?" I was thinking of inviting him out to dinner the next day.

"I'm alright." He sounded disconcerted.

"Did I catch you at a bad time?"

"You did. I'm expecting someone. I ran out of the shower and I'm dripping wet."

"Oh, I'm sorry. Go get ready then—put some clothes on. Unless he's one of *those* friends," I added without the expectation of an explanation.

"Actually, he is," he replied dryly.

"Oh." I paused. "Sorry. Call me when you get a chance."

Gary never got the chance again.

Two years later I made the acquaintance of someone who knew him well and mentioned some decorating advice he had received from Gary. Without disclosing how I knew the celebrated decorator, I mentioned that I had met him.

"He's such a whore," his dear friend said as if he were making a statement about the price of oranges in China. "He sits at that computer meeting cheap tricks, then he lines them up, and when he gets tired of them, poof!"

He snapped his fingers. "They're gone, and he's off to get hisself some fresh meat. And he'll travel to meet them anywhere between here and Virginia and between the beach and Alabama."

At a Christmas party three years after the last time I was seen in public with the cheap-trick collector, I saw Gary at a Christmas party in the company of the current addition to his worthless set. Gary was wearing a Santa cap, a red jockstrap and black boots, and left early to attend another party at the local go-go boy bar downtown.

Lesson: Alone is better than in tacky associations. Or, as the old Castillian proverb goes, better single than ill married.

Day 29:

Smooth as Silk, Authentic as Rayon

The acquaintance of married men who indulge in intimacy with other men, I used to believe, should be valued by other gay men who are or have been themselves married. It would be natural, I concluded several years ago when the intransigence and intolerance of single gay men regarding their partner's children forced me to retreat from an otherwise satisfying relationship.

As rational as some advice is on the subject of what's best for my children or the limits I should establish to the attention I give them, the unsolicited hints from Heloises frequently annoy me—with notable exceptions. They should have had their own children if they had such great ideas on raising them. Often the mere existence of children becomes an obstacle—the single partner often harbors ill feelings toward the breathing evidence of a previous breeding engagement.

Experience has shown me, however, that the possession of a current or invalidated marriage license is no insurance against biases similar to those expressed by single men. I have known plenty of gay fathers who eagerly turned over all responsibility for raising and supporting their children to a former spouse and her new husband. Some abandoned their families abroad or in other states and have never seen them again. Then again, I have enjoyed with great delight the company of a single man who has embraced my children as an extension of his own beloved partner, and has nourished a cautious but affectionate friendship with my female spouse.

Blurring the distinction between extremes we have men like Jay Morris, married to an allegedly unsuspecting woman and the father of two.

Jay profiles himself on an Internet site as married, 48 y.o., 6', BL/BL, 180 lb., 7.5 in. cut, 7 in. diam., versatile, ISO men 18-? for hot sex. For the uninitiated, this means that Jay is forty-eight years old, six feet tall, blue-eyed and blond, weighs 180 pounds, his erect penis size is 7.5 circumcised inches long and seven inches in diameter, and he is in search of men between the ages of eighteen and infinity for sleazy sex in an equally sleazy motel. With this information he has covered the widest range of interests of most men who surf the Net for sexual contacts.

When Jay and I met at a McDonald's downtown Columbia, it was clear that his profile needed amendments: under six feet tall—as that is my height and he was shorter than I—BL/dark BR, 240+ lb. He should have added that a concave surface had replaced his broad butt, and that upon visual inspection in the men's room at McDonald's it was obvious that the 7.5" x 7" measurement was exceedingly magnanimous on the much, much bigger side. Such shortcomings were ultimately of no import, but had they been, Jay would have had to defend himself in gay small-claims court.

To this day I'm not sure what other pieces of misinformation he fed me, but it seems that Jay owns his own company, a small but profitable software concern that requires frequent travel, and during his spare time he sings with a local singing group that also travels, though with far less frequency.

"You'd probably like to come to one of our parties," he said one day over lunch. I had not expected me to attend parties at his house: how would he explain me to his unsuspecting wife?

"Once a month a group of us gets together in a hotel room for a party," he added. "Most are married men."

More than the possibility of such a group's existence in the buckle of the intolerant Baptist chastity belt, it struck me as ironic that the hotel he mentioned is within the same general area as the headquarters of one of the many conservative religious groups that rule the southeastern United States.

"How is your daughter doing?" I asked him, not to change the subject, but to diversify the topics we had covered. His daughter had just graduated high school and wanted to live on campus when she went to college, although she would be no more than fifteen minutes form home.

"She's still hung up on living in a dorm. I'm sure that's going to backfire," he said with regret. "I know her. She's just like me. As soon as she has a taste of cock, that'll be the end of school. She'll just be running after cock and forget everything that has to do with school."

"You finished a master's degree, though."

"She's not as mature as I was at her age," he added in all seriousness.

Invitations started to come over my email service for the monthly hotel gatherings. Twice I confirmed that I would be attending, only to cancel later. The procedure was: early the afternoon of the day of the gathering he would send email or telephone parties interested in attending, with information about the hotel room number and the password, which was generally stated as "My name is Bob and I'm looking for Dick." Only the name of the caller usually varied.

A couple of months went by without an invitation. I wondered what had happened and called Jay. He had just returned from a trip to Puerto Rico, where he reportedly had sex in all its forms—he had recently become actively interested in what he called "serious assplay," which I understood to mean fisting, as the active partner, and he wanted to know if I'd be interested in a session sometime soon.

"I got the worst case of the runs," he told me.

"Probably from the water. The island's water reserves are quite polluted, you know," I told him. "But that should be the least of your troubles. The island has the highest concentration of HIV infection on U.S. territory, so I hope you protected yourself."

"Now you tell me!" he replied jokingly.

I, however, was very far from lightness.

Jay had also been touring Europe with the men's choir. A stop in Paris coincided with his twentieth wedding anniversary and, since his wife had traveled with him, they had been able to renew their wedding vows in the sacristy at the Cathedral of Notre Dame. He wasn't Catholic—I don't think he had a religious preference other than whatever he worshipped in the altar of fleeting sex—but, as he put it, "How many people can say they did something like that?" To which a mutual friend who heard the account third-hand replied, "But those few probably meant it more than he ever did." Apparently the rest of the choir members who knew about Jay's not-so-secret life felt deep embarrassment for the poor woman: they were all invited to witness his affirmation of vows, just as Jay's wife had invited them to his surprise fiftieth-birthday party without knowing that more than half of the choir had had in its mouth what she had enjoyed farther down in her anatomy.

"I married because I never fell in love with a man," he told me one day when I asked him the reason for his choice earlier in life. "I had only had sex with men, and lots of it, before I met my wife, but I never fell in love with any of them. Then I met her, and we had sex, and I reckoned I could do that as good as anyone, and I liked her, so I decided we could get married. But we'd been married for about three months, and we had done all this fucking, and I started to wonder, 'Hey, is this all there is?' So I started to go out again with men, and I haven't stopped yet."

Why stay in a marriage like that?

"We have social and business commitments. It wouldn't be wise of me to get out of the marriage. For one thing, it would surprise the hell out of her, because we have no problems."

None that a blood test couldn't reveal, anyway.

Months went by and I continued to come up with excuses to skip the parties. However, just in case I ever got the nerve to go, I asked him to keep me in mind.

One fine day in late August I decided it was time to find out what this gathering of married men was all about. I drove down a road lined with car dealerships and took a turn at the corner where the Southern Baptist

Convention Headquarters building stands. At the appointed time I knocked at the door. A man's head peeped around the edge of the door.

"I'm Rick and I'm looking for Dick."

He unchained the door and suddenly the buzz of a roomful of naked men started again. Throughout my stay at the party I realized that everyone went instantly quiet whenever someone was knocking at the door.

I walked into a half-darkened suite furnished with two double beds, each of which were occupied by multiple partners engaged in various types of sexual activity. Most of the men in the room were in desperate need of an exercise program; more than half were probably retired, and wedding bands shone on many hands, though not all.

I stripped to my briefs, which I intended to wear at least until I had become accustomed to the room's dynamics. I left my pile of clothes on the floor by the bathroom door and stepped into the room. Someone had hooked up a television set and a cassette player; a male porn film was playing. Several body types were mixed in one bed, in contortions that covered faces, in some cases, and other body parts in others. A chunky man was straddling another heavy man in the other bed.

"Hey!" Jay yelled at me from the side of the more heavily occupied bed, then walked over, kissed me on the lips and pulled off my briefs. He was going to see very little: the novelty of the spectacle and my discomfort had inhibited any external reaction to the view.

"How are you?" someone who was standing by me asked. When I looked I recognized the manager for the grocery store where I shopped every week.

"Oh, fine. You?"

He didn't say anything. Instead he tugged at my genitals and started to pull my nipples.

I looked toward the bed, where one of my neighbors, a young man who had moved south from Wisconsin, was taking a break from fellating activity to look up and wave at me.

The room went totally quiet when another knock was heard. "Hi, I'm Rick and—"

In walked a man I had met at a small gathering some years before, a very large man who worked with the state's Law Enforcement Department and on Sundays sang in the choir of one of the most famously conservative churches in the city.

I stood against a wall, resisting hand signals and verbal remarks meant to encourage me to overcome my shyness and join in the festivities.

One very drunk man—we could bring our own bottles if we wished, since the five-dollar attendance fee would only cover the room—stood by me, and Jay went down on his knees to put the man out of his misery.

"Well, folks," a deep voice said suddenly. "It's been fun, but I got to get going. See you next time." It was a corpulent man in fatigues.

"He's a captain in the Army," Jay said to everyone after he left. "And he can salute my pole anytime." He had arrived earlier than most other guests, and had been in the shower during the time I had been there, since he had already taken care of business. "He's been having problems with his wife, so he had to leave early," Jay added.

My curiosity had been sufficiently sated, but I didn't dare leave. I hadn't been there long enough and didn't want to be talked about after I left. I had to wait until Jay was busy enough not to notice my departure.

Eventually Jesse, my neighbor, approached me.

"I'm so embarrassed," he said. "I had never been in anything like this, and I can't get it up."

"You're not alone," I answered. "Did Jay invite you?"

"No, I didn't know him until I got here. David called me."

I had no idea who David was. Last names were not provided at introductions, but I was too self-conscious to pay any attention to anyone's first name either.

I had arrived at five, Jesse at four. I had been there for little over an hour when another knock at the door muted the room. I suppose that if anyone else's heart was like mine, it leapt every time someone was at the door, scared to death that it could be someone other than a guest.

Gary Winmore walked in, effusively grabbing a butt here, a penis there, and patting the large church-choir singer's back. I knew it was time to leave.

"I'm leaving," I told Jesse.

"Can you give me a ride? I walked here from home, but it's so hot I don't really want to walk back. Do you mind?"

"Of course not." I was glad to have someone else leave with me. Maybe it would look as if I had picked someone up there and we were going elsewhere to enjoy each other in private, rather than being seen as the provincial boors whose sophistication was not enough to deal with the freedom that ruled the room.

"Come back when you can stay longer," some old, emaciated man by the door said when we were leaving.

"Had you ever seen so many old farts tugging at their limp dicks in the same room?" Jesse joked on the way home.

"Had you ever seen so many ugly old farts in one room?" I joked back.

I don't know whether my departure and reticence were the ultimate social faux pas among the closetful of men in the room that afternoon. Jay never called or wrote again to invite me to parties or to solicit me for serious fist action.

Lesson: Never underestimate human capacity for debasement.

Day 30:

Email Fight at the It's Not OK Corral

Northerner of Hispanic origin new to the Carolinas seeks friends in the Midlands of South Carolina.

44 y.o., graying short-cropped brown hair, 6' tall, 185 lb., moderately hairy, athletic build. Married, two adult children, family aware of orientation.

Former skier, jogger, into light workouts. Ph.D., former college professor and computer scientist, recently consulting in international business. Hobbies: reading, writing, traveling. Interests: skydiving, theater, film, national politics, professional baseball (Twins fan) and football (Pittsburgh Steelers).

Do not smoke or use drugs, and prefer the same from others.

Would like to meet other gay married men for dinner, movies, walks. Not interested in a relationship; sex is not required. Discretion respected.

Email me if interested.

I posted the message on a computer bulletin board for gay men. The following day I received a reply:

I'm interested.
Timothy Paul Hathaway II

My answer to that was:

Hello. You know about me, so tell me about you!

Timothy Paul Hathaway II was a forty-three year-old educational researcher for a university in North Carolina. He was married; his son was twelve and his daughter nine. His wife was aware of his sexuality.

Before we married I told her about my previous sexual experiences with men. She said it was probably adolescent experimentation, a phase that all young men went through. I didn't tell her I was in my twenties when it happened. It started when I was in military school in Tennessee. I married her because she was from a small town and naïve, and she was less likely than others to suspect anything.

Now he was out to her. That disclosure excluded information about encounters he had been having all along with students in toilets at the university where he was employed and men he had sucked off in other public facilities, including some high-risk unprotected sexual encounters.

I'm sure that if I told her the whole truth she would divorce me. We have had our share of struggles, and it's been an extended process of ever-changing growth. Together we have discussed where we are right now and where we would like to be, trying to think outside the box. We have discovered a polyamorous network in the US that publishes a magazine, Loving More. *Let me know if you'd like to take a look at some past issue, as we can share them.*

What was polyamory?

The philosophy behind polyamory is that we are all capable of loving many people simultaneously, and it is more natural to share that love than to trap ourselves into one partner while falling into possessiveness and jealousy. Polyamorous paradigms include triads and even larger arrangements and combinations of males and females.

It sounded as if a Greek prefix were conferring legitimacy to good old-fashioned swinging.

My wife Alicia and I are founding members of our area's polyamory group. I also belong to an online discussion group for married men who are out to their wives. We had a conference in Baltimore last August. It was interesting, and I met a guy from Charlotte for private discussion. ;-}

If I had not understood before the concept of information overload, Timothy gave me a superb opportunity for full and unequivocal comprehension.

Was he bisexual, then? I was hoping he'd label himself with the abhorrent moniker, thus canceling out even the slightest possibility that I would ever have any further interest in him. A flag always goes up when someone tells me he's bisexual—or bisucksual, as my friend Hank calls it. It's not a flag, really, but a nasty rag that speaks loudly of all I can expect from this self-proclaimed pleaser of males and females. I know that bisexuality exists (or is it ambisexuality?), but most men I have met who claim to be so are usually full of emotional crap.

The truly bisexual never go about bragging about their versatility, nor are they constantly on the defensive when faced with those of us skeptical about their ambivalence. The man who operates heterosexually but feels love for a man as well suffers in the darkness of his soul for not being able to conquer the social restraints that bind him to one partner and denies the other of a fuller partnership: in that part of his heart he cannot fully reveal sits the awareness that he is homosexual, even if he feels great affection and responsibility for his female spouse. That's being a gay man trapped in a straight body of social expectations and responsibilities, not bisexuality.

People who insistently call themselves bisexuals are invariably Narcissistic jerks who get off on being capable of using males and females equally to satisfy their attention-starved egos and cannot accept the fact that given a real choice their faces would be buried in a man's groin, not trying to mask their true preference by fantasizing about a penis while penetrating a vagina. They are equal-opportunity manipulators. Or else they are boors raised in intolerantly religious homes where being queer is the worst "choice" anyone can make, and thus they develop a deep self-loathing that inhibits them from being fair to themselves or either gender. Thus they resort to the mask of bisexuality, which only deludes themselves.

I don't know that I am anything. I'm just sexual.

He and his wife had discussed possibilities, all of which excluded dissolving their marriage.

I don't want to leave my family. It doesn't feel righjt to throw away twenty years of marriage. We need to look for alternative paradigms that are satisfactory for all of us.

Our agreement is that we need to shift our paradigm to accommodate all of our needs. Our goal is to include another man who will make our family his intentional family. He would live with us, sharing our space and helping with the children.

For a minute I thought he was talking of a live-in man servant *cum* fuck buddy.

If he only wants to have sex with me, that would be okay, but we prefer someone who would also have sex with Alicia.

Oh, brother. I could tell I was still thinking inside the box.

My friend Scott, up in Virginia Beach, became the recipient of copies of Timothy's email. "Where do you meet all these weirdoes?" he asked, truly alarmed. "Please tell me you're not going to continue to write this man."

I didn't listen to Scott.

What did Timothy's children think of their father?

I came out to them and told them that they were free to share that information with anyone they wanted. Alicia and I agreed that it wasn't fair of me to come out of my closet and then put them in another one. My daughter thought it was cool. My son didn't say much. He's difficult to read. I have tried to get him to tell me what he thinks, but he doesn't say much. The other day I was checking why our computer's hard disk was so full and opened some of his files. He has been downloading pictures of women having sex with dogs. I decided it was not up to me to say anything, because I don't believe in censorship.

Is it censorship if your teenage son is obviously deriving pleasure from watching images of the debasement of women? How would he like it if the pictures were of his mother or his sister?

But they aren't. I simply don't believe in censorship. Furthermore, he has never complained when he sees me downloading pictures of naked men engaged in sex.

What in hell is he doing downloading male porn in front of his children? Didn't that assume a maturity that his children couldn't possibly have?

Had his son ever mentioned anything again?

One day I was driving him to the doctor, and he was unusually quiet. I asked him what was wrong, and he said, 'I just wish that you weren't gay.' I corrected him and told him that I was not gay. He asked, 'Don't you go to gay bars and hang out with queers?' I told him that I did, but that was mostly with my friend Ed, and he knows Ed.

Uh?

Alicia and I often rent videos of male sex and watch them together after the children are asleep. I also sit up in bed reading male porn out loud to her. She is into it also, and it often helps us become more intimate.

Oh.

"That makes him just sexual?" Scott asked me after reading a copy of Timothy's email. "Those two were made for each other, the warped voyeurs. Doesn't that woman have any shame?"

"Now, now, Scott, you're thinking inside the box. You need a paradigm shift. You have to evaluate where you are right now," I replied, trying to sound serious.

One night when Alicia and I were talking about sexual issues and reading stories in Blueboy, *she turned over on our waterbed and asked me, 'If you like gay sex so much, what am I, a warm wet hole?' Sometimes she asks these questions that I have no answer for. I have to stop and think where I am right now, and sometimes I just tell her that. She expects a more solid answer, but I tend to change my position depending on how much information I continue to receive, and all I can say is that it depends on where I am right now.*

Timothy and I corresponded for the next two years. Occasionally he would call me from work, but when he was laid off from his job the calls became infrequent. He relied more often on email to communicate with me, and I started taking longer to reply.

I have joined the temp pool at the university, but I'm hoping for a permanent job in the university system. I have talked to several people about open positions, and several of them look very promising.

His Ph.D. was apparently not particularly useful. Every job he unrealistically applied or interviewed for was given to someone else. He continued to fill temporary clerical and data-entry positions at the university.

I'm thinking of returning to school to continue my education.

More education was going to make him more employable? How about seeking a job that could support his family and take the burden off his overworked wife?

My goal is to become a counselor for polyamorous couples. For that I need a license, and getting a graduate degree in social work is the best way. Otherwise, it's next to impossible to get professional liability insurance.

This was a new goal. Some twenty years before Timothy had returned to Pittsboro, outside of Durham, to work on a doctoral degree in vocational counseling at one of the local institutions of higher learning. He had spent several years working as an assistant dean of student affairs in a small college in southern Illinois. His father had given him the old family vacation house to use until he received his degree. It was a one-bedroom bungalow in the outskirts of Carrboro in central North Carolina, a small structure with a large living area that included a small kitchen. But Timothy and Alicia remained in the house, with its rent-free advantage, years past its functionality. The children came and grew up, and Timothy divided the living area into two small windowless bedrooms for them.

"I don't know how you can stay in that nigger whorehouse," his father often said. "Why don't you get a mortgage and move somewhere else?"

At the end of two years of email exchanges, Timothy and I finally met. I had to lead a training workshop at Research Triangle Park, the intellectual oasis provided by relocated Yankees in the area, surrounded by what Scott called the *ay, ay, ay*—ignorance, illiteracy and intolerance—so characteristic of Jesse Helms country. My morbid curiosity made me tell Timothy that I was traveling to Durham. We agreed to meet the evening I got there.

Timothy did not immediately enthrall me with his looks. His gravel voice was difficult to understand, especially because of his heavy Southern drawl. Still I gave him a tight hug: this was a person who had been emptying his guts out to me for over two years, and I felt it was warranted; he stood stiffly at the door, leading me to think I had been inappropriately forward.

Two weeks later he asked me to meet him in Charlotte for lunch. While we sat in an open area at a science museum, Timothy spoke freely about his feelings since we had met. "I could really fall in love with you. I really want this relationship. I mean, you can't imagine how I want this relationship. But I can't have it if you don't want it. So that's what I'm asking you right now."

My head was full of questions. Timothy had been telling me about all his dreams, and his wife's, including bringing a man in to live with them. I was not going to be that person. Had his paradigm shifted again?

"I think," he paused as if something was choking him, "that we need to revisit our plans. I wasn't counting on meeting you when we made those plans. We're not ruling out anything," he said, as if the decision rested entirely with the two of them.

"I don't know whether I'm ready for a relationship, Timothy," I replied. "Maybe given time we could get there, but right now my life is too complicated to commit to something like that." I had already had a long-distance relationship that had ended in disaster, and the possibility of an involvement with Timothy was overloaded with my doubts that I would ever adapt to what he and his wife wanted.

"I'm begging you not to shut me out," he said, holding my hands. "I'm not pressuring you, but," he choked again, "we both must want this relationship. I really—you have no idea how much I want a relationship with you."

The tears in his eyes and the droopy expression on his face made me cave in. "Okay, let's give it a shot."

We met again twice in Charlotte. The second time Alicia joined us for lunch. When they arrived—late, as Timothy always did—I realized I had in front of me the other half of this couple that I had made the mistake of becoming involved with as if I had nothing to lose by jumping into the abyss of their lives.

My immediate reaction to her was that she better be the nicest person in the world, because if her looks were the best part of her, she was not much. Her unplucked eyebrows and the complete absence of makeup gave her the severe countenance of a wicked wench in a Grimm tale. Her hair, which she said she cut herself, needed a decent cut, a good brush and a touch-up: she was supposed to be in her early forties, but her hair color was closer to late sixties. Her undersized frame was further handicapped by a disproportionately big pair of breasts over a very unsightly pouch, which she had tried to cover with an oversized wool top. Her stretch leggings gave her the appearance of a troll.

Alicia was not particularly chatty at lunch, but she said enough through her teeth.

"This is weird," Timothy said.

"What is?" I asked.

"The wife and the husband having lunch with the husband's lover," he replied.

Alicia nodded in agreement. I just blushed and continued eating my salad.

That evening after they returned home Timothy sent me email.

Alicia says you're very handsome, but not really butch. All in all I think you met with her approval.

It struck me that I had believed this to be an inspection trip to size up the competition, but actually it was more of an assessment Alicia was making to determine whether she would eventually want to jump into bed with her husband and me.

Alicia sent me email the following day to thank me for picking up the tab for lunch and to tell me how much she had enjoyed the visit. "I approve of you," she wrote with unmatched gall. "You should know that I have veto power over Timothy's choice for a partner," she added, "and if I had not approved of you, he would not have been able to see you again." I didn't know whether I should laugh or simmer in the hot bile rising to my mouth.

I immediately wrote Timothy. What if she had disapproved of me, what then? My willingness to enter into a relationship with him meant nothing, since, after all, if Alicia had not approved of me, then I would have been history? So I could have given my unwavering intent to make our relationship work, to surrender to him my affection and loyalty, only to find out later that Alicia could have put an end to us?

You're overreacting. The truth is that I had forgotten anything about that veto stuff. Back when we were still discussing alternative paradigms and talking about bringing another man into our household, Alicia mentioned something about having veto power over my choice. I didn't pay much attention to it. Please don't put me in a bad space because of it.

So what was it, what she wanted carried weight in his choice, or what she said was as important as hot air?

Don't overreact. You are at a disadvantage, because you have entered our lives at a time when we have discussed many options and considered several models, and we can sit up in bed at night and talk about this, whereas you are down in South Carolina unaware of what we are saying. But in my heart I know that I would not make any fundamental decision without telling you about it.

And if the decision were detrimental to me, was that the risk I was taking in exchange for a long-distance relationship that was already showing signs of strain and wear before it ever started?

I decided to trust the sincerity of his will and repressed my ill feelings.

Time for a secret: Alicia told me last night that she would like to have sex with you and watch you and me having sex. Close secret. We talked about you last night before and during sex, and it enhanced both our orgasms tremendously.

Oh, mine.

I traveled to Durham to save Timothy the expense of driving down to South Carolina. He was in financial straits due to his minimum-wage situation, and I didn't want to add to his trouble.

"If he doesn't have money with which to support a relationship, then he should bow out," Scott wrote me. "I don't know how you're looking at it, man, but to an impartial party it looks like you're paying for sex. You don't need to pay for that, bud."

Perhaps Scott did not understand the extent of my generosity. If this relationship was going to fail, it was not going to be because I had been selfish with my money.

The trend began a period during which the Holiday Inn became my home away from home—naturally, staying at his house was out of the question, although I never really knew, since I was never invited to it and never saw it. Timothy made reservations and chose restaurants. I paid. It became a given that I would be paying for hotel accommodations, meals and entertainment, whether we met in Durham, Greensboro, Salisbury—yes, the home of the steak of the same name and Elizabeth Dole—or Charlotte. It was also the case in Atlanta and Charleston.

Alicia was very upset when I came home last night from spending the weekend with you. She feels that we are going out and having a good time, and she stays home having none. Perhaps we could consider having her join us for dinner the next time you're in town.

Alicia became a permanent fixture for dinner on Friday night when I'd arrive in Durham.

Alicia has season tickets for University Players performances. She bought three, so that the three of us can go together. I'm sending you the schedule, so that you can choose what dates are best for you.

We started going to the theater in Alicia's company. Invariably she would sit next to Timothy and get all over him, holding his hand, putting her arm over his shoulders, playing with his hair. I was very uneasy. I had not seen Timothy for two or three weeks; she had him in bed every night. Why did she need to indulge in such public displays of affection, as if they were teenagers in heat? Was she marking her territory—when was she going to start pissing around him? Was she sending me a hardly-subtle message that this was hers and I could only have Timothy when she allowed me to, when she gave him permission to come out and play with me?

You're overreacting. Sometimes when I read what you write I wonder if you have been taking hard drugs. If you want to hold my hand during the performance, you can do it. She wouldn't object.

I didn't want my hand to find hers when I tried to hold his.

Alicia just wants to be your friend. She wants to be respected and included in my relationship with you. But if what you want is for me to get down and give you a blowjob when the lights go out, that's not going to happen.

No, it wasn't what I wanted, and his crassness mortified me. My opinion, which I kept to myself, was that if she wanted to be respected first she needed to attain a level of self-respect and dignity that I had not perceived.

You have to understand that this is very difficult for her, and she's in a bad space right now, with pressure at home and at work. She has had to see our marriage evolve in the past twenty years from her vows to a STR8 man to a bisexual husband.

Bisexual? My judgmental little mind, in its usual box, began to whirl, purr and hum. He was married and his guilt made him search for a solution to his life that wouldn't leave his wife stranded. That was not bisexuality; this character was more in denial of the core of his being than in command of a sexuality that allowed him equal satisfaction from a man and a woman.

When had he become bisexual?

You have a very limited view of the many manifestations of sexual desire. I don't believe that labels should confine us into inflexible modes of sexual expression. I love both my wife and my male partner. I don't know why that is so difficult for you to understand.

Oh.

Well, I loved my wife as a decent human being who had had to tolerate more than most spouses in this world, and who had still stuck by me, sharing a house with me and respecting me as a human being. She, however, had not expressed any interest in going to bed with Timothy and me, and I doubt she would ever feel any love for him.

Neither would most of my friends, for that matter. He had made himself odious even to my married gay friends. They were waiting for me to return to my senses. I was reminded that Timothy and Alicia had made other attempts to ensnare gay men to share their unique view of the sexual world, and all had fallen flat when the self-respecting men fled in disgust.

I had always believed that everyone who had expressed and demonstrated some interest in me deserved the benefit of the doubt. I had some ability to tolerate certain things if I thought that eventually something positive would evolve. My patience was constantly tested in this case, but I was willing to continue. Maybe deep in me I refused to believe that these people were actually serious and that what seemed like humiliation and financial abuse was just a sacrifice I had to make on my way to a more optimistic future.

Our relationship survived, but it was approaching a chronic state of endangerment. My interest had diverged. I was holding out, waiting for him to finally admit to himself that he was gay, not bisexual. I was on a mission to prove that to him and bring him to face the facts. I didn't want to traumatize him or lead him to abandon his family—I had realized myself many years before that taking such a step could lead to boundless regret when it was done for the wrong reasons. In Timothy's case, I would have been the wrong reason, because I would never leave my family again, and if he did, he would do so to be alone. What I really wanted Timothy to do was to stop having sex with his female spouse, share her life and his children's as a gay husband and father if they so wished, and to make himself sexually my exclusive province.

The truth was that I resented his wife, I wanted him to love me more, even if she were also someone he cared for, and I wanted her to disappear from the midst of our relationship forever. It was not looking good.

I didn't know how to play Alicia's game: I had never played it before. We'd see who was going to be left standing when all was said and done.

Alicia's birthday came up. She wanted to go to Myrtle Beach for the weekend, and she asked that both Timothy and I be there.

"Would you have any objections to all of us staying in the same room?" he asked me one night when he called.

"Yes. Severe. As in no way, no, no, no."

"Well, I guess that takes care of that," he said with a chuckle. "We were planning to take a two-bedroom suite in a hotel right on the beach."

I didn't want to stay under the same roof, I explained to Timothy. I'd feel extremely uncomfortable. First of all, we had the issue of who was going to sleep in what bedroom. If he slept with his wife, I'd feel slighted. If he slept with me, I'd feel selfish. I preferred to stay in a hotel and get together with them to go to the beach and for meals. I was very explicit: if I were to go, I'd have to stay elsewhere.

I talked to Timothy the following day.

"Did you make your hotel reservations?"

"Yes." He choked. "We're going to be staying in a two-bedroom suite on the beach. You'll have one of the bedrooms."

"I told you that I didn't want to do that," I said angrily. My objections had meant absolutely nothing.

"But it's her birthday, and that's what she wanted. She said it was just a matter of simplifying logistics."

I feared another display of metaphorical pissing to mark the boundaries of their relationship, to make it clear that I was excluded when she was around. If I had made the choice to keep her out of my sex life with her husband, then I had to stay out of her play time with him. Or maybe she was just acting out her exhibitionist side. Either way I really did not want to be around them in their hour of heat.

As usual, however, I fatalistically drove out to Myrtle Beach. Earlier in the day I had been in a state prison in McCormick, on the eastern end of the state, to conduct a language interpretation for an attorney and his incarcerated client. I drove back through Columbia and out to what is generally referred to in South Carolina plainly as "The Beach." I arrived in early evening, my eyes sore and reddened. I had developed a cataract and the strain of driving at night was more than I had really wanted to experience that night.

The hotel on the beach was a dilapidated wood structure with outdoor steps leading to the second—and top—floor. Its appearance explained its availability and eighty-dollar daily rate, other than the fact that it was off-season. The second bedroom was actually the living room, furnished with a double bed. The other bedroom was in the back, accessible through a strangely designed indoor hall closed off from the living room by a door.

Around midnight I decided I had had enough. We had gone to dinner, which I paid for, and then driven to an all-night Wal-Mart to buy latex-free condoms—Timothy was allergic to latex. I didn't know that's what we were shopping for. When I asked why we were going there Alicia replied, "To get some stuff." She obviously knew what the reason for the trip was, and when I realized that she knew I felt horribly embarrassed.

While we were in the living room, Alicia and I had been sitting in a sofa facing the side of what was supposed to be my bed. Timothy was laying on his side in bed and suddenly complained of soreness in his feet.

"Let me have them," Alicia said. She grabbed his foot and pulled it right against her crotch while she massaged his toes. Timothy was moaning. It was time for me to call it a day.

Alicia retired to the bedroom. I took a shower and, when I came out, Timothy was in her bedroom. Were they going to sleep together?

I got into my pajamas and jumped in bed. The bedroom door opened and closed. Timothy came out in his underwear. He sat on the side of my bed and ran his hand up and down my back; I was facing away from him.

"Are you okay?"

"I guess I'm just tired," I lied. I was so sorry I had come.

He left to take a shower.

Timothy was clinically impotent. He could not take an oral medication to help him with it, because it interfered with some other drugs he was taking. Therefore, he had to inject a medication called Trimix into his penis. The shot dilated the vessels inside his penis, making it unnaturally erect for an indeterminate period of time: it could last anywhere from one to four hours.

When he came out of the shower it was obvious he had given himself the shot. In the shadows occasionally broken by light filtered through the cretonne drapes from a lamppost outside the room and the sordid atmosphere that in my mind had already overtaken the whole evening, he looked obscene, with the rock-hard erection that responded to no natural arousal and two uncommonly big testicles that hung in a sack beneath the small but hardened appendage. He walked around the room searching for a mug in which to pour some diet beverage. He opened the small refrigerator in the corner and the light from it shone around him, profiling him as a bundle of flesh that disappeared when he shut the cooler's door.

He went back into Alicia's bedroom. Was he going to sleep with her? What were they plotting in there?

I felt like a lap dog, brought along for entertainment, except that I was also the money man, paying to be tortured by these two freaks who had God only knew what designs.

Was a view of our lovemaking going to be her birthday present? It wasn't entirely impossible: she had already expressed an interest in peeping, to which I had objected strenuously. Judging by the effect that my opposition to sharing a room with her had had on Timothy, who knew whether my objections to her voyeurism would yield any respect from either of them.

What the hell was I doing there?

He stepped back into the living room and sat in bed with me.

"What's wrong?" he asked.

I turned around. "I feel very uncomfortable here. This was a mistake."

"Relax. This is what she wanted." Was that supposed to make me feel better? "Please, look at me."

I looked into his eyes that I wanted to scratch out. Then I heard Alicia going into the bathroom and instinctively covered myself to my neck with the blanket.

"Are you going to sleep here, or with her?"

"I was hoping we could have some sex. You and me."

"I don't know that I'm going to be up to that tonight. I don't like the idea of your wife walking in on us."

"She's not going to do that, don't worry about it."

"I can't."

He said he understood, then lay by my side. I pretended to be snoring. He stood up quietly and walked into Alicia's bedroom, I supposed to prevent wasting one perfectly good erection.

I lay there wide awake until early morning. When I was sure that they were both snoring, I got up and repacked the few items I had taken out of my travel bag. I left a note on the kitchen counter: "I'm sorry, but I really don't feel comfortable here. I hope you understand." I walked out. It was five in the morning. A Waffle House nearby was open, and I stopped for breakfast before going back on the road.

When I arrived home my answering machine had two messages from Timothy. They were confused about my actions. Alicia was very hurt. They were returning to Pittsboro, and hoped I had made it home safely.

"Are you convinced now that these people are creeps?" Scott said when I narrated the experience.

During the next few days Timothy and I exchanged bitter messages.

You have to apologize to Alicia. I am hurt too. This is not the first conflict we have. You must consider going to therapy. You need counseling to help you resolve those issues that keep coming up, like your insecurities. You should go to counseling for at least six months.

I reminded him of the goal he and his wife had before I came into the picture; it was clear to me that we would never be able to reach that goal, that I seemed unfit for them—a constant source of mortification for me.

You don't understand, or maybe you just don't want to understand. I explained to you that we had shifted our paradigm. You are too narrow-minded, still thinking inside the box. Don't you trust me? I have told you that I love you, but I also love Alicia. I don't see a conflict in that. You seem to think that it's a matter of degrees: I would have to love one of you more than the other, and all I can tell you is that my love for you and my love for her are different. That's where I am right now.

I felt that he had changed his mind so many times that I really didn't know who he was or what he would believe from one day to the next.

You ask me to commit to something, and all I can tell you is where I am right now. Maybe that sounds wishy-washy to you, but it's different for me. I have learned that people's feelings change as they gather additional information. The person I am today is not the person I was two months ago.

That was supposed to make me feel better? What if the person you become tomorrow is someone who doesn't want to be with me?

That is a risk we all take. I can only tell you that you have my heart. Don't you trust me?

Where did he think he would be five years down the road? Was his wife always going to be in the middle of decisions we took, so that we could never plan anything that did not include her feelings and her need to cling on to a man who had shown repeatedly that his preferences lay elsewhere? Why couldn't she be like my wife, who accepted me for who I was and respected herself enough to know that her place was outside the boundaries of my romantic involvement with another man? Why couldn't she? Because she needed to feel an importance she didn't have in my life, and because he encouraged her meddling.

What did the word commitment mean to him? That I had to trust him blindly? What makes a person trustworthy? Aren't reliability and flexible consistency the marks of character? I felt that the reason he wouldn't commit to a belief about where our relationship would eventually go was that he wanted the benefit of being able to change his mind at will and not have to deal with accusations of violating his previous commitment, but instead he was nothing more than a selfish flake. And this business of polyamory? What if tomorrow he would decide that our gay monogamy was not where he wanted to be and that it wasn't true to what human beings should allow themselves? Would I be expected to go there with him? What if his wife found a lover that would also take on her husband? What would my place be then? If it went against my unreasonable inflexibility, would I have wasted my time and emotional energy?

He and his wife were constantly picking up the tent of their relationship and pitching it deeper into their own forest. They had to, because he was guilt-ridden and she was a sadly codependent fool. I had already built my psychosexual edifice on solid ground. I had spent a lifetime of April firsts kissing frogs in hope of finding the prince, and had ended up scarred with warts and bathed in pond scum: if I were to establish a relationship again it would have to be with someone who knew who he was. It didn't matter whether he didn't want me next to him every waking moment of his life: in my declining years I had learned the value of being alone—not lonely, alone—and had learned to appreciate what giving space for my partner to grow eventually meant to both of us. But I wanted someone who was mine sexually as I would be his, someone who had fallen to the same depths I had and realized that he knew damn well what he wanted, to the sexual and emotional exclusion of others. Someone who understood that all I really owned was myself, and if I were to surrender my self to another he had to care for my self the way I nurtured his, who in return would reward me with exclusive rights to his body. That didn't make me a pathological fool. It made me human. Jealousy is only pernicious when our insecurities smother our partner with unreasonable demands of even visual fidelity. I didn't need someone who was still struggling with his identity and sinking himself in psychobabble to rationalize his self-loathing while accusing me of being a worse human being for feeling jealousy: I had no time for it. What I did have a right to was to sit down with my partner, set conditions we felt were important to the two of us, negotiate the ones we could and, if objections were strong, realize that we were not meant to be. And whereas our biological families, if we had any, were as important to us as we were to them, we would also know where the boundaries lay.

I was under no obligation to continue to torture myself hoping that something would change, while Timothy and Alicia insisted on squeezing her in through a backdoor that they denied even existed, but opened at every opportunity.

One fine day when I had too many other things to concern myself with, I told Timothy we were off.

"I thought you loved me. It has been easy for you to dismiss me and our relationship."

No reply was necessary to that.

Several weeks after the breakup Timothy sent me email that summarized what had been happening in his life during the time we had not communicated.

I went to the gay pride parade in Greensboro. I met old friends and made new ones. I had a chance to explore the S&M world, and may be doing some of that soon. I also realized that I am not bisexual, and that queer is my true nature.

Months later he again insisted on providing me an update on his extraordinary life. *John was here this weekend. I don't know why I get involved in these long-distance relationships, except that there is an excitement that comes with them.*

Timothy: I'm so happy you're happy. John: I hope you have deep pockets and unwavering patience.

Lesson: Invest your emotional and financial assets in ventures that promise a return on your investment, not on conning losers and their psychobabbling propositions.

Day 31:

Don't You Know Your Months?

April Fool! April is a thirty-day month.

When I thought that life, not just a month, was full of April firsts, along came Lloyd Cleveland. He brings joy to living not far south enough from both Bob Jones University and the only Ku Klux Klan museum in the world, and a stone's throw away from the two-street metropolis that denied a stage to The Indigo Girls because they were lesbians. This happiness is particularly important at this point in my life, because I live in— tenebrous organ music, ghostly moans and groans, crow chirps—the Deep South, not the most suitable place for a glackie.

Glackie? From GLAC: Gay, LAtino, Catholic. (Oh, stop it already: it's better than GYLA—Gay, Yankee, LAtino.)

Before I go tiptoeing down the primrose path, let me clarify that my negative stories are not an indictment of same-sex relationships, but rather a testimonial to my own poor taste in men. A paean, if you will, to my paucity of common sense. It's been a long road this one I have traveled. My flaws, opinions, hangups, insecurities and neuroses have generally made everything worse than it should have been. I blame no one but myself for the bumps, though sometimes it seemed that I had plenty of help inching my way down the cliff.

Along the way I have also met some marvelous people who have become great friends I would trust with my life. Yes, some were *that* kind of a friend, others weren't, but nonetheless it's the family I have put together to substitute the one that didn't particularly care for me once they knew the bitter truth.

A couple of those friends also included two who will forever live in my heart. We had differences that prevented us from remaining at a physically intimate level, but the bonds were so strong in so many other significant ways, that we salvaged what, in the long run, was worth the most.

That does not make us so too different from the rest of humanity.

www.ingramcontent.com/pod-product-compliance
Lightning Source LLC
Chambersburg PA
CBHW061341280526
45784CB00001B/89